IMAGES
of America

SILVER CITY

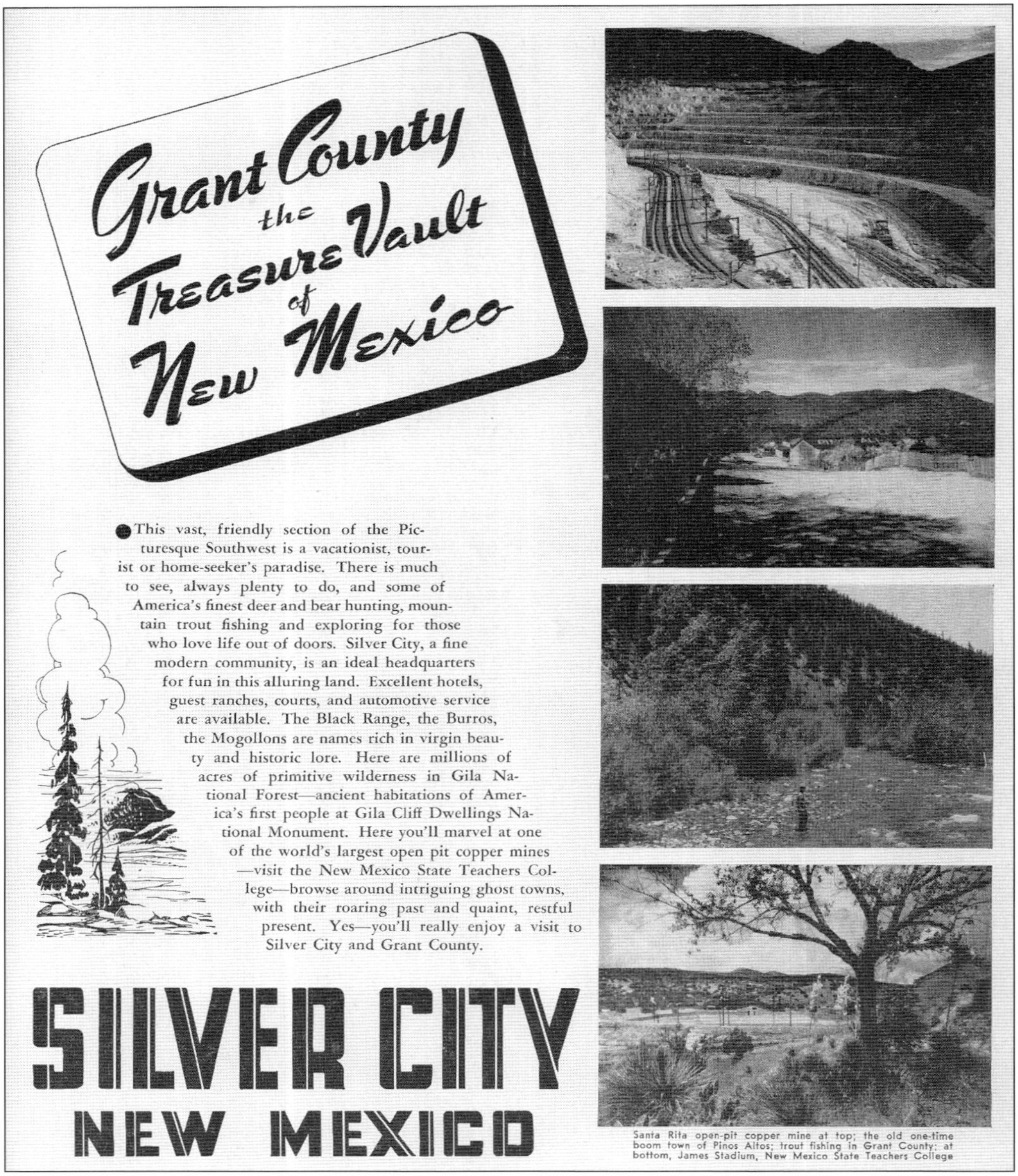

This vintage flyer extols the attractions of Silver City and Grant County, New Mexico, calling the area a "vast, friendly section of the Picturesque Southwest." Mentioned in the advertisement is the Gila Wilderness, offering excellent fishing, hunting, and other outdoor sporting opportunities, as well as the Gila Cliff Dwellings, mining history, and the college—attractions that still lure visitors to Silver City today.

On the Cover: When Silver City town leaders mandated concrete sidewalks in 1907, businesswoman and property owner Elizabeth Warren decided to pave the sidewalks in front of her properties herself in order to save the expense. Warren purchased a steam engine and a rock crusher and eventually began her own construction business. This 1930s view, looking south on Bullard Street, shows one of Elizabeth Warren's sidewalks, still in use today. (Courtesy of Don Turner.)

IMAGES
of America

SILVER CITY

Carolyn O'Bagy Davis
and Terrence M. Humble

ARCADIA
PUBLISHING

ISBN 978-0-7385-9994-6

Published by Arcadia Publishing
Charleston, South Carolina

Printed in the United States of America

Library of Congress Control Number: 2013936752

For all general information, please contact Arcadia Publishing:
Telephone 843-853-2070
Fax 843-853-0044
E-mail sales@arcadiapublishing.com
For customer service and orders:
Toll-Free 1-888-313-2665

Visit us on the Internet at www.arcadiapublishing.com

To the memories of Dawson "Doc" Campbell, C. Burton Cosgrove, Jean Eckard, Patrick Humble, Margaret Little Hunt, Stewart Pinkerton, and Otho Woodrow. Thank you for the stories.

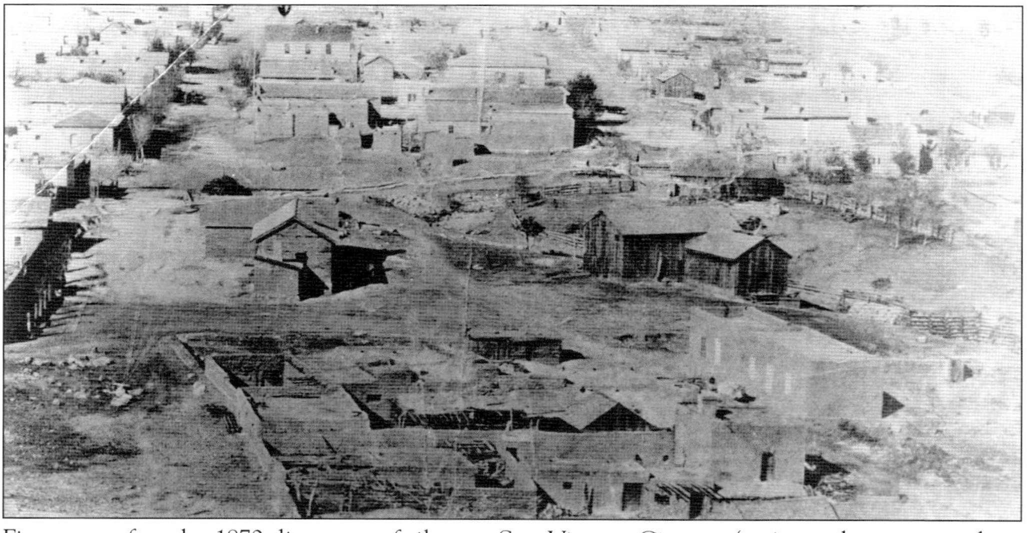

Five years after the 1870 discovery of silver at San Vicente Cienega (a *cienega* being a marsh or boggy area), prospectors flooded into the region, living in tents or in shelters of brush or adobe. Looking northward on Bullard Street, it is apparent that buildings were going up quickly. Among the adobe buildings in the center foreground, Lorenzo Carrasco built adobe furnaces to process silver. (Courtesy of Don Turner.)

Contents

FOREWORD

Personality of place is an elusive essence—more than the sum of a community's parts, its people, and its past, but still reflecting all of these elements. With echoes of vanished cultures and a continuing, complex human heritage, Silver City has personality-plus. Set in the ruggedly beautiful landscape of southwest New Mexico, this town of some 12,000 residents is a richly textured living collage with a unique character shaped by geographic, human, and historical elements.

The region's deep Hispanic and Native American roots are reflected in distinctive foods, architecture, and celebrations. The Southwest owes its ranching and mining traditions to the Spanish, who introduced cattle to the New World and launched the ongoing quest for precious ores. Westward expansion in the 19th century drew soldiers, miners, and settlers of widely ranging backgrounds. Along with their material goods, they brought their perspectives, traditions, and cultural values to the frontier. The early 20th century saw a huge wave of influence from health seekers desperately hoping our congenial climate would provide relief from consumption (tuberculosis). Many who recovered remained here with their families as contributing members of their adopted community. Even as mining—the region's dominant economic force for two centuries—began to wane in the early 1980s, Silver City entered yet another period of discovery, this time by cultural tourists, artists, retirees, wilderness enthusiasts, and other assorted adventurers. That chapter is still unfolding, but its profound influence on area life and character will provide rich material for future researchers. Each historical layer—some eras deeply scarred by conflict, others enhanced by collaboration—has contributed something to the Silver City area of today.

Unlike the many Western boomtowns that have vanished into memory, Silver City was established with the future in mind. Frustrated in its early efforts to establish local government and a public school system, Grant County threatened to defect to Arizona in 1876, prompting a profound change of heart in the territorial legislature. As a result, Silver City is New Mexico's oldest incorporated community (the only one still operating under a territorial charter) and boasts the earliest public school system in the state. Our citizens pursued a university for Silver City with the same determination, landing the New Mexico Territorial Normal School in 1893. Several name changes later, this institution continues today as Western New Mexico University. Silver City was a town built to last, and it is rich with surviving historic neighborhoods that reflect the stories of its visionary founders.

Many fortunes have been made and lost in the boom-and-bust economy of southwest New Mexico, but the region's most consistent—and valuable—resource has always been its people. Silver City has a deeply ingrained volunteer ethic (our 1878 charter required all able-bodied men to donate labor for street maintenance each year). That spirit lives on in countless ongoing efforts. Quality of life is a local product transcending economic conditions, continuing in the spirit of the early miners who pieced together the first silver-crushing mill and the women who established our hospital.

Selecting images to capture this region's rich history and distinctive personality had to be a challenge for the authors. I believe they were extraordinarily successful in their choices from the wealth of pictures offered them. Along with wonderful Silver City photographs, their book contains many views from the surrounding area. This is appropriate, because Silver City has always been about relationships. It is a hub, a "commons," a trade center for a wide area, and its history has unfolded within this larger context. The authors, each having spent decades steeped in Southwestern lore, possess the broad perspective and historical background to understand such connections.

A compelling storyteller, Carolyn O'Bagy Davis has authored numerous books exploring widely ranging aspects of heritage and culture in New Mexico, Arizona, and northern Mexico. With a remarkable knack for finding good stories, she has profiled such diverse personalities as Silver City heiress-turned-archaeologist Hattie Cosgrove and Gila Wilderness mountain man Nat Straw. Carolyn has also served as guest curator of numerous exhibits at the invitation of museums throughout the Southwest. Terrence Humble, known to his friends and associates as Terry, is often described as a "human encyclopedia" of southwest New Mexico mining lore. He is, without question, the authority on the now-vanished community of Santa Rita, having coauthored two important books on its history. Terry was recognized for his contributions with a well-deserved national award from the Mining History Association in 2010. Both Terry and Carolyn were valued colleagues over the many years I served as director of the Silver City Museum. Each of them generously shared time and knowledge to enhance the museum's programs, exhibits, and research projects. I consider them both living treasures and special friends, and am honored to contribute this foreword to Images of America: *Silver City*, their first collaborative publication.

Readers should, however, be warned: continued exposure to historic photographs can have life-changing consequences. Speaking as a visual learner who was drawn into a history career through immersion in such images, I can assure you they do not lose their power over time. In fact, if you are lucky, they can compel you to learn more!

Susan Berry
Silver City, New Mexico

ACKNOWLEDGMENTS

Many people shared photographs and information, and the authors wish to thank Billie Jean Behrens, Cecilia Bell, Judy Billings, William Bishop, W.E. Bullard, Holm O. Bursom III, Ida Campbell, Kathy Campbell, Ysabel Campbell, Burton Cosgrove, Deily Crumbley, Jan Devereaux, Jean Eckard, Angela Fischer, Lynn Geyer, Laura Howell, Genevieve Johnston, Michael Kiner, Richard G. Luna, Connie McCauley, Leon C. Metz, Anthony Romero, Dutch and Cherie Salmon, Gary Sinclair, Roy Sinclair, Retta Smith, Dillon Stone, Jean Uhli, Peggy Wright, Steve Riley and Rodney Sauter of the Gila Cliff Dwellings National Monument, Kenny Libben and the Glen Redd Fisher Museum in Loudonville, Ohio, and the Fort Bayard Historic Preservation Society. Special thanks also to Bob Alexander; Jane Bardal; Jan Blackwell; and Pat McDaniels, director of the Haley Memorial Library and History Center in Midland, Texas; and Andrea Jaquez and Neta Pope, authors of *The Fort Bayard Story 1866–1899.*

This book would not have been possible without the help of Don Turner. He generously shared his pictures of early Silver City, many of which were taken by his grandfather Leslie K. Goforth.

In addition to the above-mentioned individuals, Susan Berry was a mentor and supporter of this project. She shared her encyclopedic knowledge of Silver City history and, in addition to her contribution of the foreword, added important information and suggestions. Many thanks, Susan.

Photographs that have no citations are from the authors' collections.

Introduction

New Mexico is called the Land of Enchantment. The natural wonders, pine-covered mountains, white sands, and historic communities hold great allure. But the southwestern corner of the 47th state, which now constitutes Grant County, holds a special attraction that reaches back into prehistoric times. It is a place of jagged mountains, sheer cliffs, and mysterious, deep canyons, and in spite of centuries of human occupation, this region still holds remote vistas to be explored and enough wild country to please everyone who is enchanted with the majestic Southwest. James A. McKenna came to New Mexico Territory in 1877, and loved the country from his first sight of the rugged mountains with "mighty piles of rock splashed with colors that would shame a rainbow."

At 5,900 feet in elevation, Silver City is bounded by the Continental Divide to the west, the Pinos Altos mountain range to the north, and the Burro Mountains to the southwest. The high Chihuahuan Desert plain spreads southward into Mexico. The nearby Gila Wilderness and the adjoining 3.3 million-acre Gila National Forest are the largest uninhabited regions in the lower 48 states. The Gila Forest Reserve was created in 1899, setting aside this vast area as public domain. The forest contains several peaks above 10,000 feet in elevation and serves as the watershed for the Gila, Mimbres, and San Francisco Rivers. In 1924, the forest area was declared the first national wilderness area in the United States.

The earliest evidence of human habitation points to nomadic hunters and gatherers in southwestern New Mexico about 7,000 years ago. The first permanent residents were the ancient peoples classified by archaeologists as the Mogollon culture, thought to have grown out of an earlier Desert Archaic culture. The Mogollon people were named for the Mogollon Mountains east of the San Francisco River valley, which in turn were named for 18th-century Spanish colonial governor Juan Ignacio Flores Mogollon. There is evidence that these early people lived and farmed in the area of the San Vicente Cienega (later Silver City). Local newspapers dating to the 1880s reported that ancient room foundations and burial sites, as well as pottery, turquoise beads, and grinding stones, were discovered throughout the area during the construction of homes and buildings, providing evidence of "old villages and ancient habitations."

By 1300 A.D., the Mogollon people disappeared, and Apache Indians migrated into the area two centuries later. The Apache leader Geronimo was born near the headwaters of the Gila River about 1829. The Warm Springs Apaches (also known as the Chihenne or Red Paint People), led by Mangas Coloradas, called the Gila country their homeland. Early Spanish exploration of Apacheria is evidenced by such artifacts as a 14-pound church bell, cast in 1721 and found on a bench above the Gila River in 1910; a 1770 Spanish silver coin, unearthed during construction of a home in Silver City in 1914; and an ornate Spanish stirrup, discovered south of Silver City in the 1920s.

Santa Rita del Cobre, established by Spanish colonists in the early 1800s, was the region's first non-Indian settlement. Mining of the valuable copper deposits at Santa Rita continued under Mexican governance until 1837, when danger from increasing Apache hostilities trumped profitability. With the Gadsden Purchase of 1854, the area south of the Gila River joined the US territory of New Mexico. Throughout the Spanish, Mexican, and early territorial periods, herders, farmers, and would-be settlers spent time in the marshy valley known as the San Vicente Cienega (the future Silver City), but the threatening Apache presence deterred permanent settlement. Discoveries of silver and gold, however, changed the dynamics, and miners and settlers poured in, setting the stage for years of conflict between the Apaches and newcomers.

A gold discovery on Bear Creek in 1860 proved an unstoppable lure to prospectors who flooded into the Pinos Altos area despite the danger of Apaches. In the spring-fed valley of the San Vicente Cienega, Mexican herders raised sheep and goats, and a group of Anglo prospectors began farming in the marshy area. An Apache raid in the fall of 1869 left A.J. Hurlburt's wife and child dead, but when silver was discovered the following spring, prospectors poured into the area. A Las Cruces newspaper reported that at one location at the cienega with a silver strike, "but a few hours elapsed before the hill was like a swarm of ants."

Grant County was created by the New Mexico territorial government in 1868, first with the village of Santa Clara, followed by the booming mining town of Pinos Altos, which both served as early county seats. But, when the legislature heard of the riotous antics of the first appointed judge, D.B. "Dead Beat" Johnson, who combined the bar and the court with a Mexican band, and a "crew of half drunken, shouting attorneys, gamblers and midnight sportsmen," the county seat was moved six miles south to Silver City in 1871, where it remains today.

Very soon, prospectors were digging in the hills surrounding the cienega, as well as in mining districts in surrounding areas, with Silver City becoming the supply center for the larger mining district of southwestern New Mexico Territory. By the mid-1870s, the booming town had a lumberyard, a brick plant, bawdy houses, saloons, and a number of solid citizens building a lasting community. In 1883, a narrow-gauge railroad linked Silver City to Deming, where the Southern Pacific and Atchison, Topeka & Santa Fe Railroads met in 1881 to form the country's second transcontinental rail link. An 1880 town ordinance required that buildings must be constructed of nonflammable materials, such as adobe or brick, insuring that the town would not meet a fate similar to that of many other western frontier towns built with lumber that ultimately burned to the ground.

From its earliest years, Silver City has been the anchor for neighboring communities like Bayard, Central, Fierro, Hanover, Hurley, Santa Rita, Tyrone, and even Mogollon, approximately 70 miles (and 14 hours by wagon) to the north. In a metropolitan city, those communities would be considered suburbs, but in the vicinity of Silver City, they are still distinct settlements with separate identities and histories. The reasons for this clustering are apparent when considering the landscape spreading outward from Silver City. Nearly impassible mountain ranges create barriers to the east, north, and west, and the arid Chihuahua Desert plain stretches south into Mexico. So even though these distinct towns have separate identities, they are considered to be a part of the greater Silver City community.

In recent years, the location, climate, and culture of Silver City have provided a rich and rewarding lifestyle. Mining provided an early attraction to the area, but by the 1900s, health seekers flocked to Silver City, where the clear air and nearby hot springs offered promising cures for numerous ailments, including (most importantly) tuberculosis. With the construction of many sanatoriums, Silver City enjoyed a reputation as "the World's Health Resort." Today, the climate, the nearby Gila Wilderness, and the rich history and culture of Silver City have come to the attention of people around the country, and the town draws newcomers and visitors each year. It has been named one of the 100 best small art towns in America and also ranked third in a list of the best small towns in the country. With good reason, Silver City has been called the Treasure Vault of New Mexico.

One

Mimbreños and Mountain Men

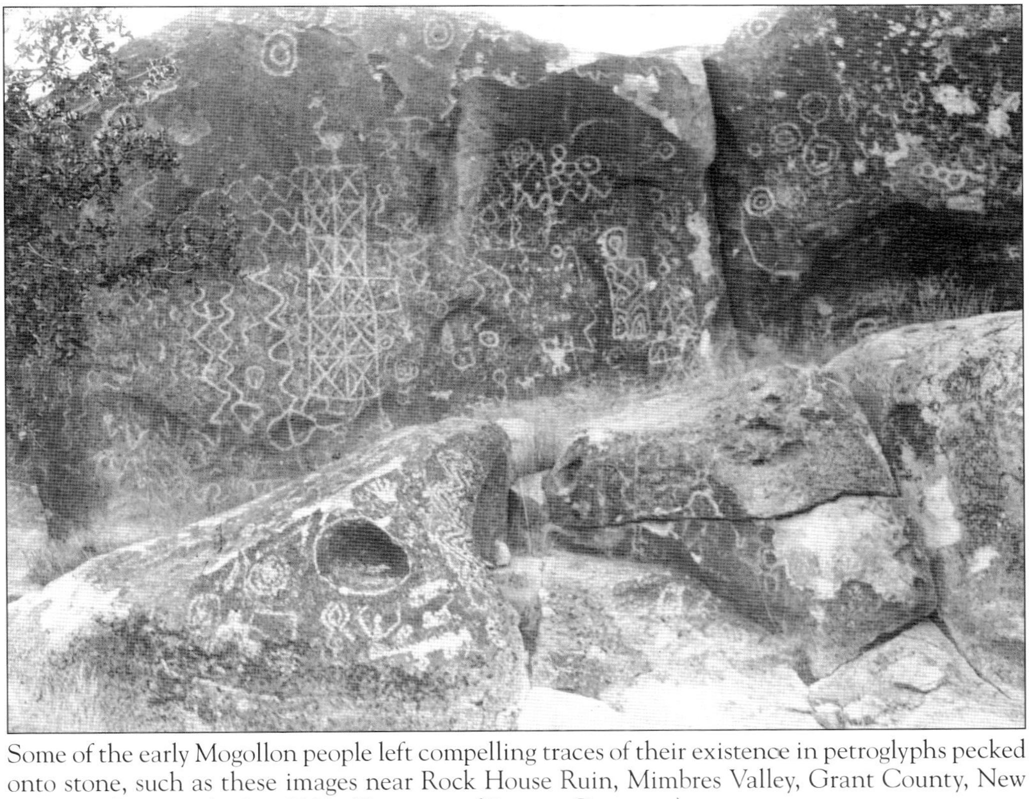

Some of the early Mogollon people left compelling traces of their existence in petroglyphs pecked onto stone, such as these images near Rock House Ruin, Mimbres Valley, Grant County, New Mexico, photographed in 1920. (Courtesy of Burton Cosgrove.)

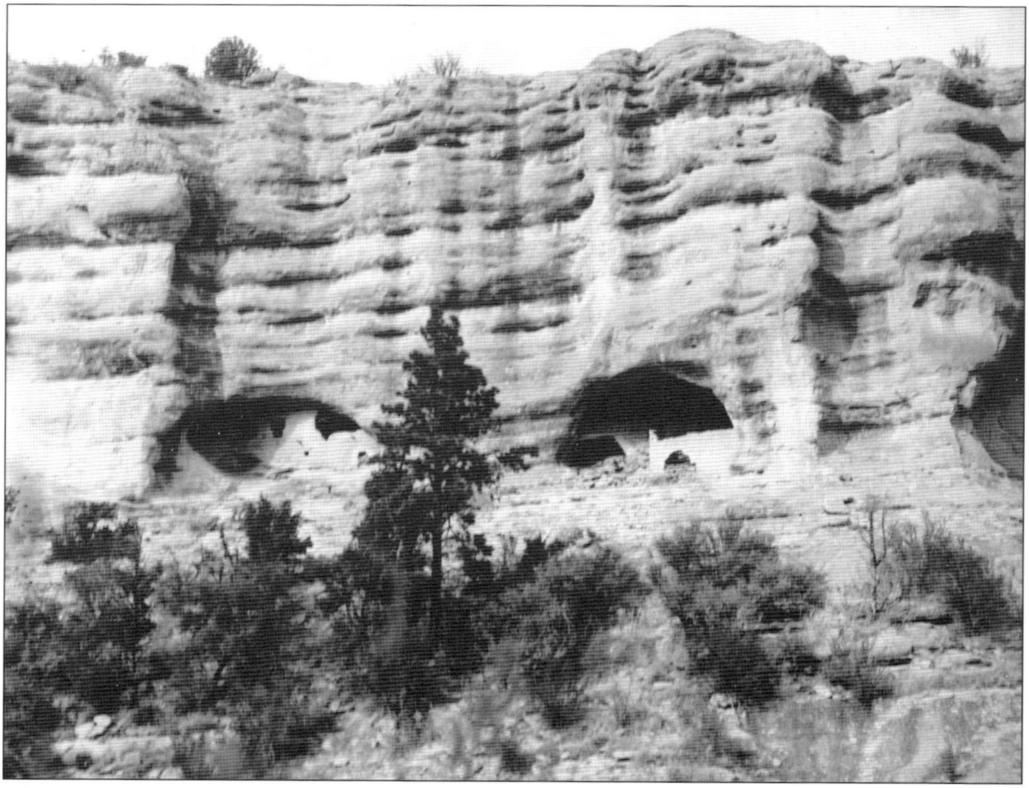

The Mogollon people built dwellings in natural caves in the cliffs formed by volcanic activity, called Gila Conglomerate. The Gila Cliff Dwellings on the West Fork of the Gila River (44 miles north of Silver City), were designated a national monument by Pres. Theodore Roosevelt in 1907. Approximately 40 mortared-rock rooms were constructed in the sheltered caves around 1270 A.D. and were abandoned by 1300 A.D. The Mogollon people farmed the land along the river, hunted game, and gathered local plants. They wove sandals of plaited yucca fibers and also wove mats and baskets. Reed cigarettes were found in the caves, as were macaw feathers from Mexico and many stone tools. (Above, courtesy of Burton Cosgrove; below, courtesy of Jean Eckard.)

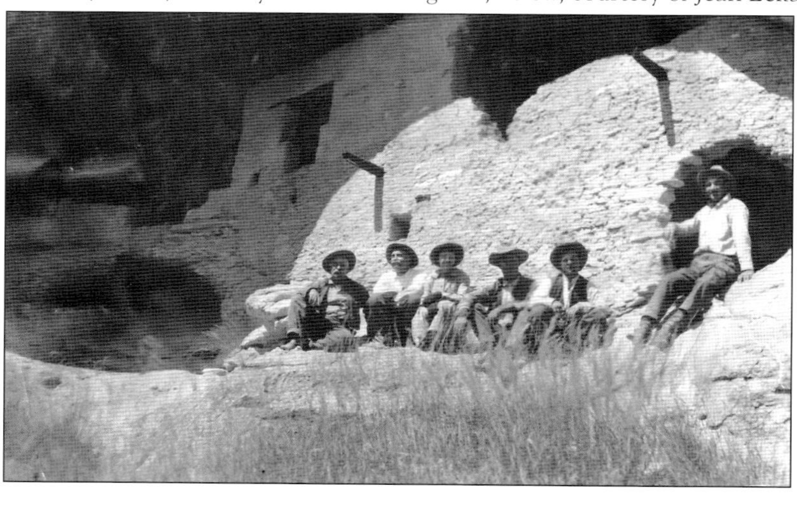

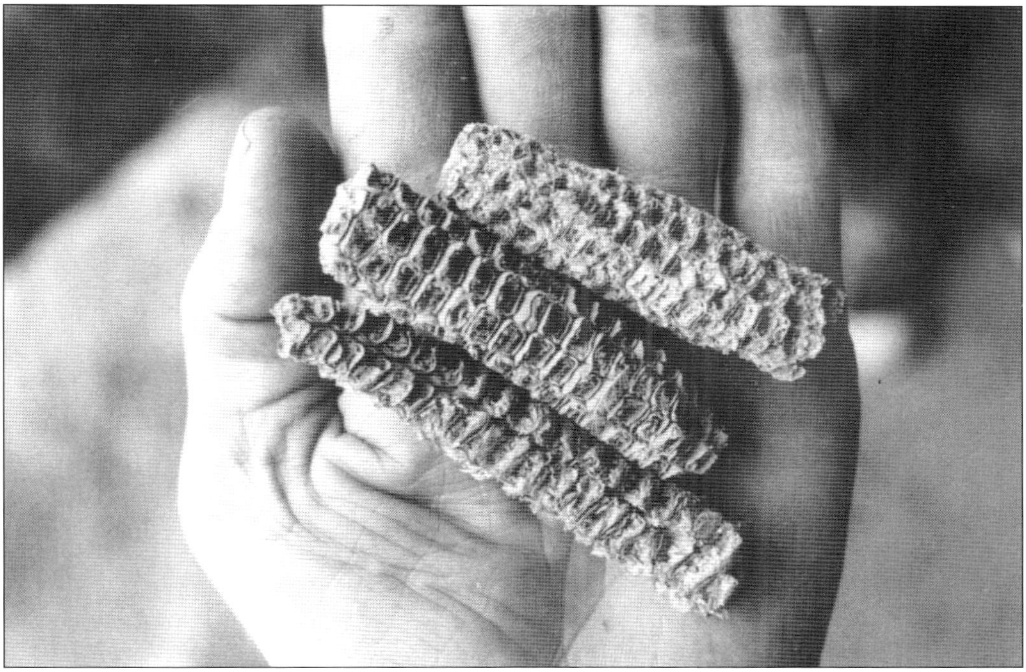

Ancient corncobs, left behind 600 years earlier, were found in a storage chamber in the Gila Cliff Dwellings by H.B. Ailman, the first visitor to record his trip to the site. He found the corncobs while searching through the abandoned rooms in 1878, and described them as being "very small, four to five inches long, and only in thickness about like your largest finger." Today, a visitor to the cliff dwellings may spy a rock storage bin filled with similar small corncobs. Below, many caves and rock shelters in the Gila country have traces of painted walls and evidence of ceremonial use. Other small ruins, rock walls, and storage chambers still exist in the canyons, evidence of an earlier people who walked these lands. (Above, courtesy of Gila Cliff Dwellings National Monument; below, courtesy of Burton Cosgrove.)

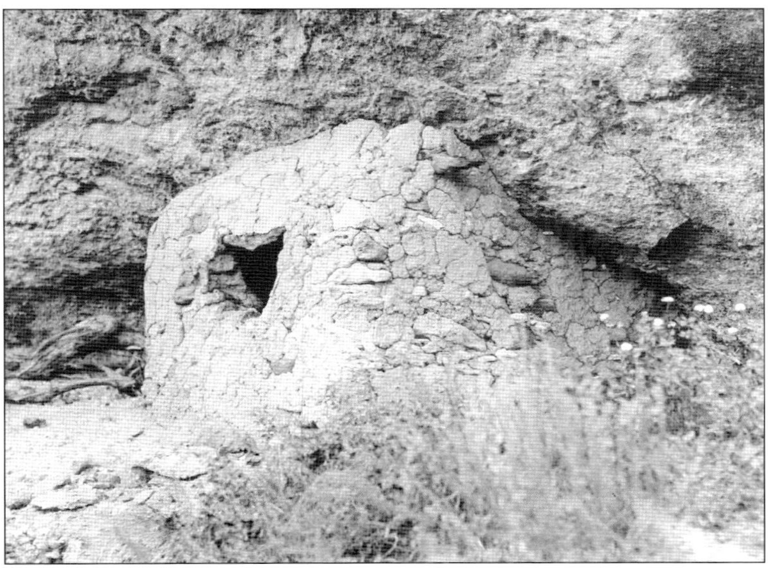

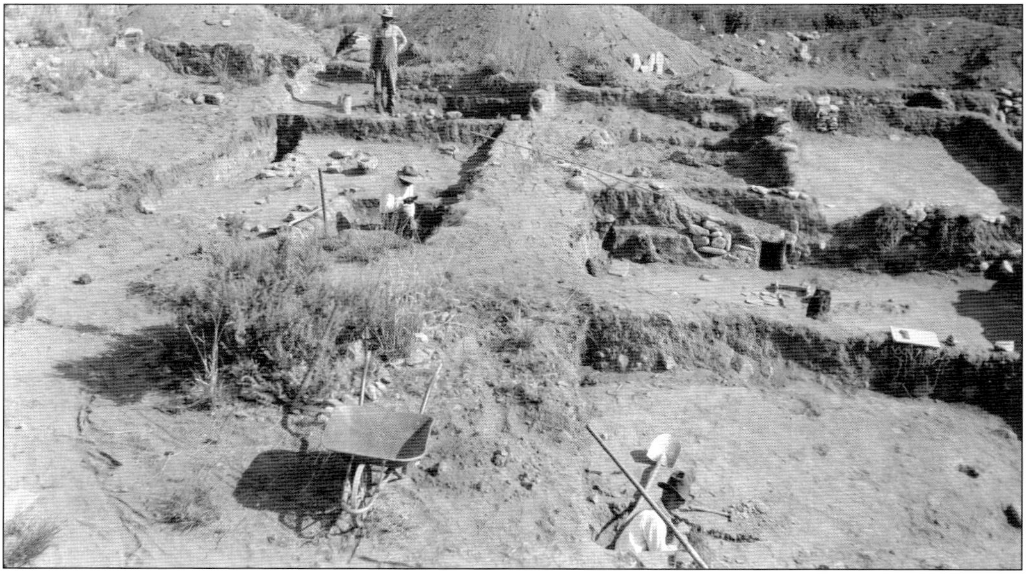

Silver City couple C. Burton Cosgrove and Harriet "Hattie" Cosgrove became interested in Mimbres archaeology in 1915, actively working to preserve and document local sites. They were hired in 1924 by the Peabody Museum at Harvard University to conduct excavations at Swarts Ruin in the Mimbres River valley. The Cosgroves worked at Swarts, pictured above, for five seasons; they also documented numerous ruins and rock-art sites in southwestern New Mexico and mapped the ceremonial caves of the upper Gila. (Both, courtesy of Burton Cosgrove.)

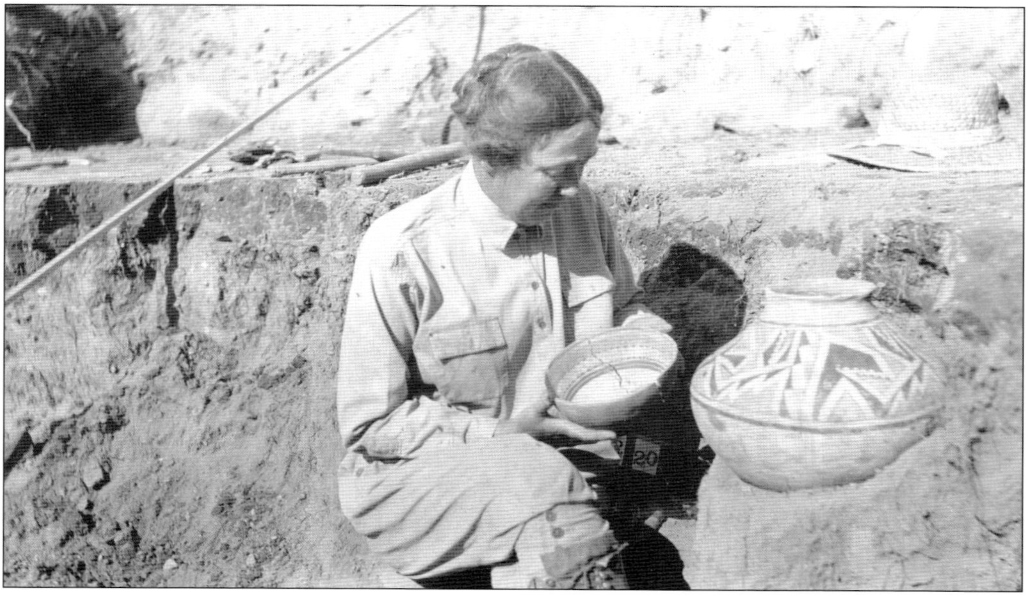

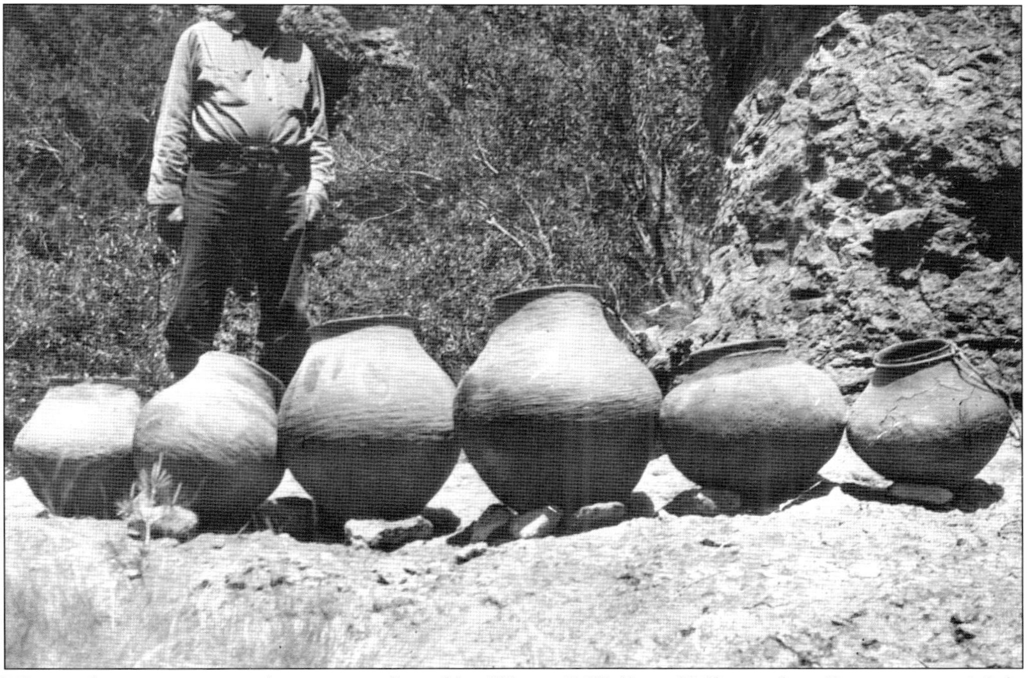

These plain-ware pots, above, were found by "Young" Wells in Yellowjacket Canyon near Mule Creek, northwest of Silver City. Pottery bowls found in Mimbres sites depict amazing black-and-white images of people, ceremonies, fish, animals, insects, and complex geometric designs. In addition to excavating Mimbres sites for the Peabody Museum, Harriet Cosgrove drew the images of hundreds of those excavated bowls, below, preserving forever the amazing life and art of the Mimbres people. The paintings discovered on Mimbres pottery are considered some of the finest examples of prehistoric art in North America. (Above, courtesy of Gila Cliff Dwellings National Monument; below, courtesy of Burton Cosgrove.)

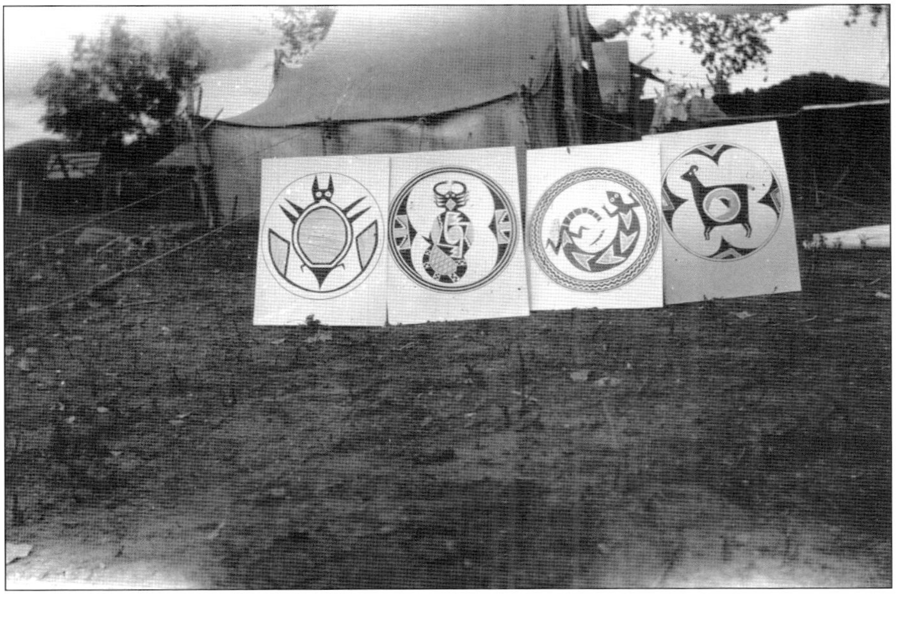

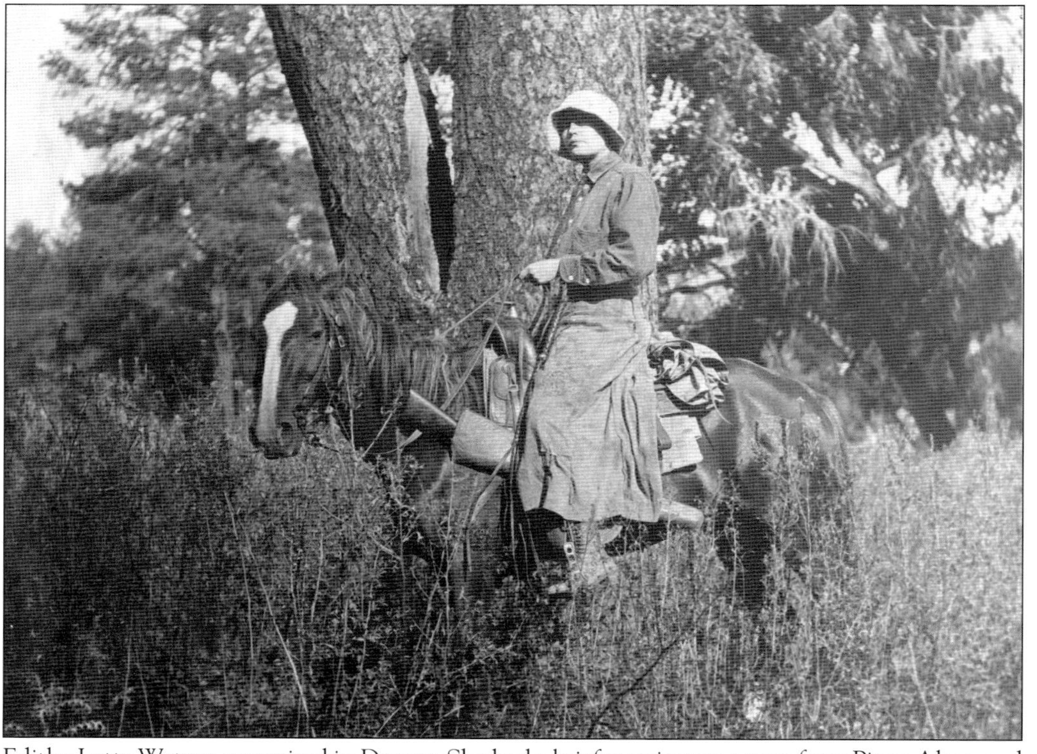

Editha Latta Watson was raised in Denver. She had a brief marriage to a man from Pinos Altos, and it was there that she developed a lifelong interest in Mimbres archaeology, spending hours exploring the Gila country. Her surviving notebooks are filled with photographs of ruins and drawings of Mimbres bowls. Later in her life, thanks to a friendship with anthropologist Ruth Underhill, Editha spent her career working with the Navajo tribe. Jesse Walter Fewkes, below, from the US National Museum, was an expert on the American Southwest. After his visit to the area in 1914, he wrote *Archaeology of the Lower Mimbres Valley*, an account of Mimbres art that introduced prehistoric Mimbres painting to the outside world. In 1922, Fewkes and his wife visited Editha in Pinos Altos, where they studied her photographs and collections. (Both, courtesy of Jean Eckard.)

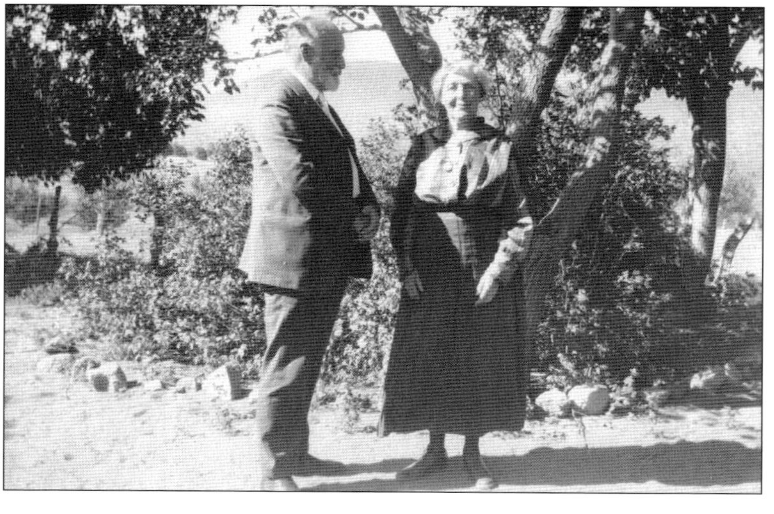

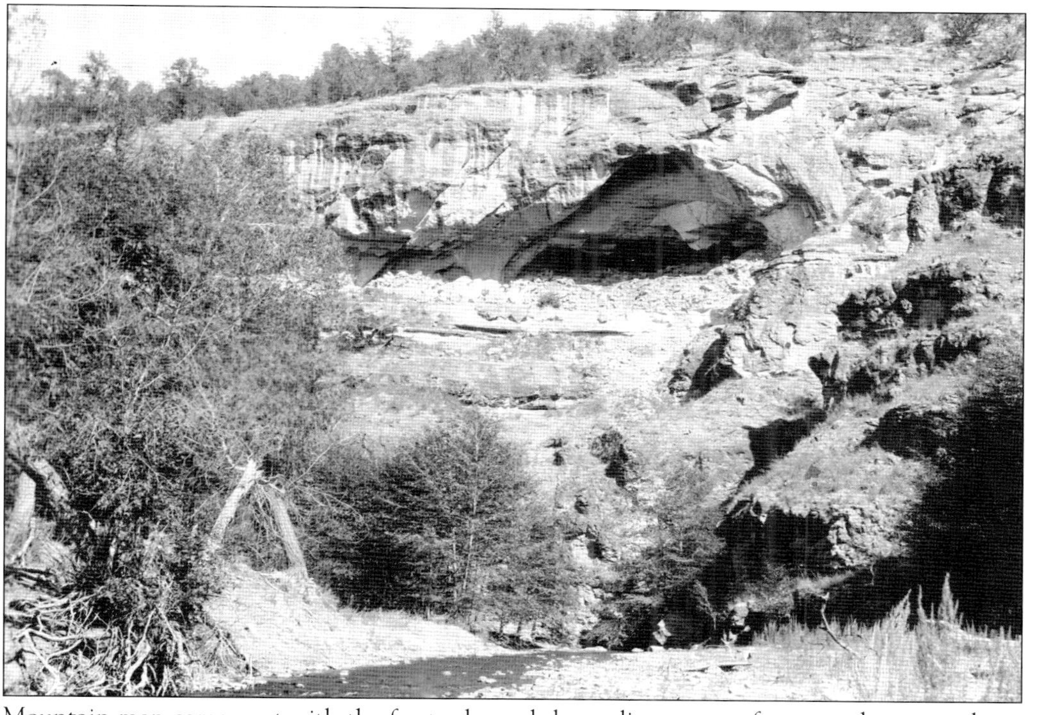

Mountain men came west with the fur trade, and the earliest group of trappers known to have arrived in the Gila included James Ohio Pattie, who trapped along the Gila River, above, in 1824. Pattie later wrote a book describing the trip, including encounters with a grizzly bear and a panther. On that ill-fated journey, the group lost their pelts and one member of their party to the Apaches. (Courtesy of Burton Cosgrove.)

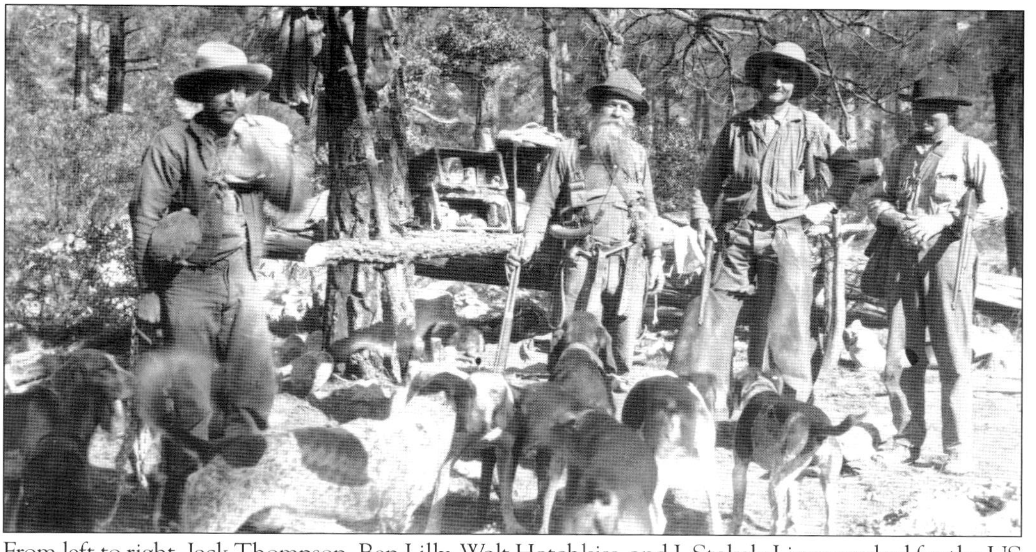

From left to right, Jack Thompson, Ben Lilly, Walt Hotchkiss, and J. Stokely Ligon worked for the US Biological Survey, mostly as predator hunters in the Gila Wilderness in 1920. Lilly, the bearded man, was a renowned bear and lion hunter who once guided Theodore Roosevelt on a bear hunt. He lived in the woods with his hounds, but never hunted on Sunday. (Courtesy of M.H. Salmon Collection.)

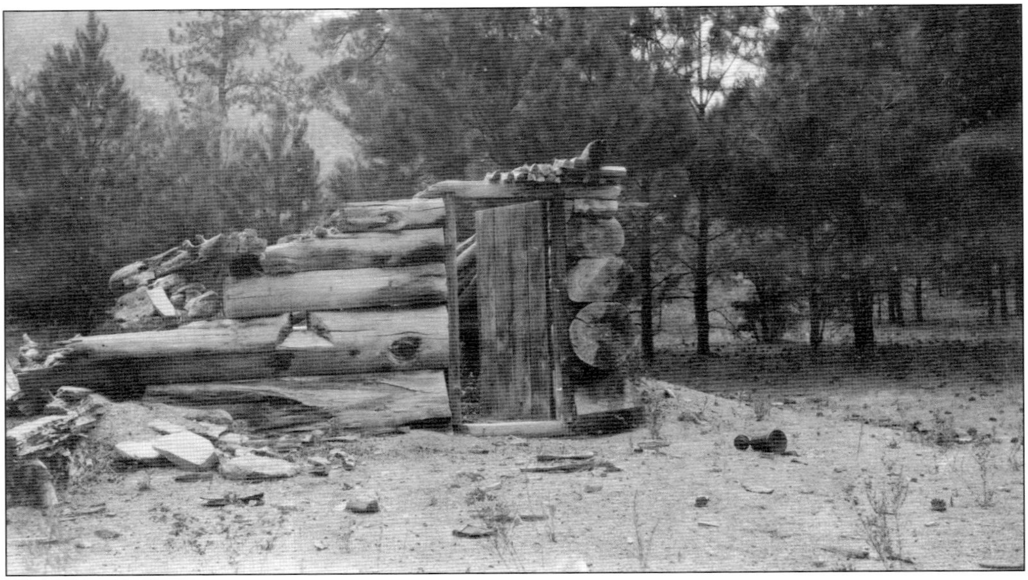

James "Bear" Moore arrived in southwestern New Mexico about 1880. In a fight with a grizzly bear, Moore defended himself with only a knife. He managed to kill the bear, but he also was left nearly dead, with one eye and half of his face and chest ripped away. He lived as a recluse in a cabin on the West Fork, above. The V-shaped hole to the left of the door was a rifle porthole, in case of Indian attacks. Moore hated grizzly bears, and he built massive log bear traps, like the one pictured below. In the winter of 1924, Moore fell and broke his leg. He burned all the downed trees within reach, but eventually, he froze. Cowboys found his bones the following spring and buried him under a piñon tree, carving his name on a rock at the head of his grave. (Both, courtesy of Ida Campbell.)

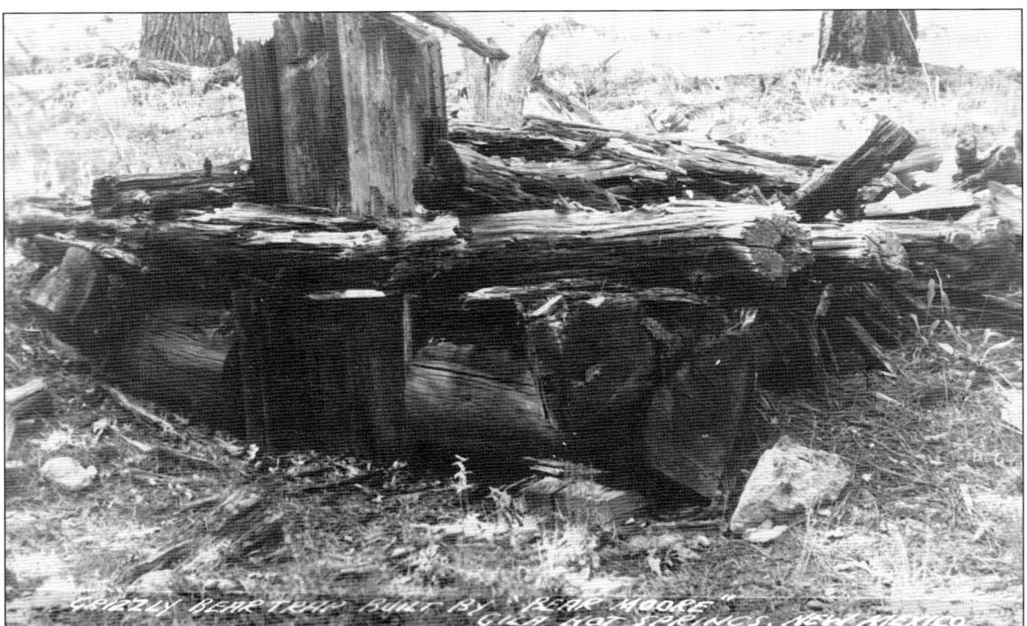

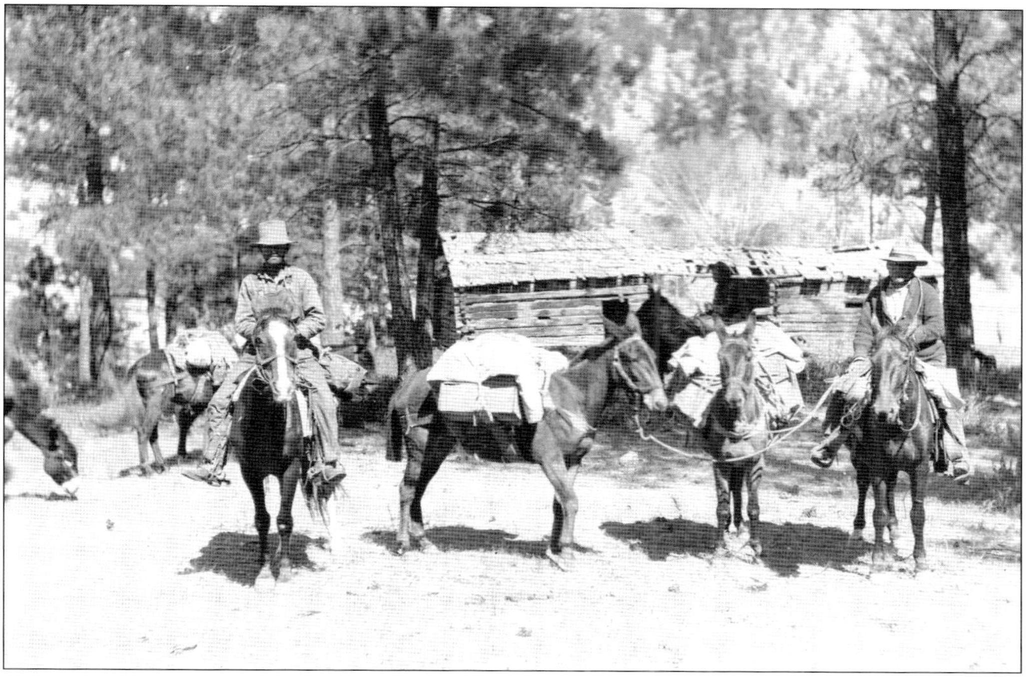

Jason Baxter came west in 1884, prospecting for gold. He built a cabin at the mouth of Double E Canyon on the West Fork of the Gila River (above, photographed by a member of the Dornbusch hunting party who camped near Baxter's cabin in 1914). The night before he was killed by Apaches, Baxter is said to have wondered, "What lies over on the other side." (Courtesy of Ida Campbell.)

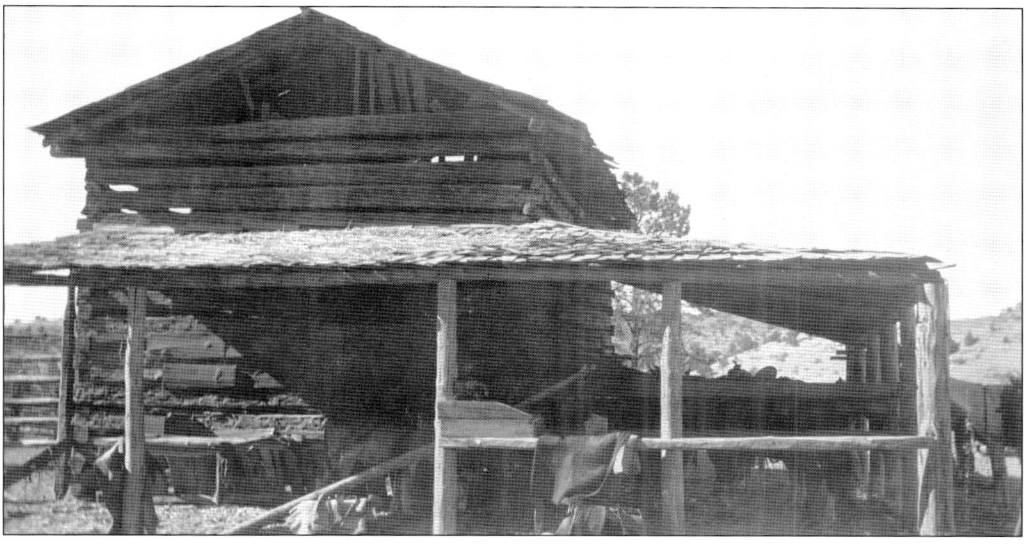

The McKenzie brothers built their cabin (later known as Jenks Cabin) at White Creek on the West Fork. By 1910, the structure was collapsing. It was here that Jason Baxter was killed by a band of Apaches, having stayed at the cabin alone the day his partners went fishing. The bullet that went through his body made a hole in the bean pot next to the campfire. (Courtesy of Jan Blackwell.)

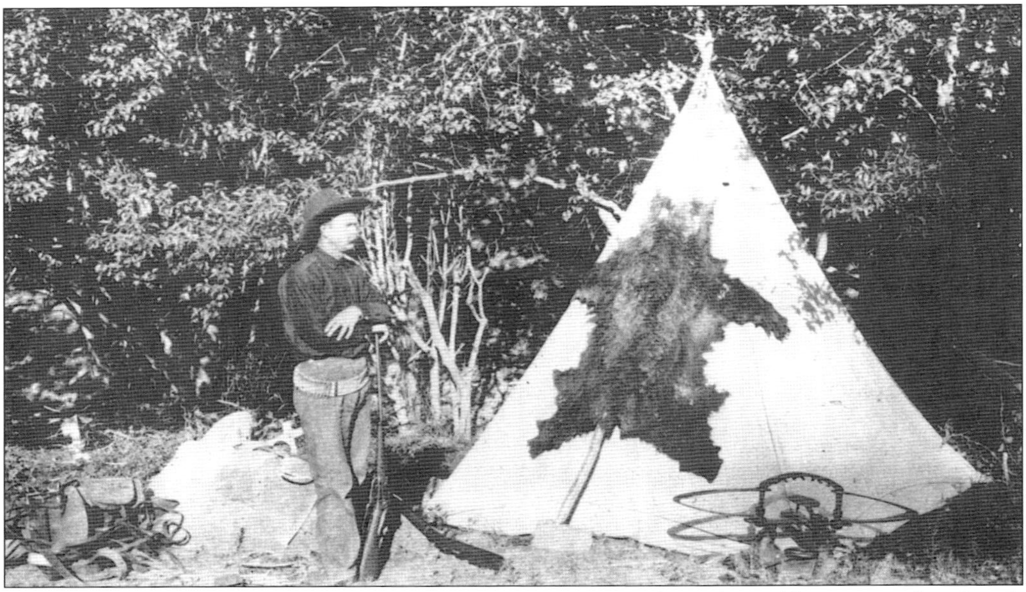

Nat Straw (1857–1941) was the last of the mountain men in the Gila Wilderness. He lived with the Navajos, prospected for gold, and hunted predators for sheep and cattle ranchers. Known as a likeable man, Straw's stories of his adventures and wilderness skills are legendary in the Gila, although the tale of his "saddle bear" he bridled and rode through the hills is sometimes looked upon with skepticism. (Courtesy of Ellen McFarland Saige.)

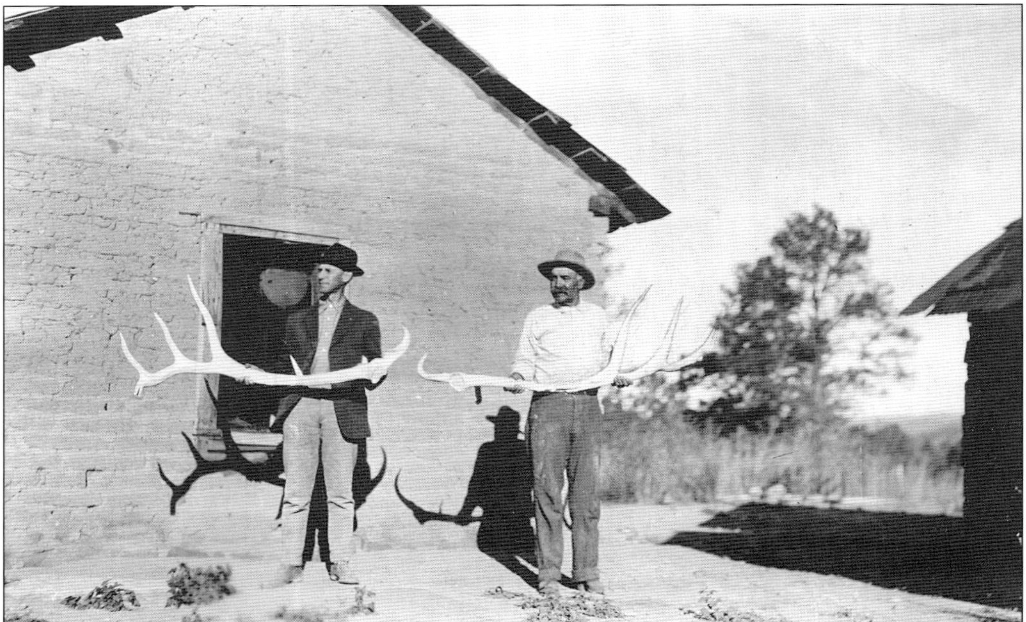

Mr. Glenn and Moss Watson hold the antlers from a Merriam's elk at TJ Ranch at the confluence of the West and Middle Forks of the Gila River. Merriam's elk were believed to be extinct by 1906, and only three pairs of shed antlers are known to exist. This type of elk had a smaller body and larger antlers than did the Yellowstone elk introduced in 1913. (Courtesy of Ida Campbell.)

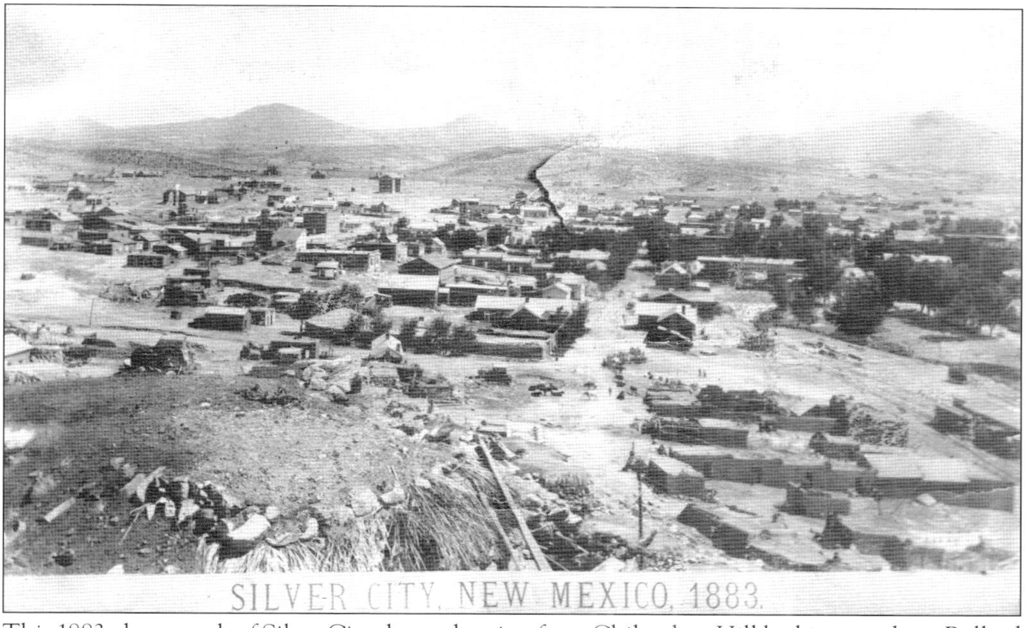

This 1883 photograph of Silver City shows the view from Chihuahua Hill looking north on Bullard Street. To the lower right is Lorenzo Carrasco's hacienda and smelter, enclosed with an adobe wall. Carrasco had mining experience in Chihuahua, Mexico, and knew about smelting silver with adobe furnaces. He produced the first silver bullion in the area. (Courtesy of Jan Blackwell.)

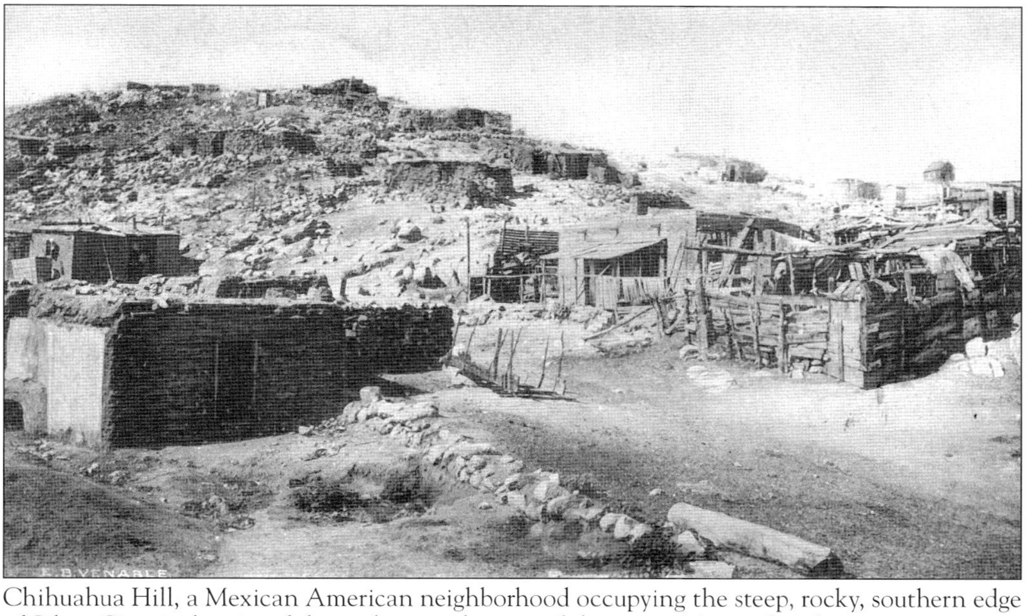

Chihuahua Hill, a Mexican American neighborhood occupying the steep, rocky, southern edge of Silver City, is the site of the earliest settlement of the town. Many of its first structures were built from stone laid in adobe mortar, eventually enlarged using adobe bricks. Mexican American residents, far outnumbering Anglo settlers in the town's early years, lived throughout Silver City and were involved in local businesses, mining, freighting, and ranching.

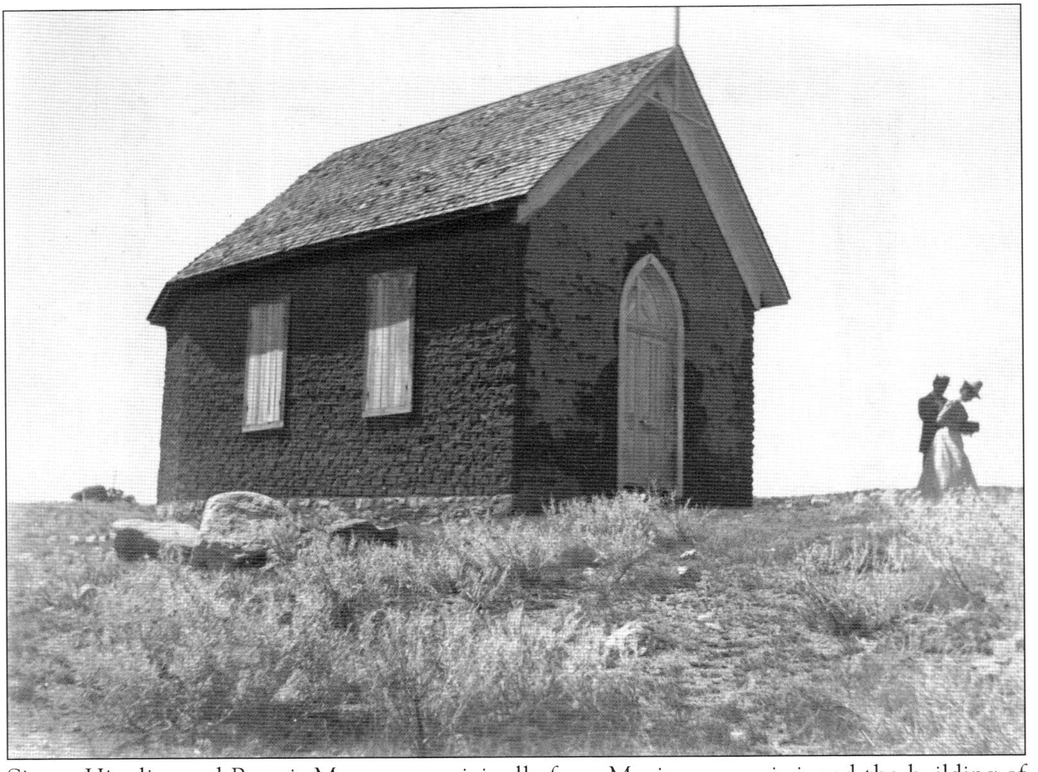

Sisters Hipolita and Beatriz Manquero, originally from Mexico, commissioned the building of La Capilla on Chihuahua Hill, overlooking Silver City. The little chapel, built in 1885, held a statue of the Virgin of Guadalupe, but it was never consecrated. Nevertheless, La Capilla was an important focus of devotion for neighborhood residents until its demolition in 1915. (Courtesy of Jean Uhli.)

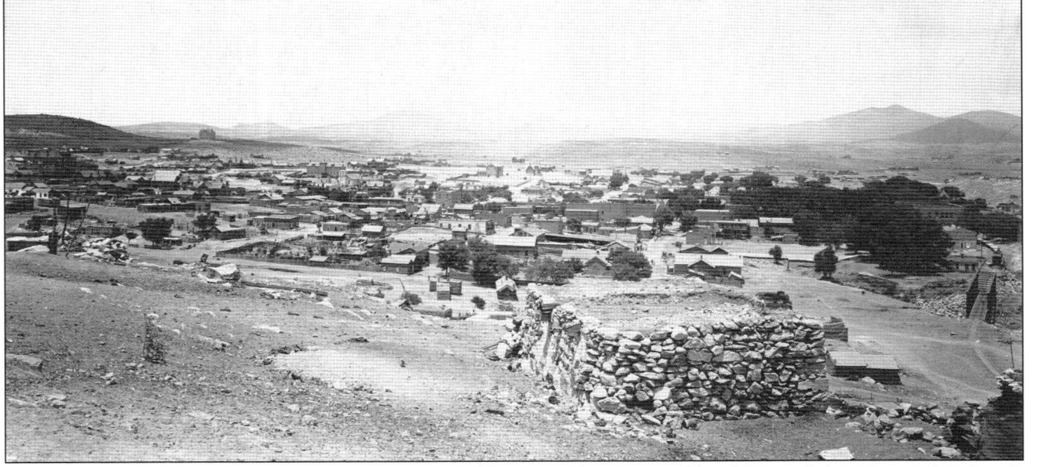

In this 1900 northward view of Silver City, Old Main, the original building of the Normal School, is the large building on the hill to the left. The Tenderfoot Corral, with its barns and stables, is just above the stone house on Chihuahua Hill. The town's early red-light district is to the left of the corral, and the railroad bridge is visible at the right. (Courtesy of Jan Blackwell.)

Two

Apache Country

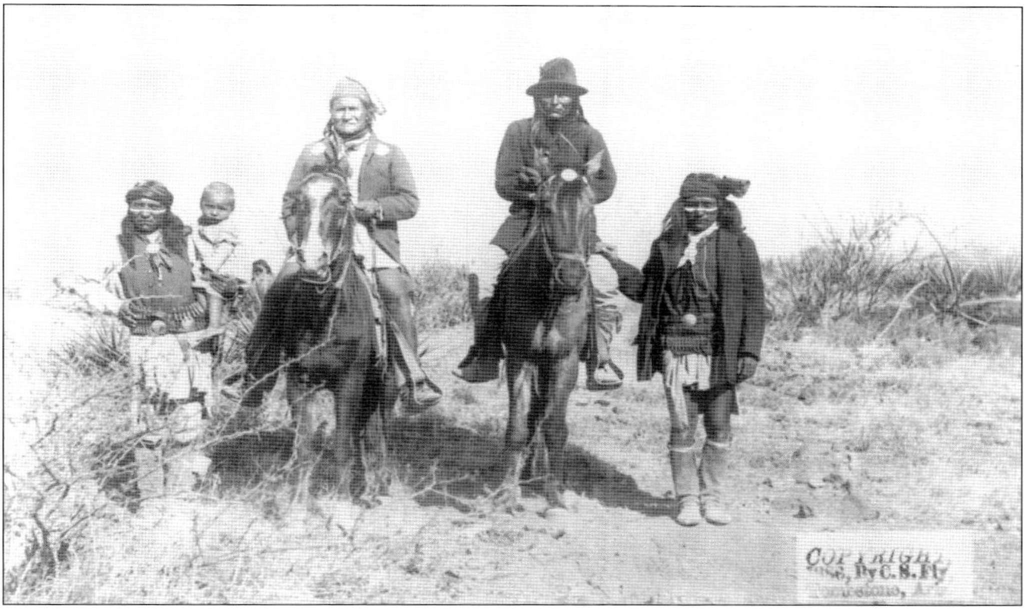

The Apache chief Geronimo was born near the headwaters of the Gila River about 1829. After years of fighting and defending his land, he surrendered to General Crook in 1886. Geronimo is mounted on the horse to the left, and his son Perico stands at his side. Naiche, second son of Geronimo, is riding the horse to the right. Geronimo died a captive at Fort Sill, Oklahoma, after being denied numerous requests to be allowed to return to his beloved Southwest. (Courtesy of the Library of Congress.)

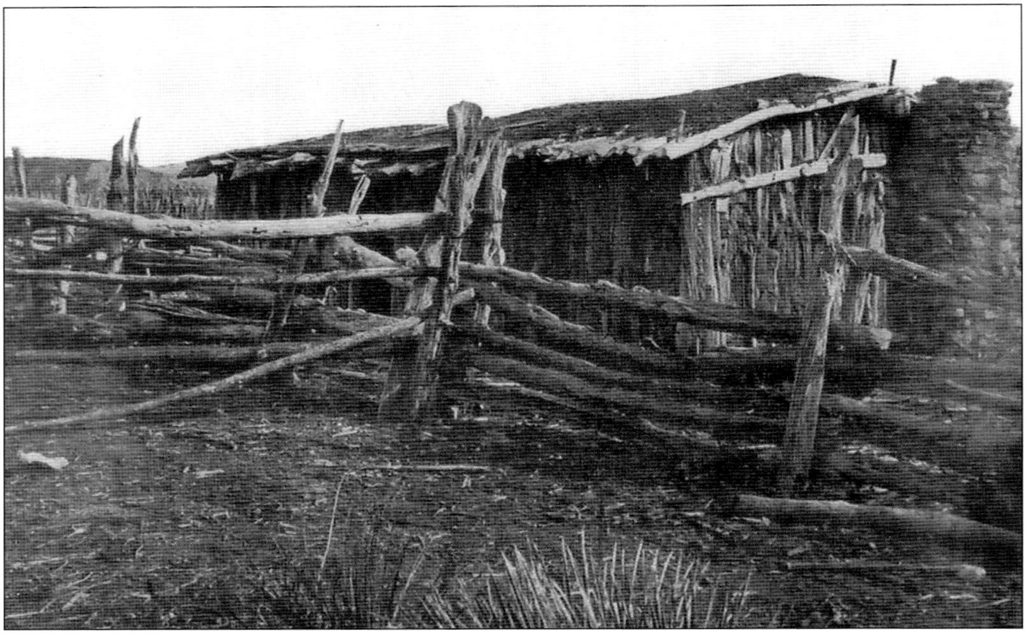

In the spring of 1880, settlers north of Silver City were warned that Victorio's Apaches were riding toward the rural settlement of Alma. The families of James Meader and John Roberts barricaded themselves inside the Roberts cabin during a 36-hour siege. Men from Silver City and Fort Bayard arrived after encountering the bodies of several of Victorio's victims. James C. Cooney had been a sergeant at Fort Bayard. He discovered silver ore on Mineral Creek in 1875 and returned to establish a claim when his enlistment was up. Cooney was killed in the 1880 Apache raid when he rode from Alma to warn miners on Mineral Creek. He was interred where he fell, inside an enormous boulder that was hollowed-out with dynamite and sealed with ore from his Silver Bar Mine. (Above, image from *The Fort Bayard Story 1866–1899*; below, courtesy of Jan Blackwell.)

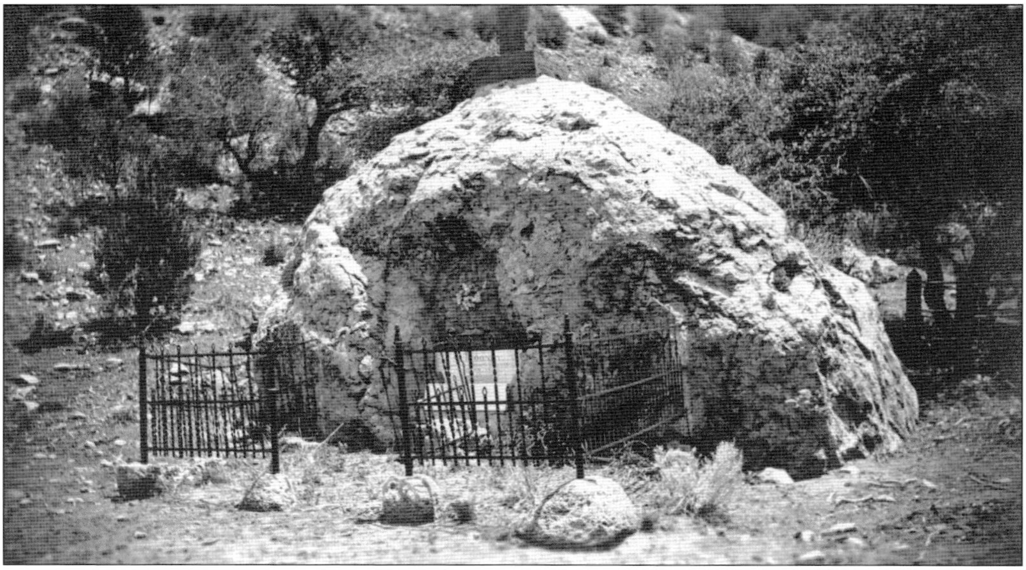

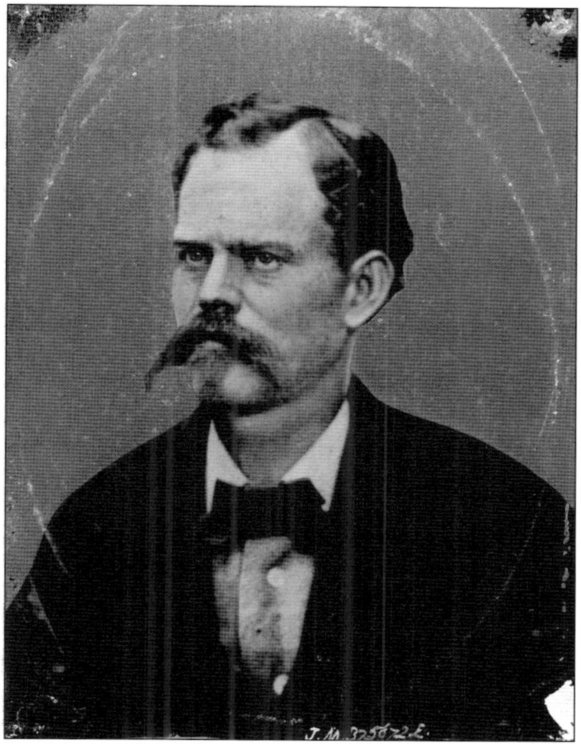

James Bullard (below) and his brother John (right) were two of the original founders of Silver City. John, who had been farming in the area, is credited with discovering silver there in 1870, and James is credited with naming Silver City. With their mining partners, the Bullards were original owners of the Legal Tender Mine. When Apaches stole some horses from Harvey Whitehill's corral in February 1871, John led a group in pursuit. During the battle, he was "shot through the heart" and killed. James sent a lock of his brother's hair to his parents in Missouri, and he always kept the scalp from the Apache who shot John. (Right, image from *The Fort Bayard Story 1866–1899* and courtesy of W.E. Bullard; below, courtesy of the Haley Memorial Library and History Center.)

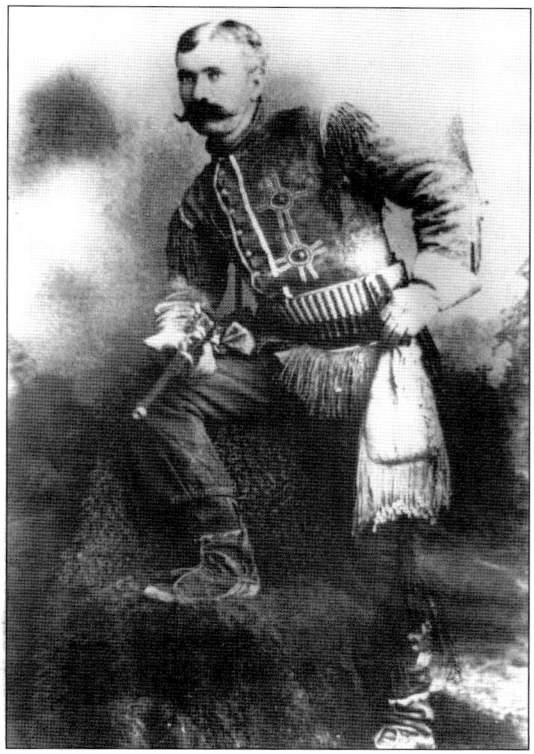

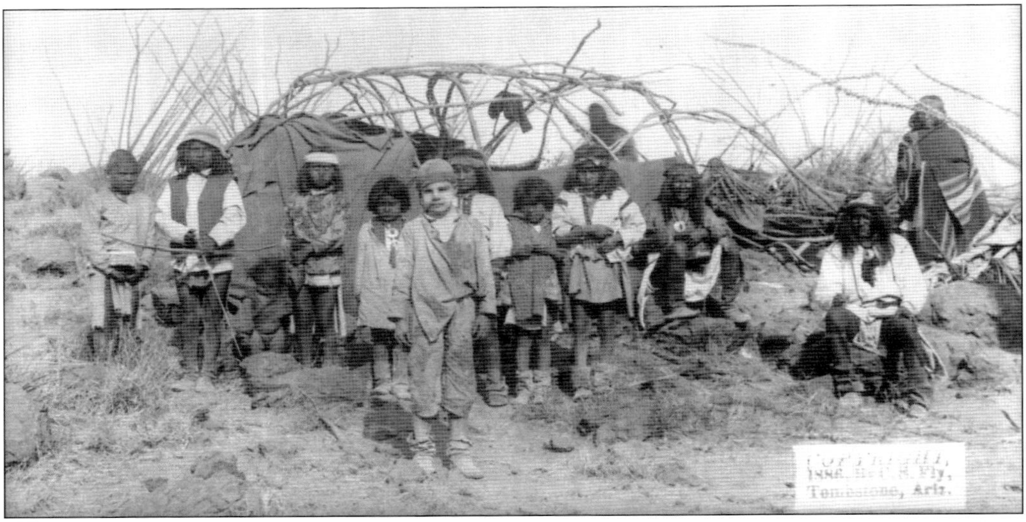

On a September day in 1885, a Geronimo-led band of Apaches raided John McKinn's ranch in the Mimbres Valley. McKinn's oldest son was killed with an axe blow, and ten-year-old Jimmy "Santiago" (shown in front) was kidnapped and taken into Mexico. Jimmy was rescued the following March by Gen. George Crook, but he seldom spoke of his time with the Apaches. He died in Phoenix, Arizona, in 1941. (Courtesy of the Library of Congress.)

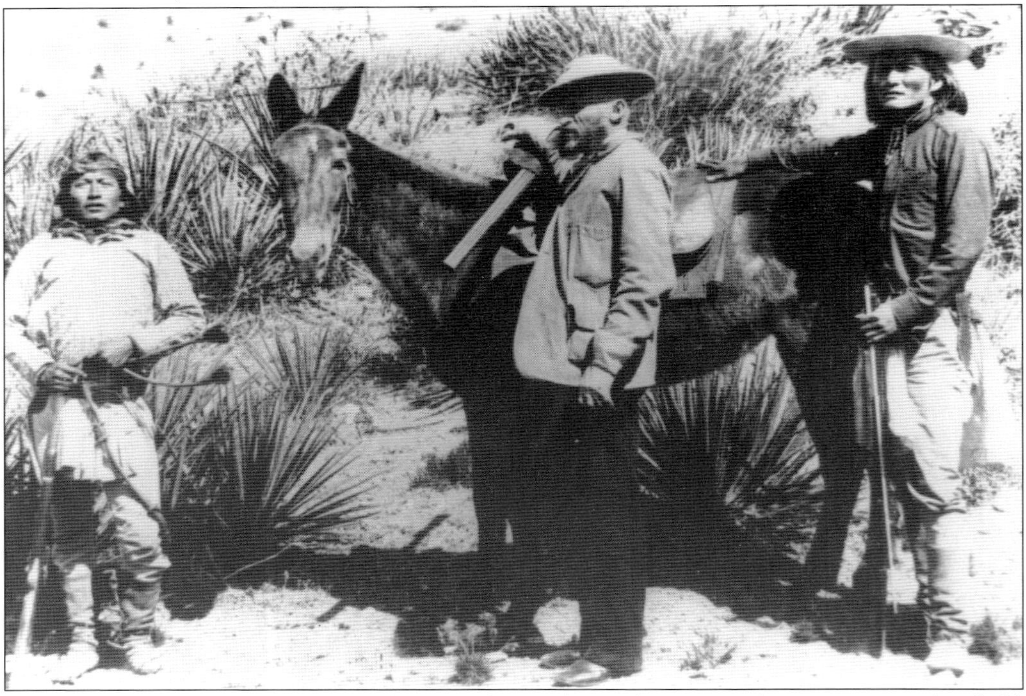

Gen. George Crook—with his mule named Apache and two Apache scouts, Dutchy (left) and Alchise (right)—pursued the Apache raiders. Crook briefly captured Geronimo's band when he rescued Jimmy McKinn, but the Apaches escaped to continue their fight until their surrender to Gen. Nelson Miles in September 1886. (Courtesy of the Haley Memorial Library and History Center.)

Silver City attorney Hamilton McComas and his wife, Juniata, rented a buggy on March 27, 1883, intending to visit a mining company near Lordsburg after an overnight stop at Mountain Home in the Burro Mountains, south of Silver City. Their six-year-old son Charley went along with them, while their two older daughters stayed behind. The McComases, armed only with a Winchester rifle, were ambushed near Thompson Canyon, south of Silver City, by a band of Apaches led by Chato. Hamilton and Juniata were killed, and the Apaches took Charley with them as they fled to the Sierra Madres. The search for Charley never ended; there were reports in later years of sightings of Apaches led by a blond, blue-eyed man. (Right, courtesy of *The Fort Bayard Story 1866–1899*; below, courtesy of the Haley Memorial Library and History Center.)

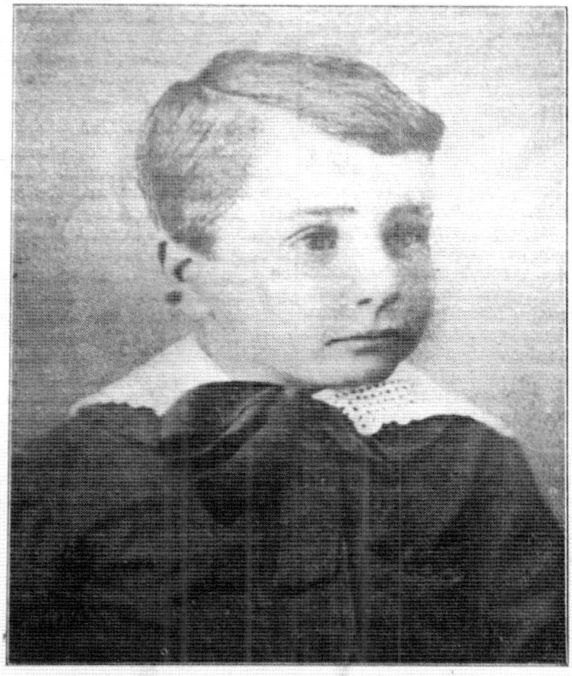

CHARLIE McCOMAS,
Captured By "Chatto's" Band of Apaches, March 29, 1883.

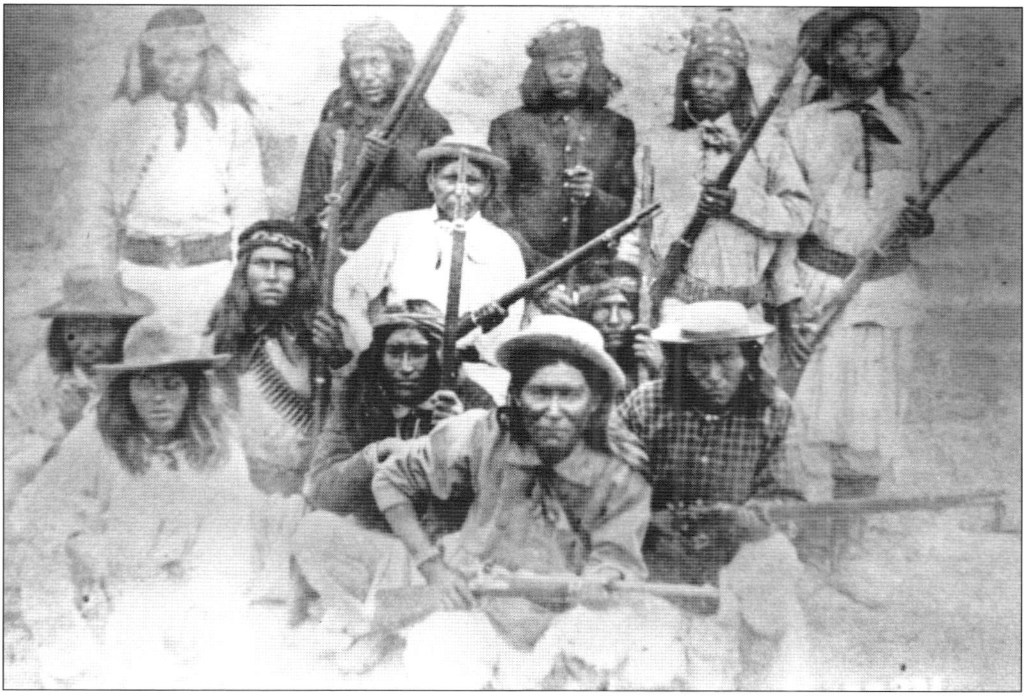

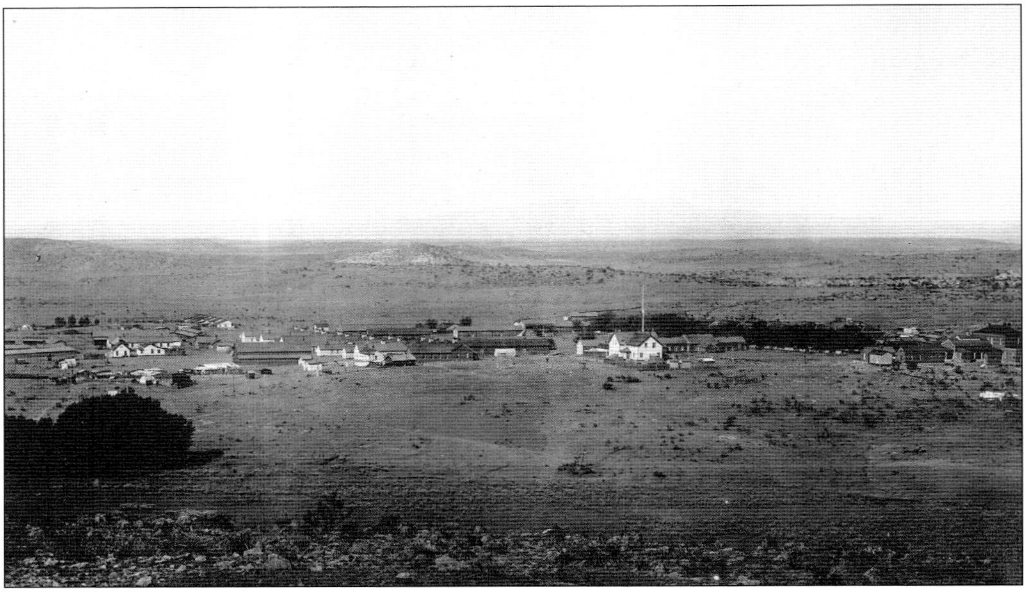

In response to repeated Apache attacks on miners and settlers, Fort Bayard was strategically located east of the mining camp at Pinos Altos (and eight miles east of Silver City). The post was established in 1866 and was manned by troops of the 125th United States Colored Infantry, the buffalo soldiers. Upon their arrival in the Southwest, soldiers initially lived in tents, later moving into log huts with dirt-covered flat roofs. The adobe sally port (seen below with soldiers in formation and a covered canon to the left) was one of the earliest buildings at the Army post. Fort Bayard has been in continuous use since 1866; today, it is a National Historic Landmark. (Both, courtesy of Dillon Stone.)

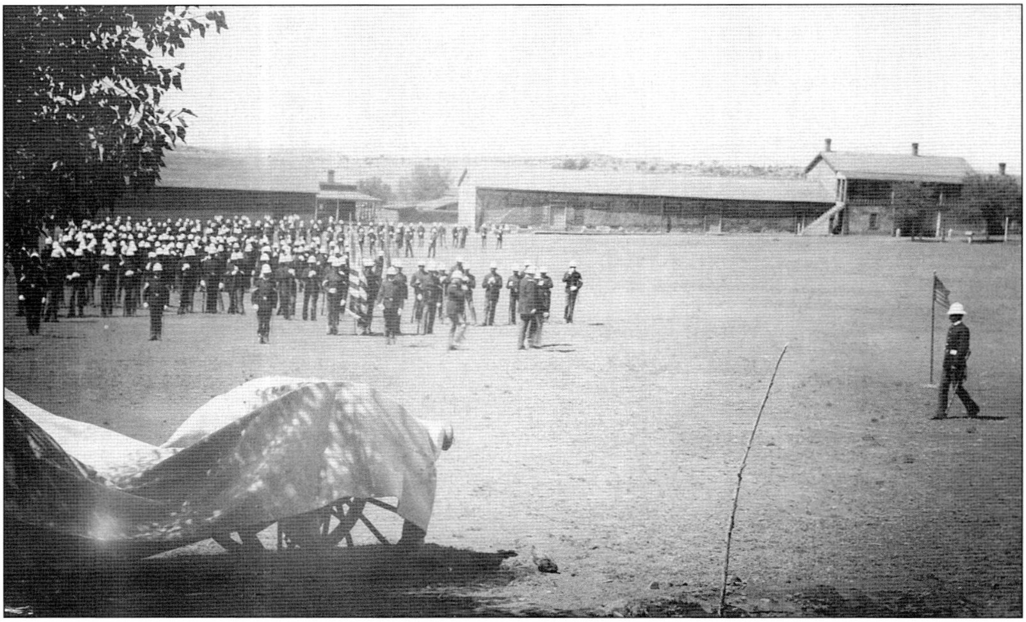

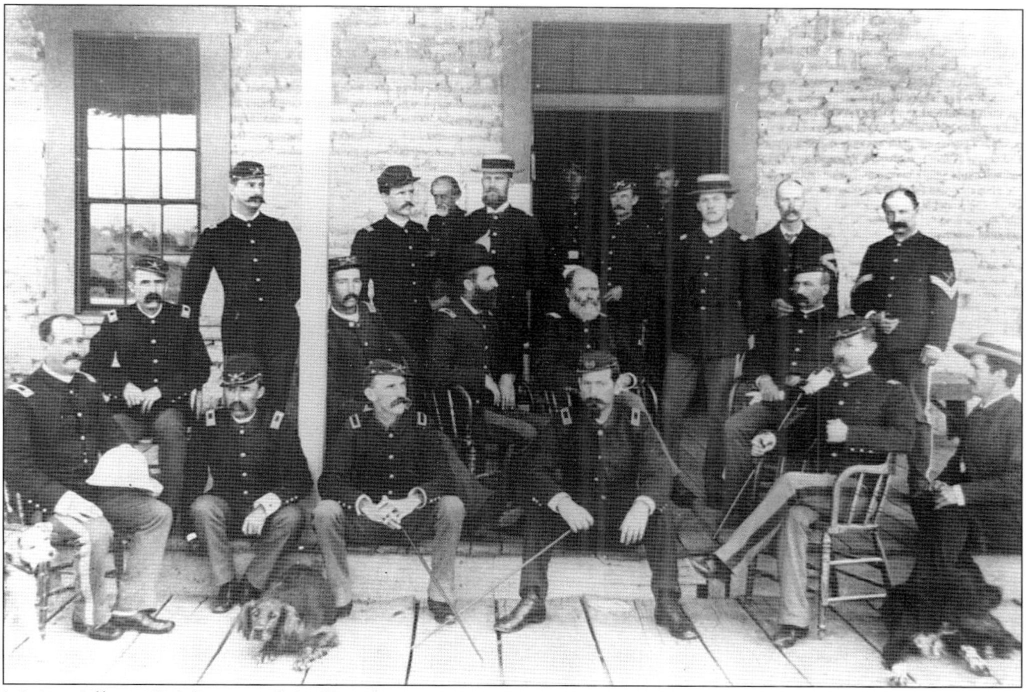

Major Albert P. Morrow, 9th Cavalry (seated in the chair to the far right), took over the command of Fort Bayard in 1876 and was head of all the military troops in southern New Mexico. Although he suffered from asthma, Morrow spent much time in the field and ordered his troops to relentlessly pursue the bands of raiding Apaches. (Courtesy of the Haley Memorial Library and History Center.)

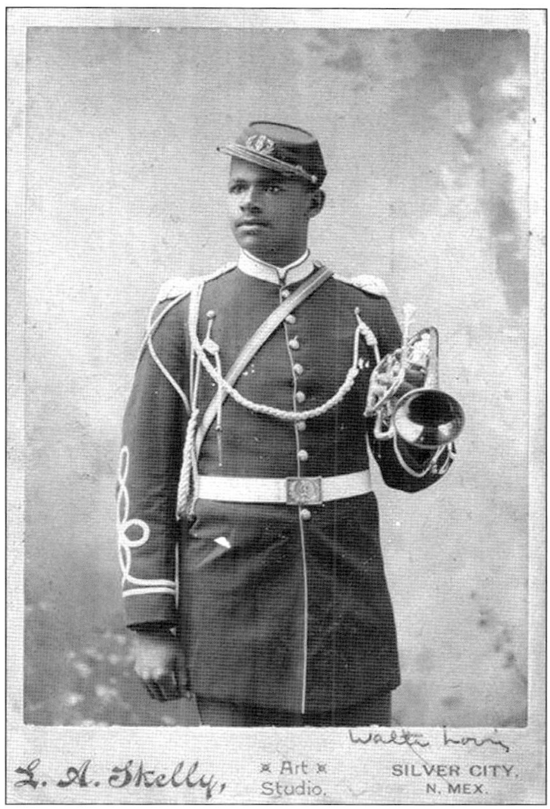

Walter Loving, an accomplished musician, was said to have had "extraordinary musical talent." He was stationed at Fort Bayard in 1893 as band director and later went to the Philippines, where he rose to lieutenant colonel and organized regimental bands. He retired after serving five decades in the military, but was captured and killed in Manila by Japanese troops during World War II. (Courtesy of Fort Bayard Historic Preservation Society.)

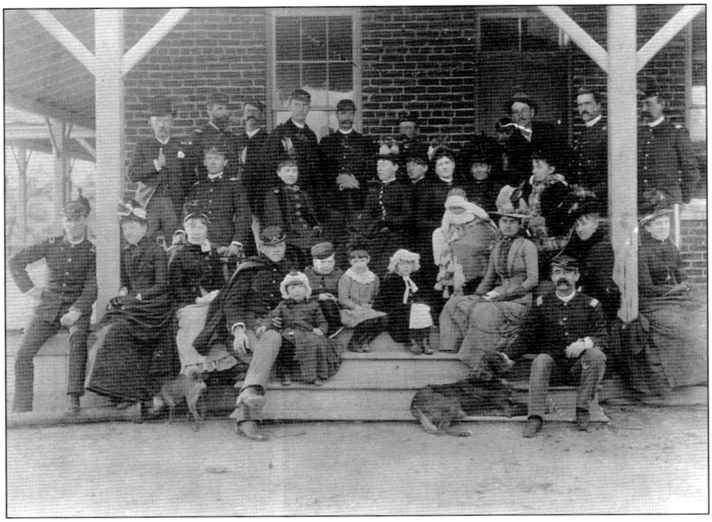

John "Black Jack" Pershing's first assignment after graduation from West Point in 1866 was at Fort Bayard. His first expedition into the mountains with Troop L was scouting for the Apache chief Mangas Coloradas. In this photograph, Lieutenant Pershing is sitting on the left side of the steps with his legs crossed. He later became a celebrated general in the US Army. (Image from *The Fort Bayard Story 1866–1899*.)

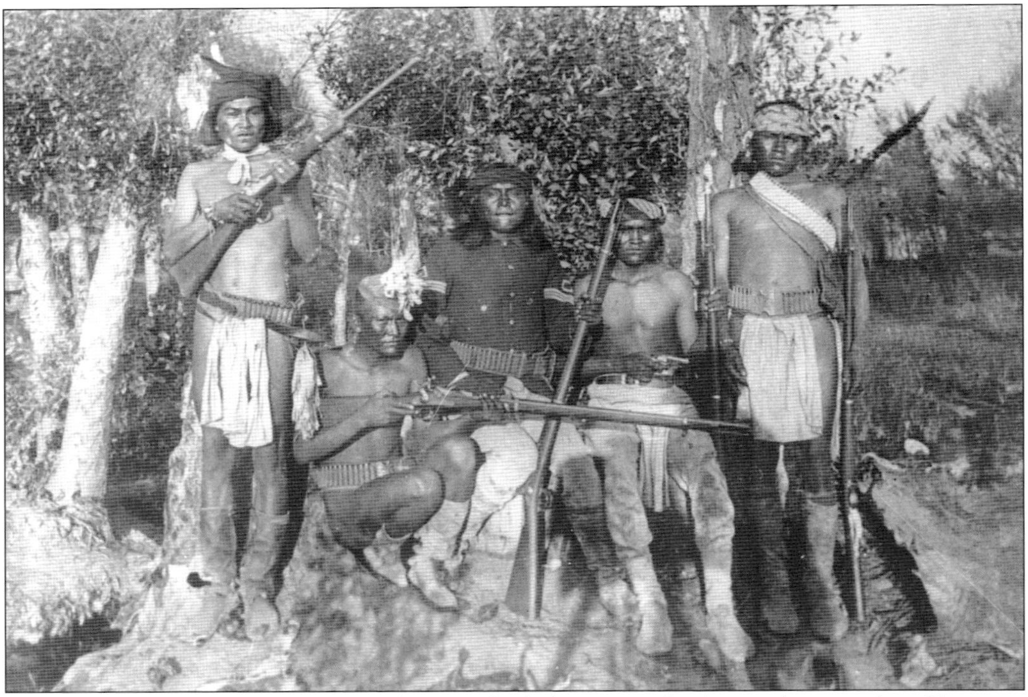

These White Mountain Apaches, photographed about 1881 by Army photographer Christian Barthelmess, volunteered to serve as scouts and were attached to the 10th Cavalry at Fort Bayard. Although they were given uniforms, they were allowed to dress as they pleased, as reflected by the mix of military and Apache garb seen here. (Courtesy of Fort Bayard Historic Preservation Society.)

Three

ONE BIG MINING CAMP

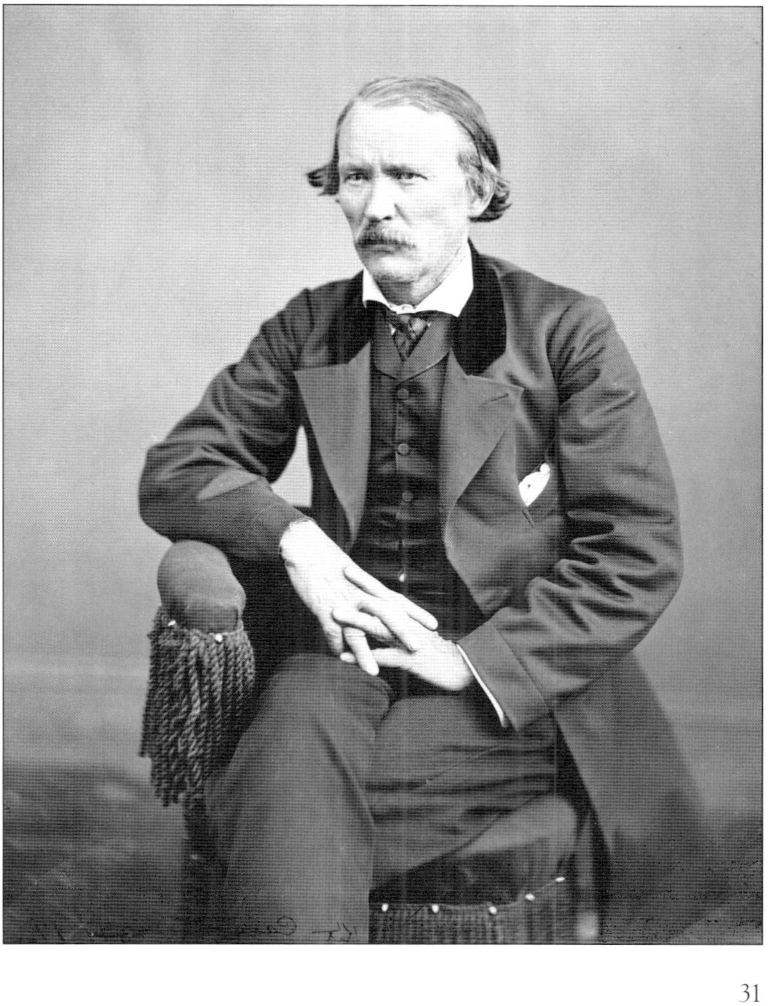

Christopher "Kit" Carson was hired by Robert McKnight in 1828 to drive a team of horses at the Santa Rita mines. Carson went on to become a famous, although controversial, frontiersman, trapper, and guide. As an Indian fighter and mountain man, he was portrayed as a hero in many dime novels. He fought in both the Mexican-American War and the Civil War and was brevetted a general. (Courtesy of the Library of Congress.)

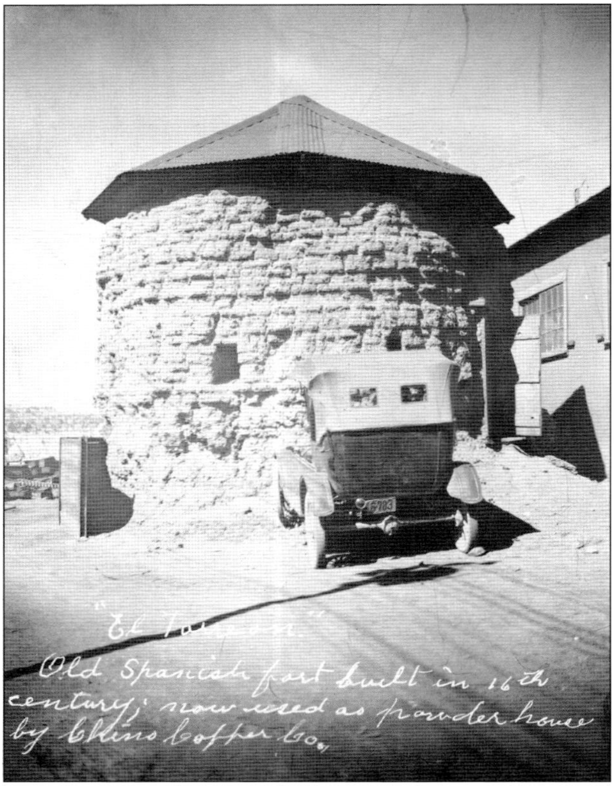

Copper was discovered in Santa Rita in 1799, although archaeological research indicates that prehistoric Indians made copper bells for trade from the outcrops. Beginning around 1804, ore shipments were carried on mules to Chihuahua, Mexico, where the copper was made into coins. In the 1830s, Mexican miners built a triangular adobe fort with a round tower in each corner, both to retain prisoners being used as laborers and to provide protection from the Apaches. Pictured at left around 1913, the last remaining tower, "El Torreon," was used for dynamite storage by the recently formed Chino Copper Company. The adobe structure was dismantled in 1951. Below, the tower is visible in this 1906 Santa Rita photograph. The Romero Mine workings can be seen in the center right, the site of the original native copper discovery.

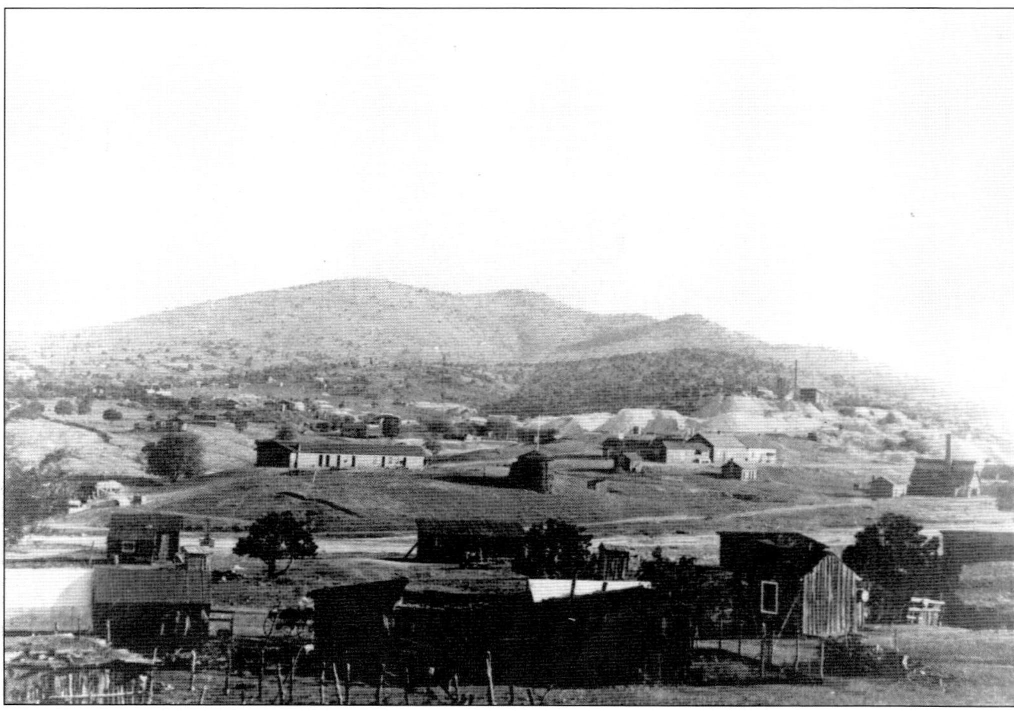

Churn drills were the first step in mining copper at Santa Rita. These Cyclone gasoline drills pounded holes into the ore body for sampling and blasting. The holes were filled with dynamite and, after being exploded, the loose rock could be loaded into railroad cars using steam shovels. Churn drills were also used for prospecting, and Chino Copper Company drillers worked 12-hour shifts in 1912, earning $5.25 per shift.

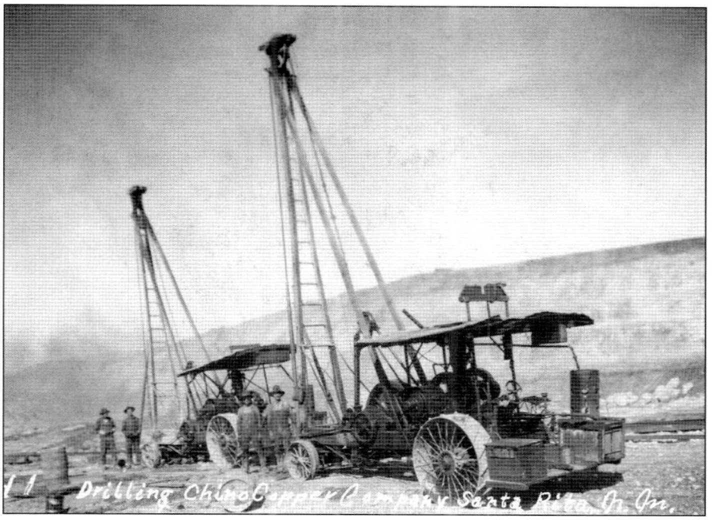

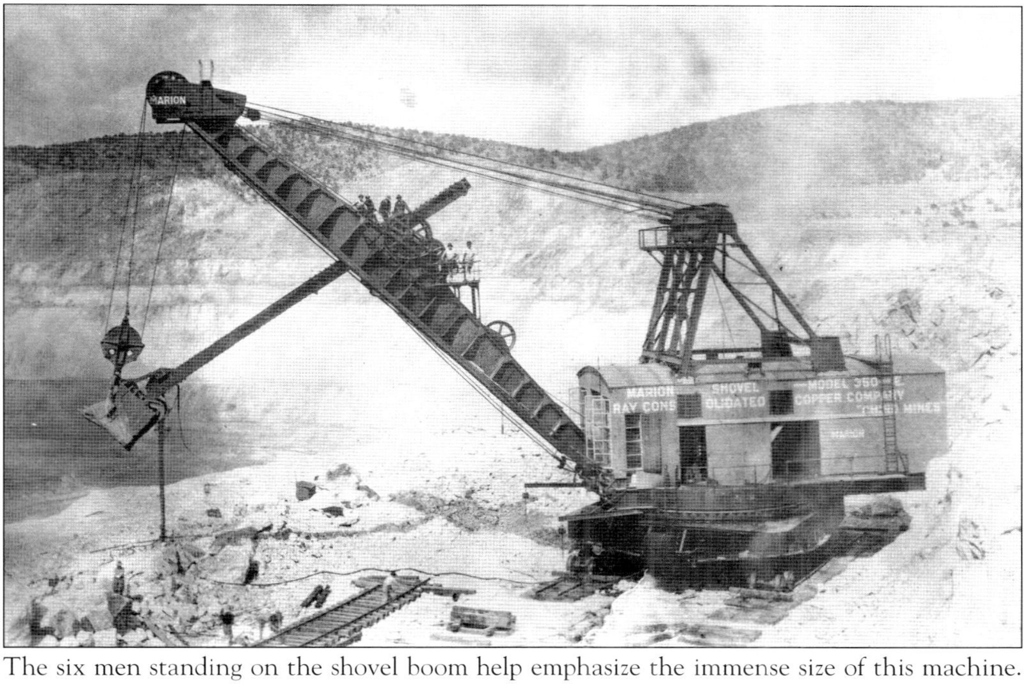

The six men standing on the shovel boom help emphasize the immense size of this machine. The Marion Model 350 shovel, purchased in 1924, had an 80-foot boom and could load railroad cars on the level above the working area. It had an eight-yard bucket and was the first electric shovel used by the Chino Copper Company. Mounted on two sets of wheel trucks, it required a double railroad track.

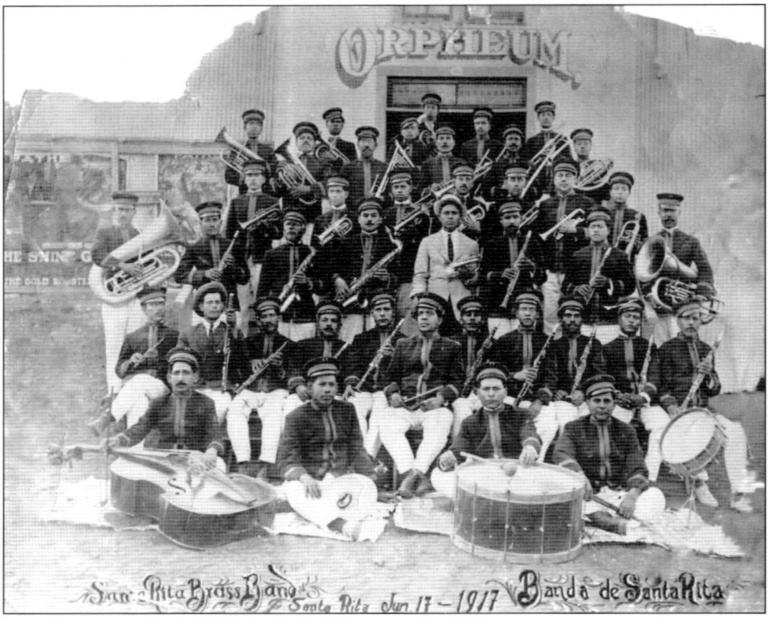

Santa Rita's brass band poses for a 1917 concert photograph in front of the Orpheum Theater, owned by Pedro Gomez. This all-Hispanic band played at celebrations and fiestas in the Santa Rita area. Many of the members worked on the track gangs, laying track for the shovels and locomotives. (Courtesy of Richard G. Luna.)

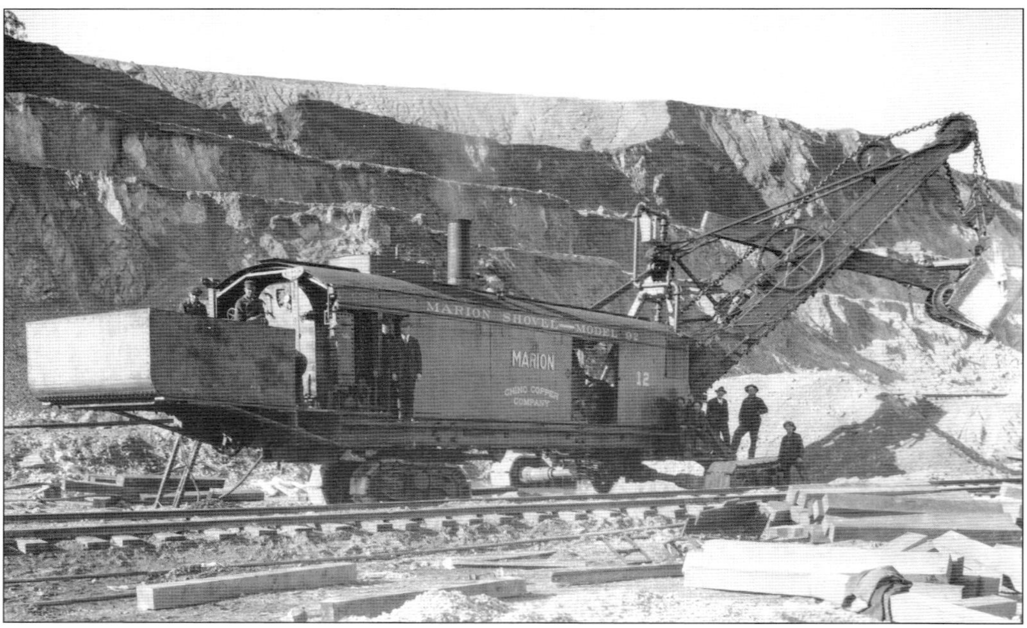

The Chino Copper Company bought this Marion steam shovel, Model 92 with a three-and-a-half-yard bucket, in 1923. Caterpillar-type crawlers were factory installed on this shovel, an improvement over the railroad wheels on older models. It also had the latest-style coal box attached to the rear of the shovel (earlier machines had pulled a separate coal car behind each shovel). The No. 12 faithfully dug copper ore in the Chino pit until 1931.

Chino Copper Company officials pose on a Porter steam locomotive around 1930. The man standing by the bell and wearing high boots is general manager John M. Sully. On the far right is mine superintendent Harry Thorne, and next to him, in the white shirt and tie, is general mine foreman Harold "Tuff" Moses. Note the man on the far right edge of the photograph who is drilling a boulder for blasting.

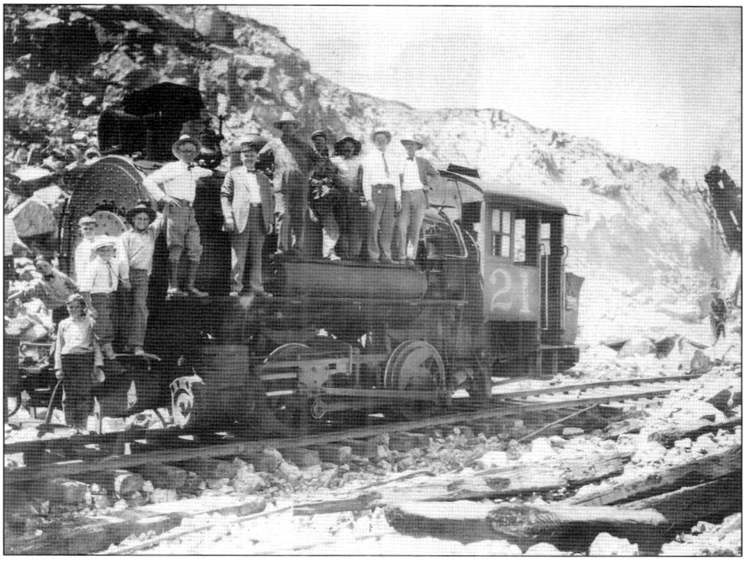

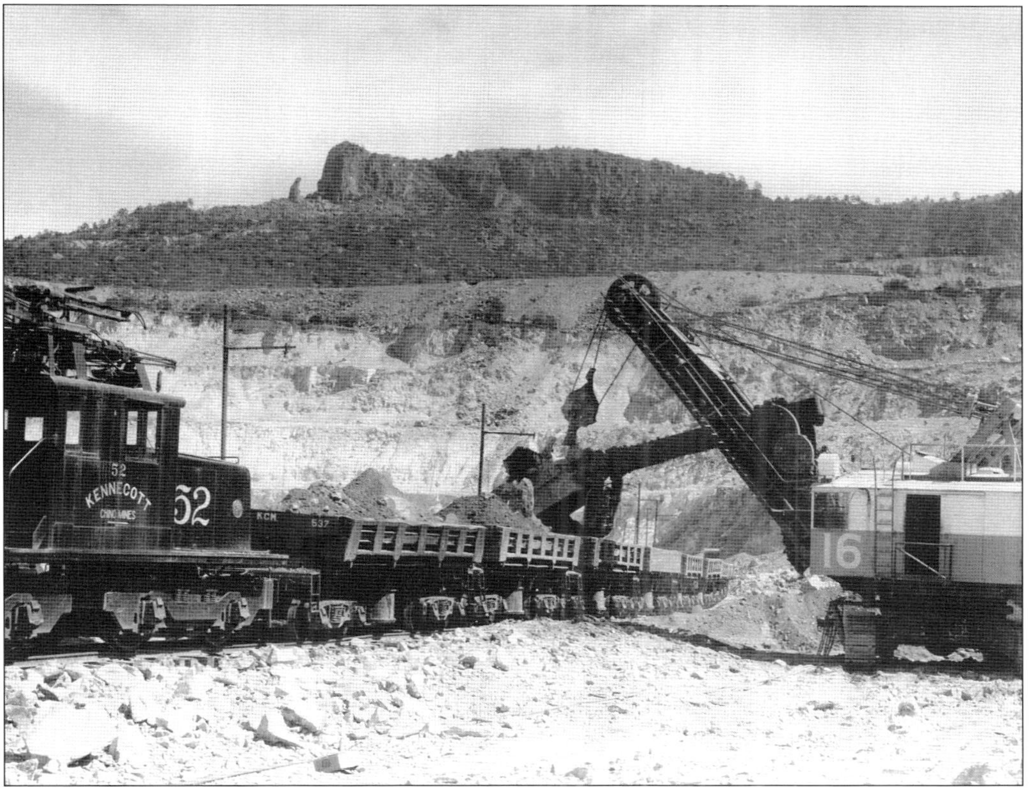

In the 1940s, electricity replaced steam at the Chino mine. This Marion electric shovel is loading waste rock into railcars, pulled by an electric locomotive. The shovel dipper holds eight tons of material. Each railcar has a pneumatic cylinder underneath, and the rock is dumped on piles surrounding the open pit and then leached with sulfuric acid to remove the copper. Kneeling Nun Mountain is in the background.

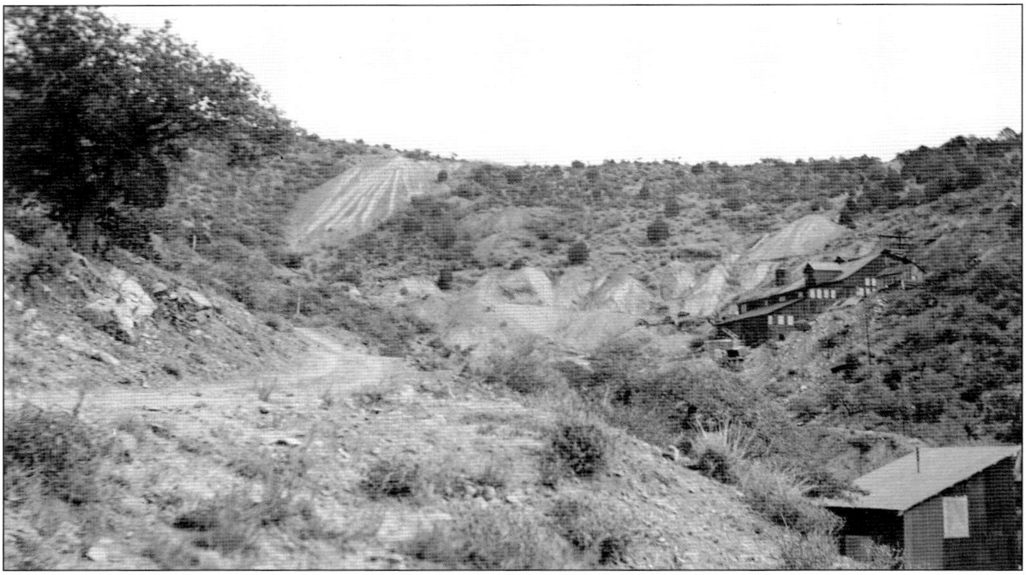

Gold was discovered in Pinos Altos by early Spanish miners, but it was not until 1860 that Anglo prospectors came to the area after discovering gold on Bear Creek. The original settlement was known as Birchville, but problems with warring Apaches kept people away. By 1866, the lure of gold, along with the organization of the Pinos Altos Mining Company, overcame the fear of Indian attacks. Now with more settlers, the town became known as Pinos Altos. Above are the Gillette Mill and dumps, and below is the Manhattan Tunnel. (Both, courtesy of Ida Campbell.)

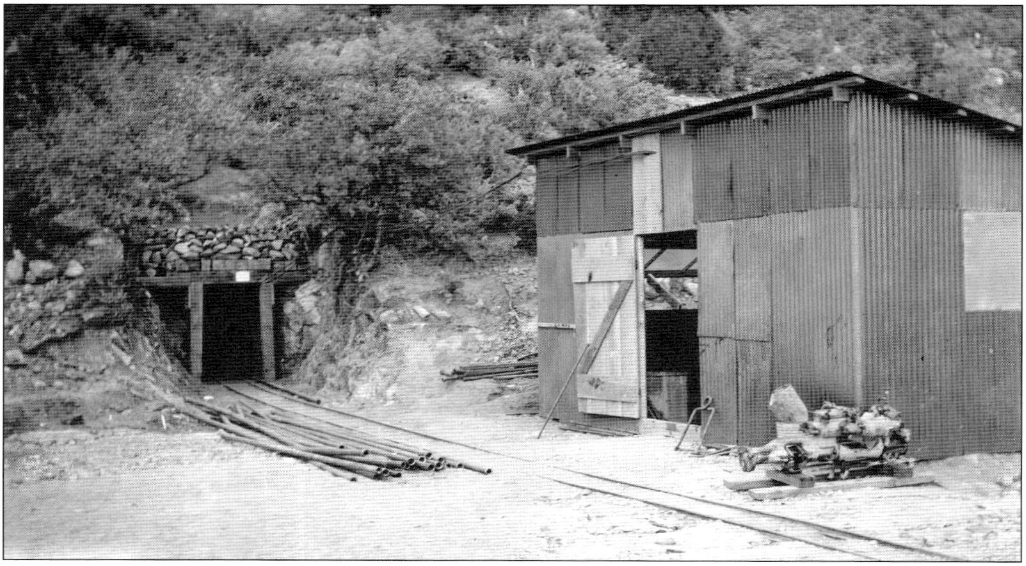

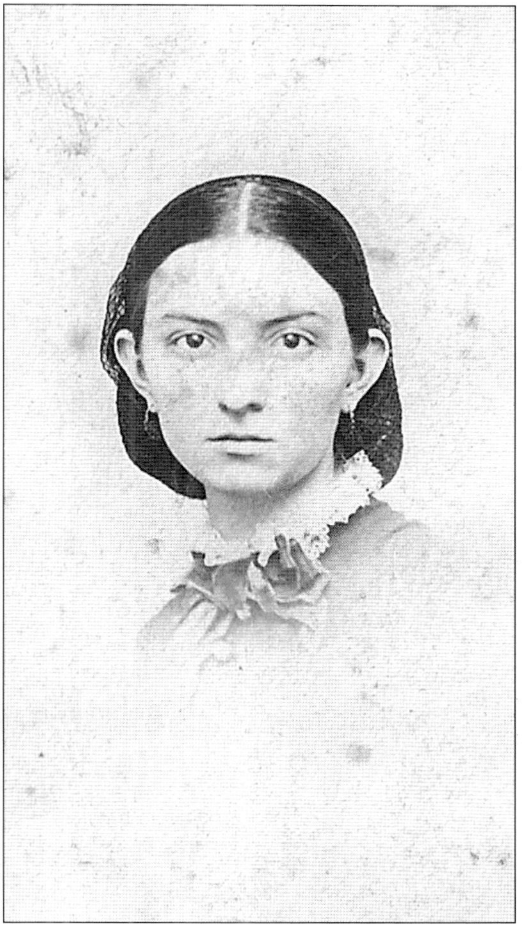

Jennie Bull Culver came to New Mexico in 1869 with her husband and two-year-old son. The family lived at Pinos Altos, below, and Fort Bayard, while Enos prospected for gold (usually with little success). Jennie was homesick and terrified of the Indians who attacked anyone leaving the settlement, but, in spite of her fears, she had a touch of gold fever. She dreamed of going home, but hoped to bring with her a bottle "filled with pure gold." Jennie noted in her letters home that men were brought in every day wounded or killed by Indians. Jennie contracted tuberculosis and grew weaker and weaker. She hoped to return home in the spring, but sadly died on November 7, 1871. She was the fourth person to be interred in Silver City's first cemetery. (Right, courtesy of the Glen Redd Fisher Museum; below, courtesy of Jean Eckard.)

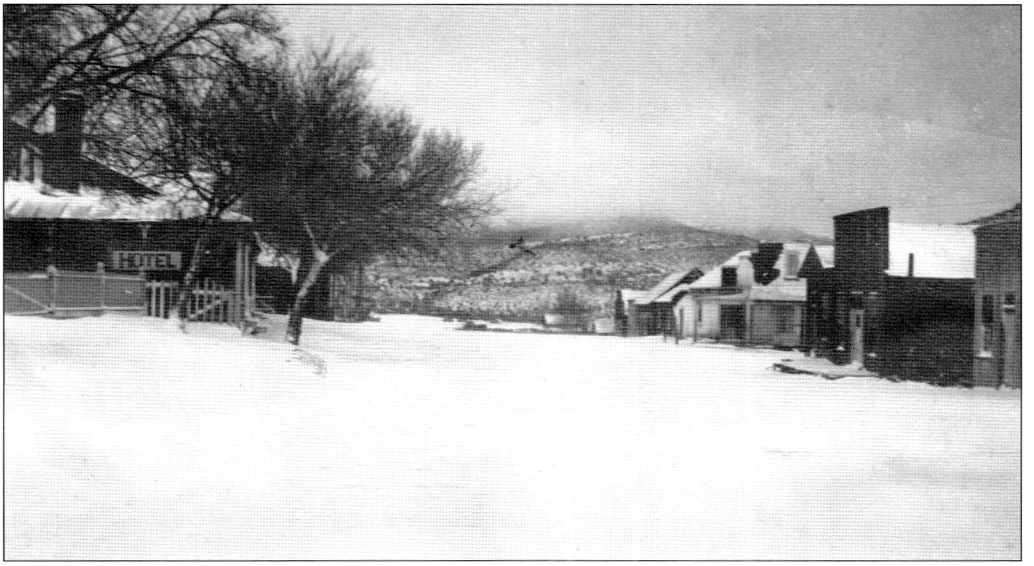

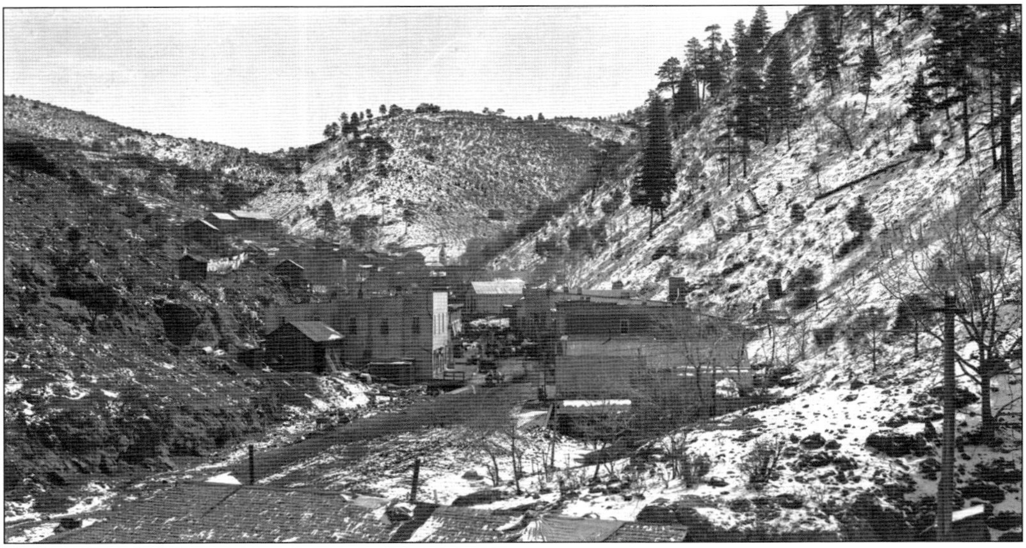

In 1876, gold and silver were discovered in the creeks around Mogollon, about 70 miles north of Silver City. Rich mines were located in the hills, but the town was built along the banks of Silver Creek, which flooded with every big rain. The Little Fannie Mine, pictured below in 1912, was one of the richest mines in the area. Discovered by Frank Vingo in 1887 and named after his wife, the site produced millions of dollars worth of gold, but when it closed in 1942, people left Mogollon, and it became a ghost town. Today, it is a picturesque village with shops and historic attractions. (Above, courtesy of Anthony Romero; below, courtesy of Jan Blackwell.)

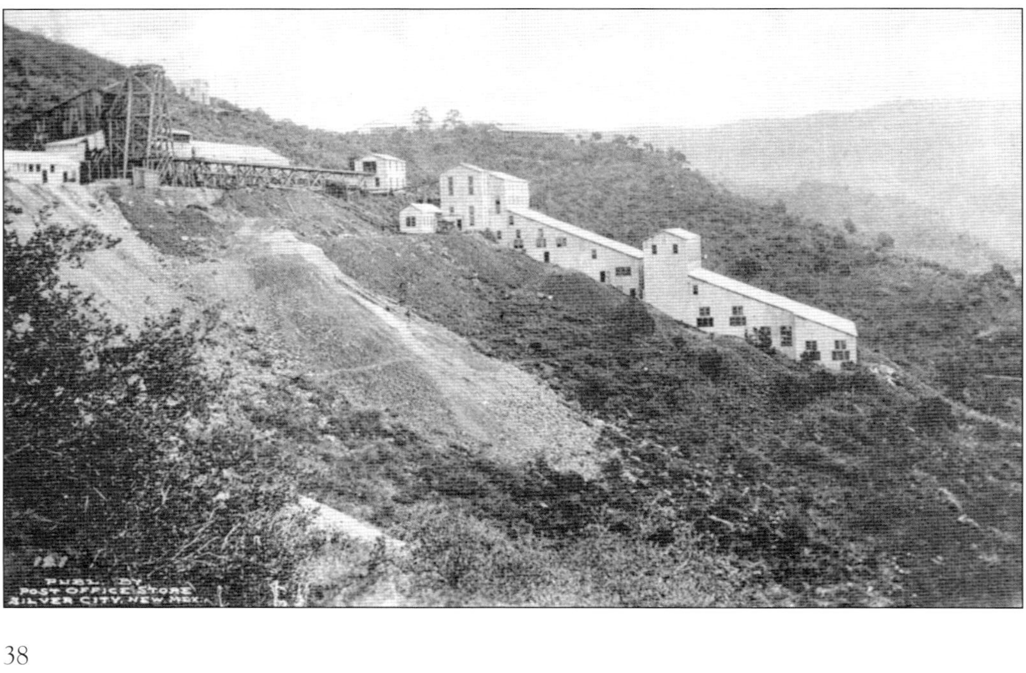

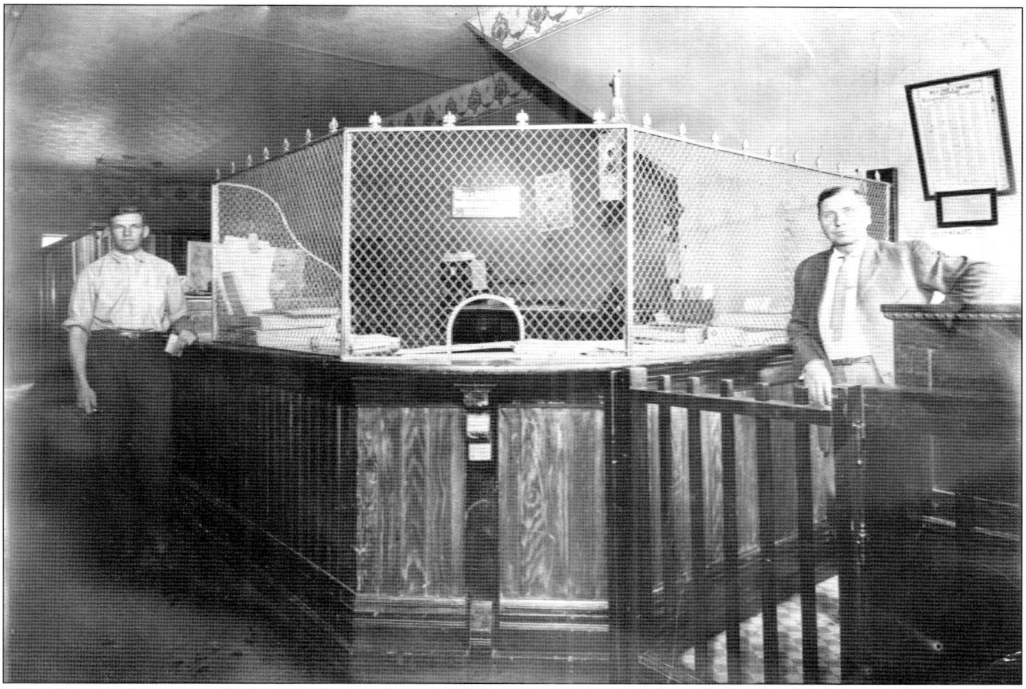

Charles William Marriott worked for Wells, Fargo & Company and went to Silver City in 1890 to manage the local office. Above, Marriott (right) stands in his office around 1906. After securing the mail contract on the Mogollon route, he was responsible for transporting money for payrolls and silver and gold bullion from the mines. Below, Marriott stands third from the left with his hands in his pockets, wearing a dark hat, beside a stack of silver bars in front of the Wells Fargo office. The money and bullion proved a tempting target for bandits, and drivers were held up (and sometimes killed) on the journey between Silver City and the mining towns. After a driver was killed by a group of Apaches who left the reservation, Marriott supplied the remaining drivers with Winchester rifles. (Both, courtesy of Jan Blackwell.)

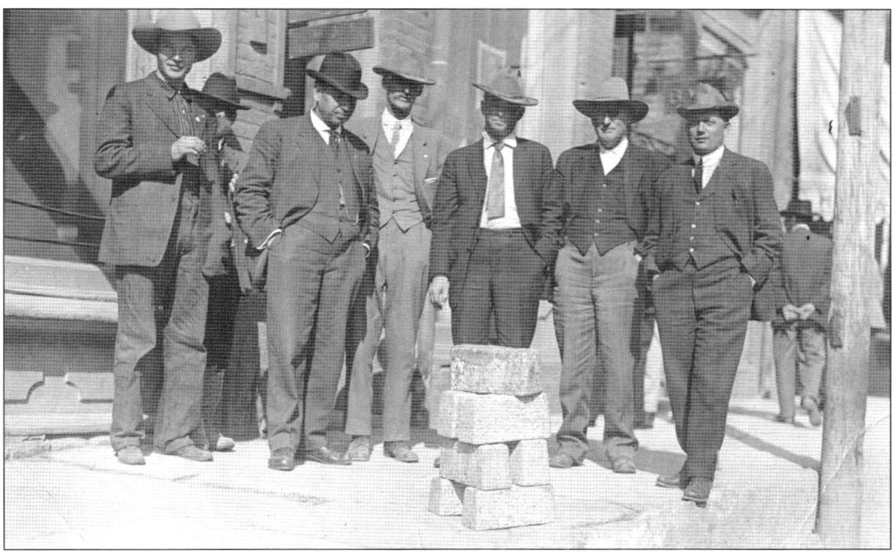

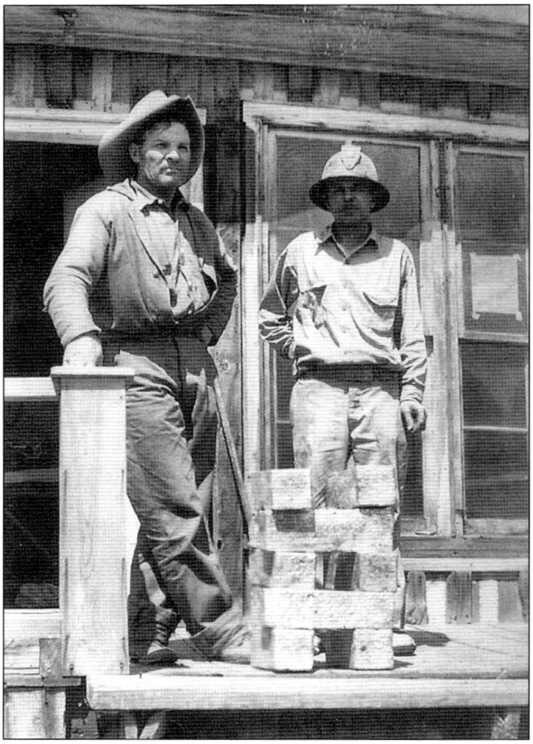

Clarence Tipton (left) was a rancher whose brand was Cross Open A Bar. In addition, he was a saddle bronc rider and a boxer. He also hauled supplies to Mogollon, carrying gold and silver back to Silver City. He was drafted in 1918 while working at the GOS Ranch. Because 18 cowboys came up on the draft list, the GOS owner talked the draft board into giving them an extension until after roundup. (Courtesy of Deily Crumbley.)

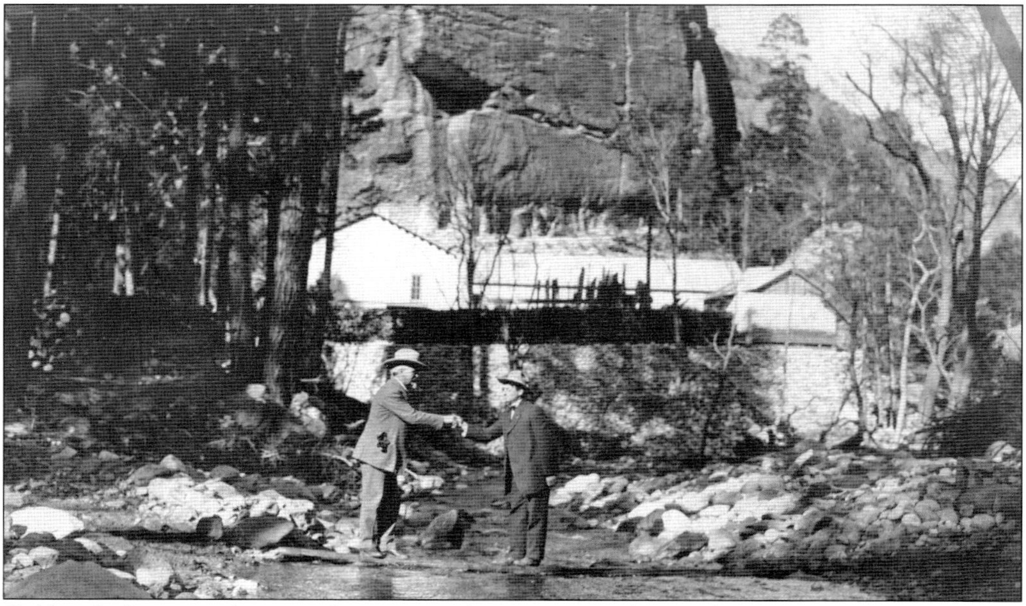

Gold and silver were discovered in 1889 in the mountains above Whitewater Canyon, northwest of Silver City. Because of the narrowness of the canyon, John T. Graham constructed a mill at its mouth. To bring water to the mill, a pipe was installed along the canyon walls, 20 feet above the floor. The narrow, elevated pipe ran for three miles and was called the "catwalk." (Courtesy of Jan Blackwell.)

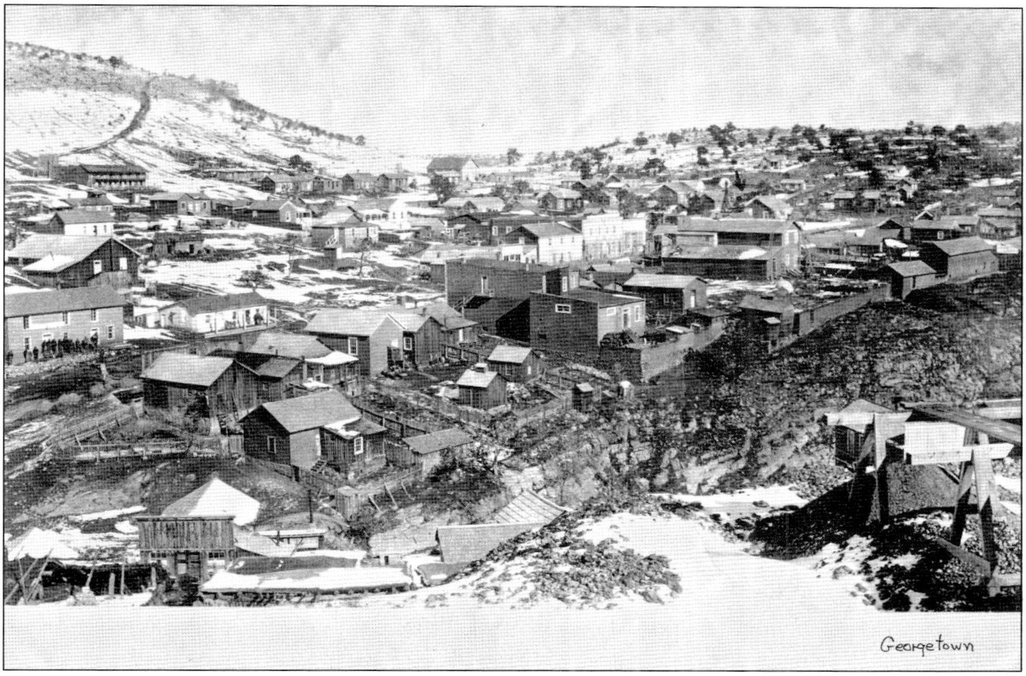

Georgetown was thought to be named for George Magruder, vice president of Mimbres Mining and Reduction Company. The region east of Silver City was rich in silver, and prospectors were working in the area as early as 1866. The McGregor Mill, pictured here in 1884 and located to the southwest on the Mimbres River, used water from the river to process the ore from Georgetown. The town boomed in the 1880s, but a fire destroyed several buildings, and by 1893, when the price of silver dropped, the town went into a decline. Other than the cemetery, very little remains today of Georgetown. (Both, courtesy of Don Turner.)

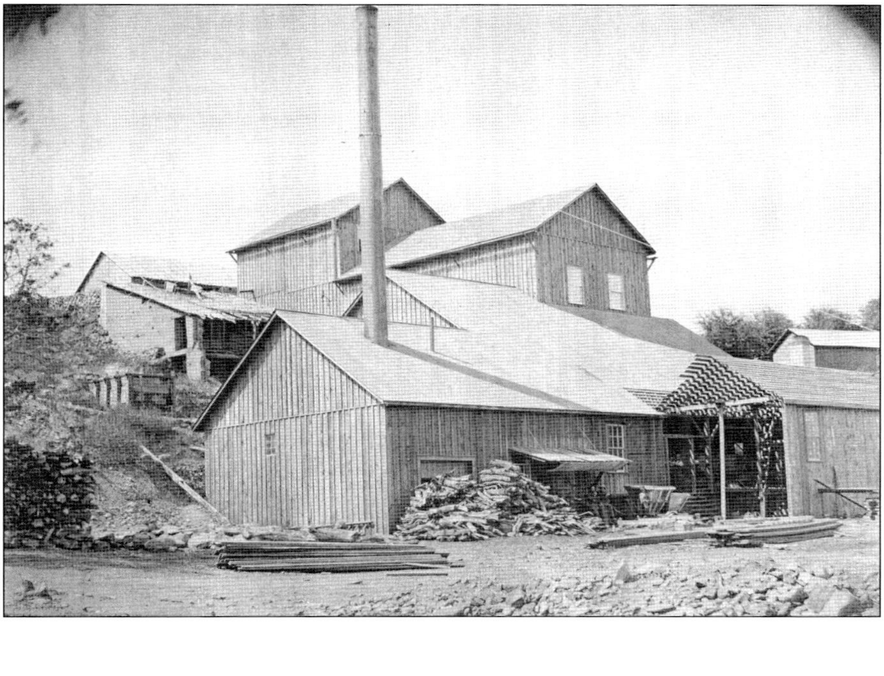

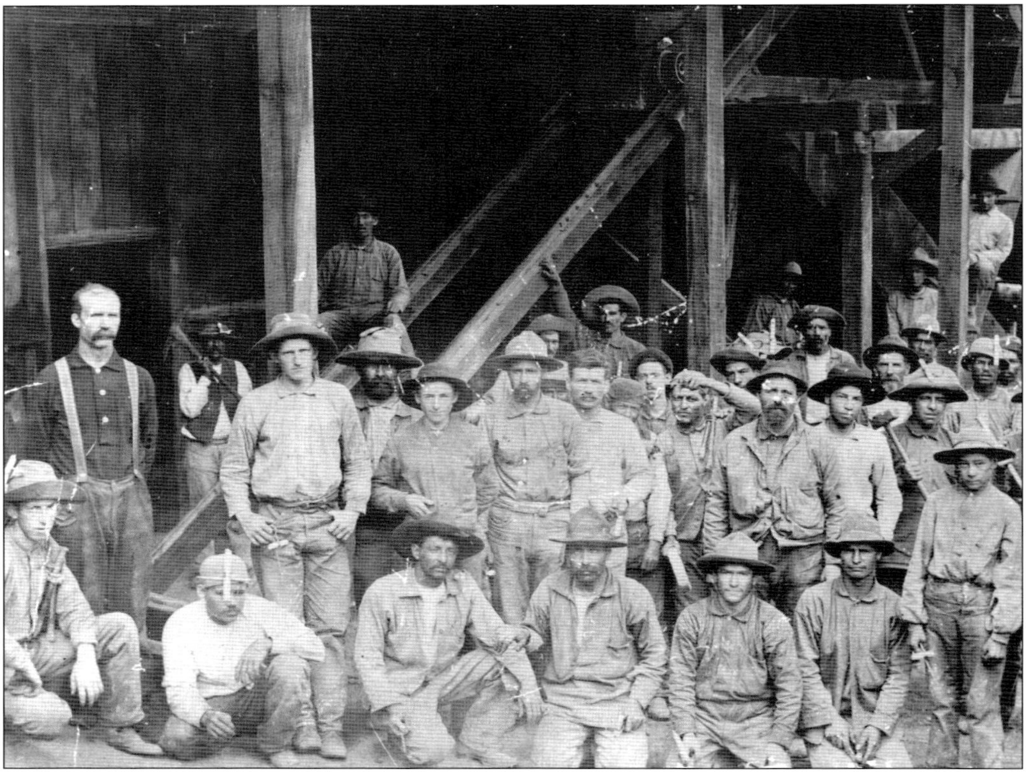

These hard-rock miners worked in the 600-foot-deep Texas Mine in the 1890s. Many of the men have attached a candle to their hat brims to serve as a meager light source in the deep tunnels. The Texas Mine, which closed in 1906, was located west of Central (now Santa Clara), on Twin Sisters Creek. Above, the man standing to the far left is Lewis Sherman Goforth, great-uncle of the donor of this photograph. The cable on the diagonal shaft can be seen in both images. (Above, courtesy of Don Turner; below, courtesy of Dillon Stone.)

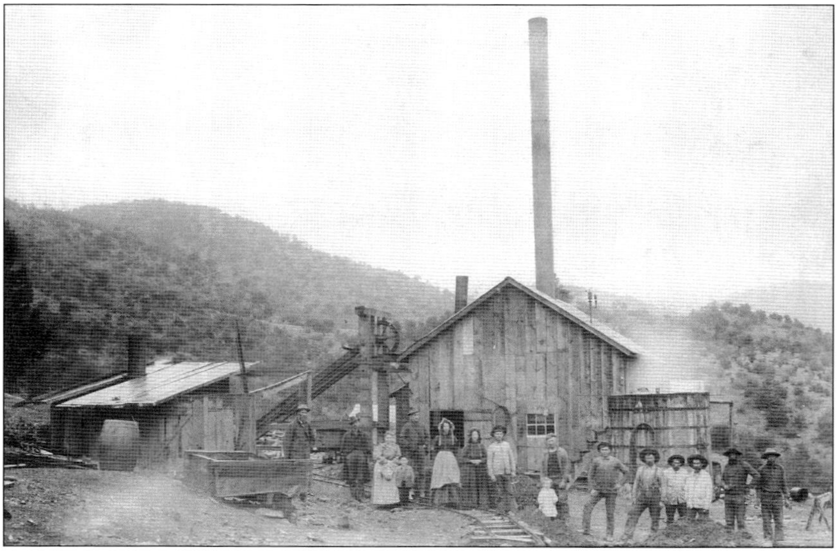

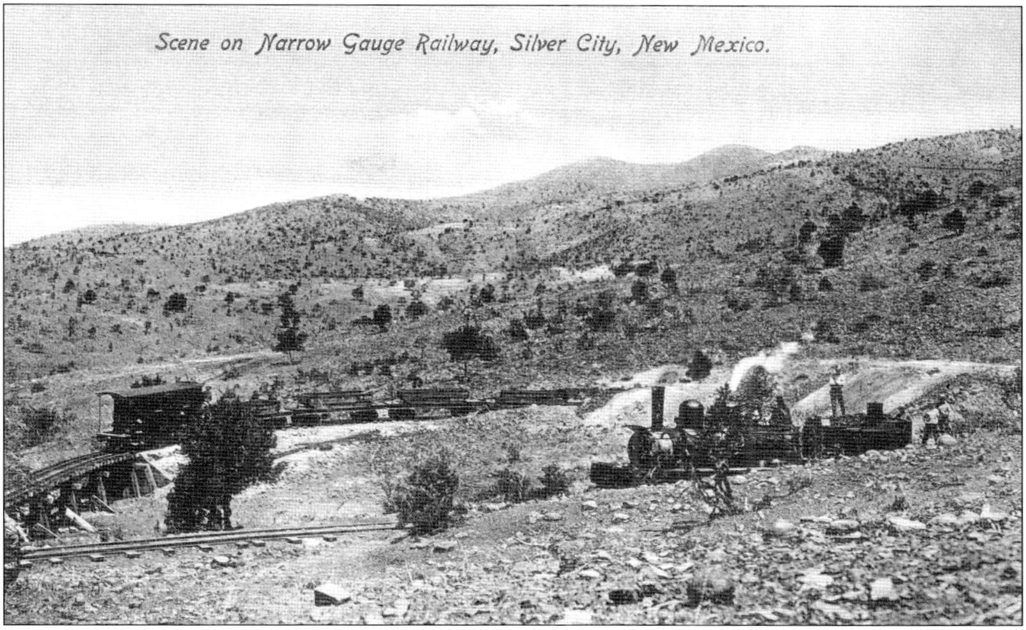

The narrow-gauge railroad operated intermittently between 1906 and 1913, carrying ore from the mines at Pinos Altos, around W Mountain, past Chloride Flat and Boston Hill, and down to the Silver City Reduction Works. The steep grades required several tight, treacherous turns, such as Hairpin Loop and Horseshoe Curve. (Courtesy of Jane Bardal.)

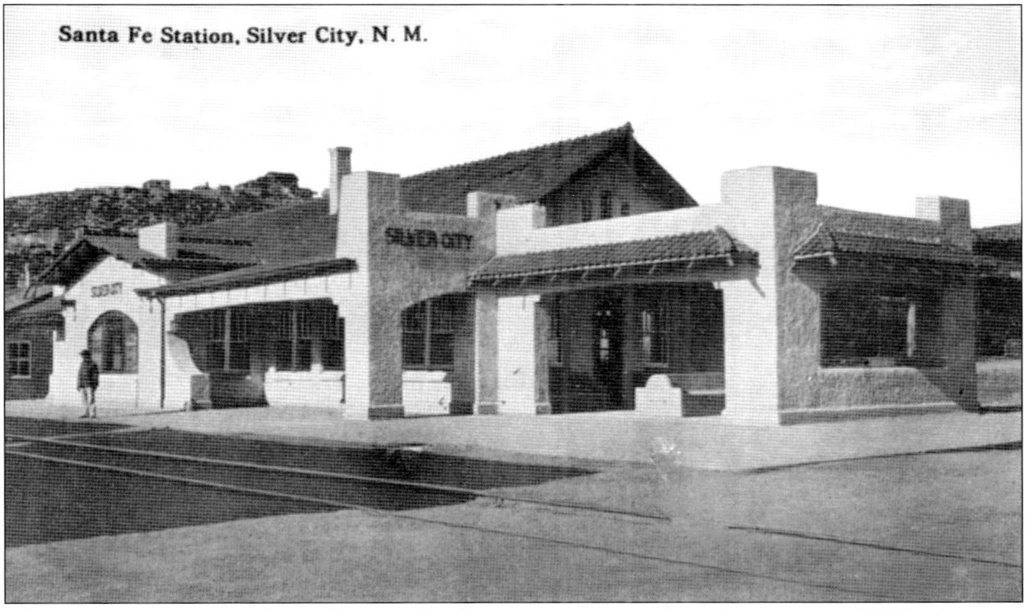

The new Atchison, Topeka & Santa Fe Railroad station opened in the summer of 1915, adjoining the older depot that was later used as a baggage warehouse. The new station was located near the south end of Bullard Street, just east of Chihuahua Hill. The station cost the town $25,000 and was considered a beautiful edifice that would welcome newcomers to Silver City. (Courtesy of Jane Bardal.)

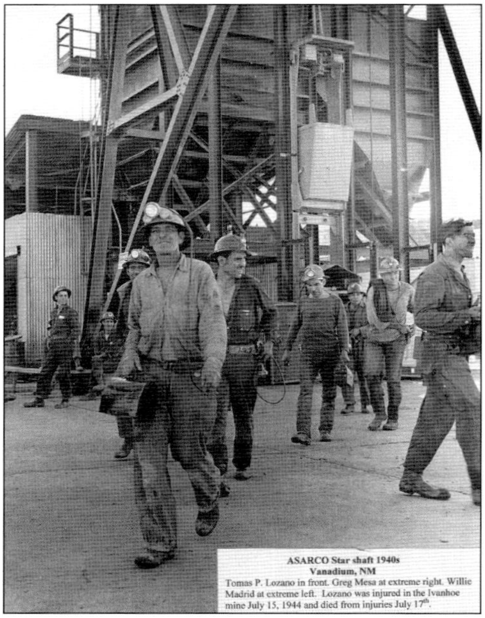

This group of underground miners was photographed as their shift ended at the ASARCO Star shaft in Vanadium. Mining has always been a dangerous occupation. Tomas P. Lozano (foreground) was injured in the Ivanhoe Mine on July 15, 1944, and died from those injuries two days later.

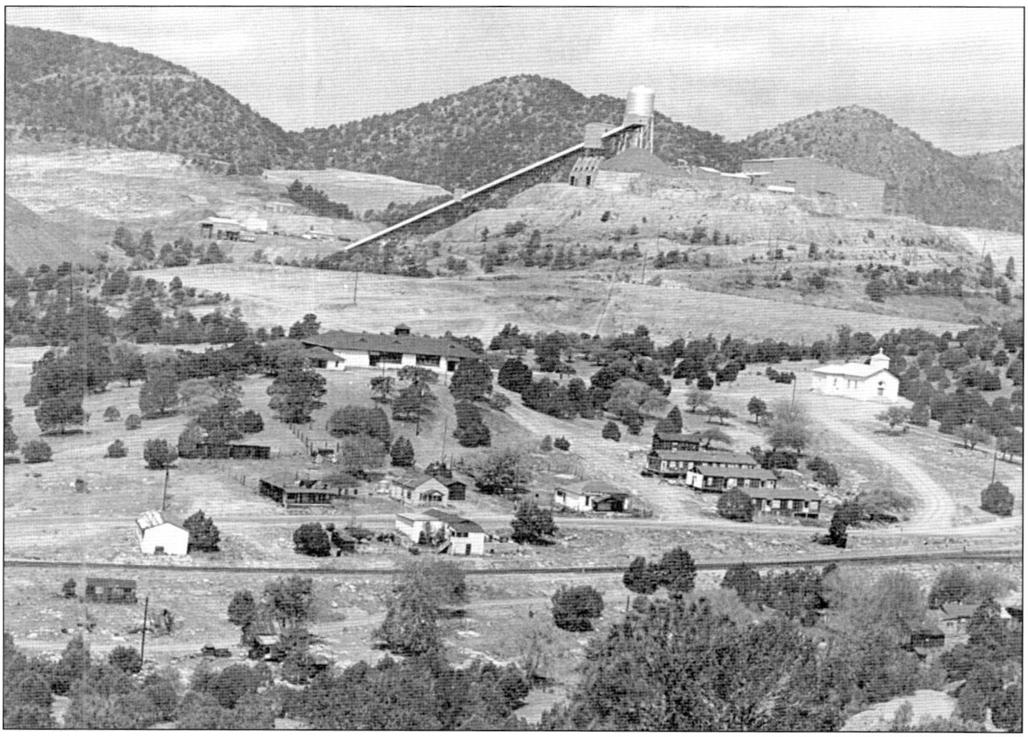

The town of Fierro (Spanish for "iron") was named for one of the metals discovered there over 150 years ago. The older part of town is in the foreground, and the 1916 St. Anthony's Church is visible to the right. The large building in the center is the Fierro School, and behind it are the open-pit copper mine and the underground workings of the Continental Mine, opened in 1964 by the US Smelting, Mining & Refining Company and now owned by Cobre Mines.

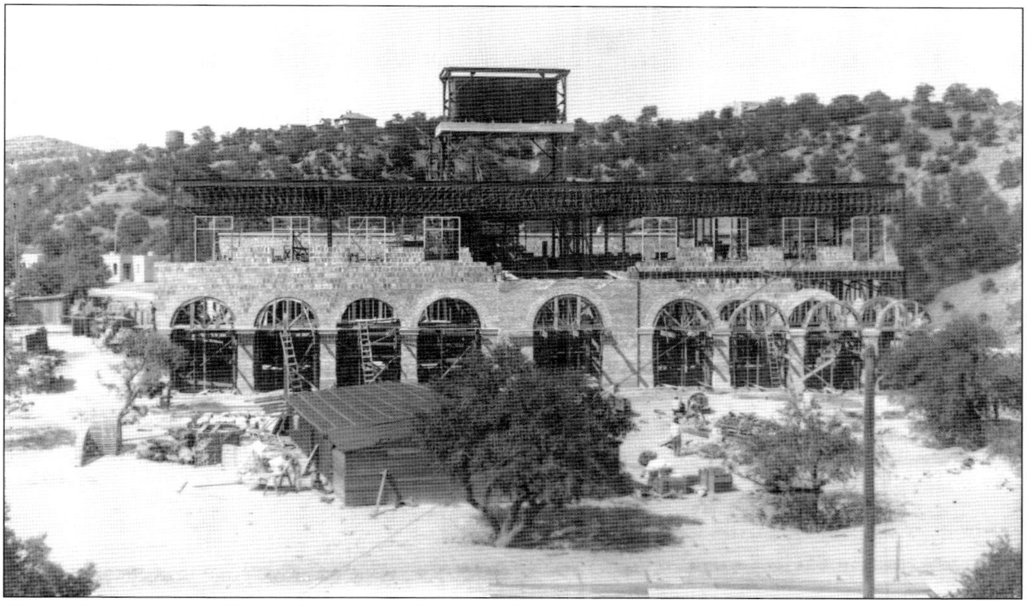

Turquoise was mined by prehistoric Indians in the area southwest of Silver City, later known as Tyrone. With discoveries of copper, the Phelps-Dodge Company built a million-dollar town that was completed in 1915. Designed by architect Bertram Goodhue, with direction from Margaret Douglas and Grace Parish Dodge, it was known as the "most beautiful company town in the world." In addition to homes there was a railroad station, a department store, a hospital, a bank, and a school; however, it was the only town in southwest New Mexico with no saloons and no brothels. By 1921, copper prices dropped, people moved away, and Tyrone became known as the "million dollar ghost town." In the 1970s, it disappeared completely when copper mining started up again and the open pit was expanded. (Above, courtesy of Anthony Romero; below, courtesy of Don Turner.)

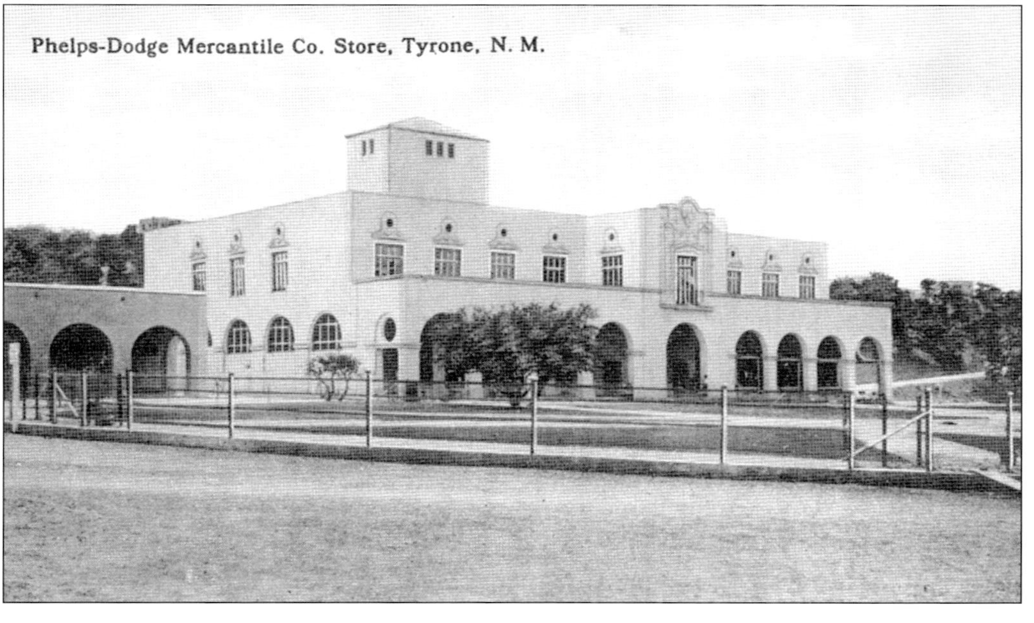

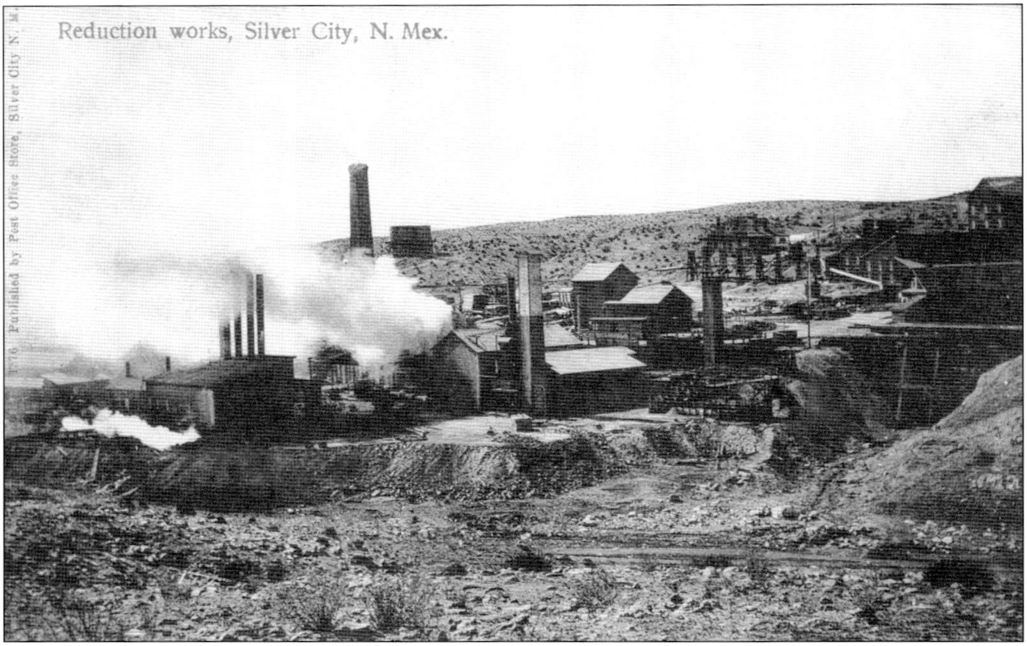

The Silver City Reduction Works were located south of Silver City, next to San Vicente Arroyo. The narrow-gauge railroad, which brought ore to the smelter from the Pinos Altos mines north of town, ran through the city to the smelter and then south to join the Southern Pacific Railroad and the Atchison, Topeka & Santa Fe Railroad at Deming, New Mexico. (Courtesy of Don Turner.)

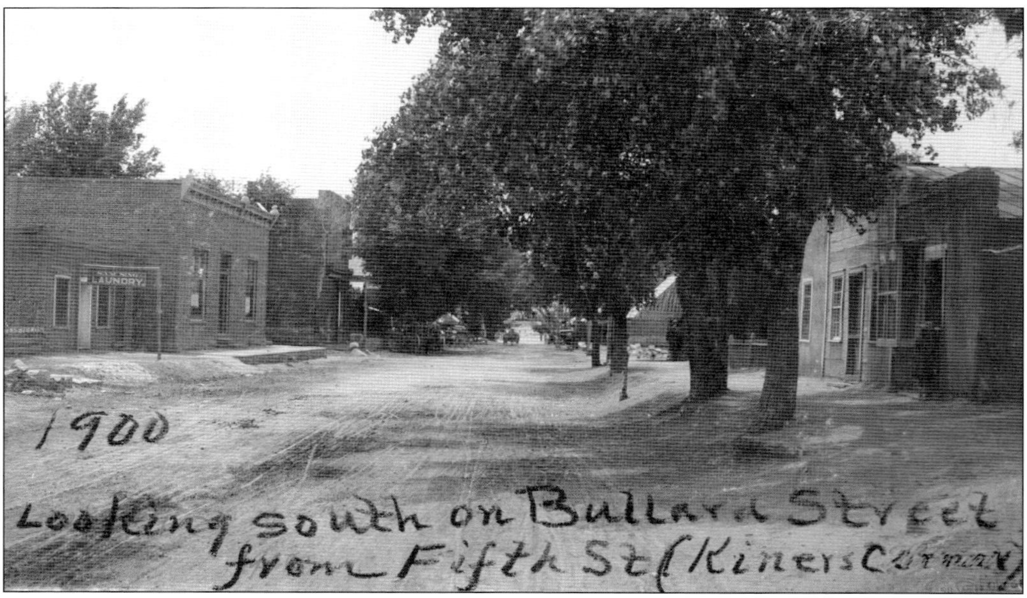

Silver City was a thriving community, as seen in this 1900 photograph taken on Bullard Street looking south at Kelly Street. At the left is Sam Sing's Laundry, and next to it is Elizabeth Warren's newly constructed insurance office. It would not be until 1907 that the town required businesses to put in concrete sidewalks, and it is obvious that the rainy season would turn the streets and walkways into a muddy mess. (Courtesy of Lynn Geyer.)

Four

Settlers and Scalawags

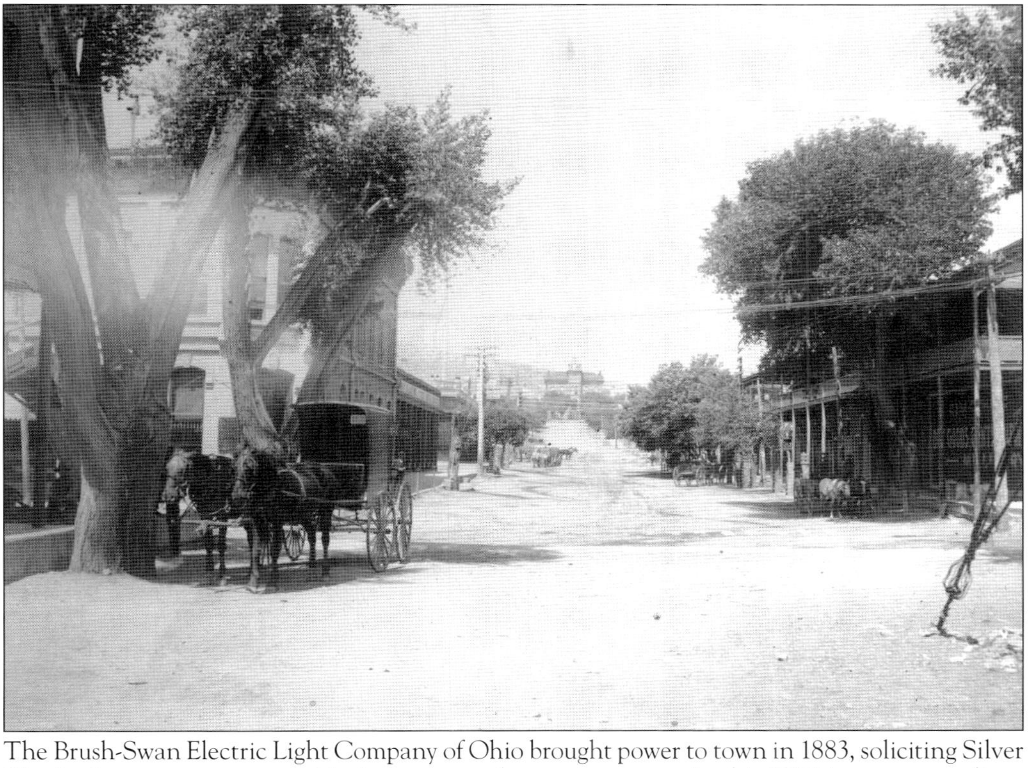

The Brush-Swan Electric Light Company of Ohio brought power to town in 1883, soliciting Silver City businesses to contract with their proposed power company. In this 1900 image, power lines are visible across Broadway. Looking up the street to the courthouse, the Silver City National Bank is on the left, and the Palace Hotel is to the right. (Courtesy of Lynn Geyer.)

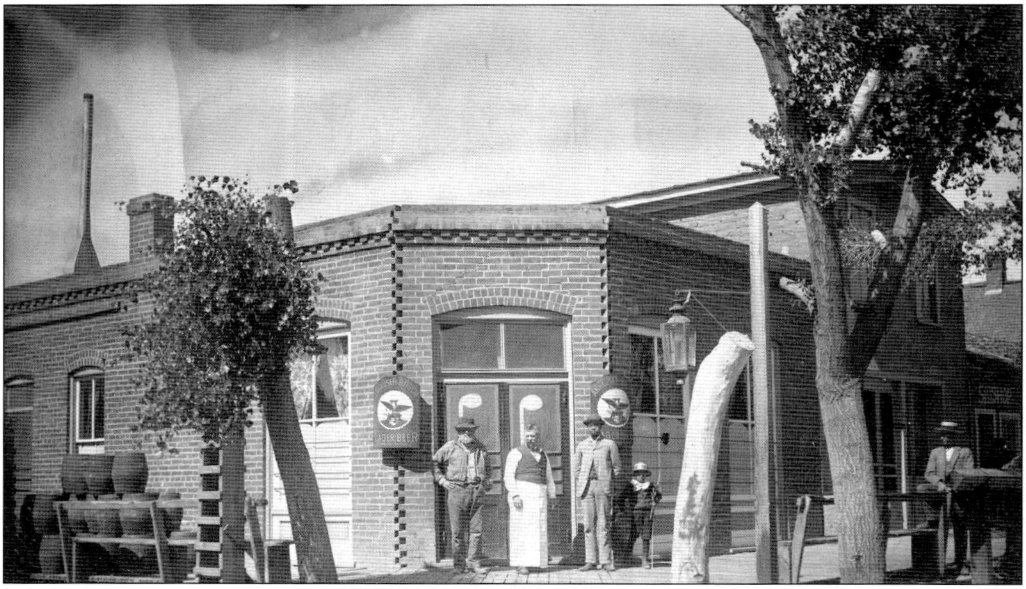

Above, Stephan Uhli (wearing the long white apron) stands in front of the Cave Saloon. Uhli came to Silver City from Germany in 1880 and worked as a butcher for McMillen's Meat Market before opening the saloon at the corner of Broadway at Texas Street. The brick wall of the saloon facing onto Broadway can be seen below, behind the wagon. To the right in both photographs is Eli Rosenberg's Shoe Shop. (Above, courtesy of Jean Uhli; below, courtesy of Don Turner.)

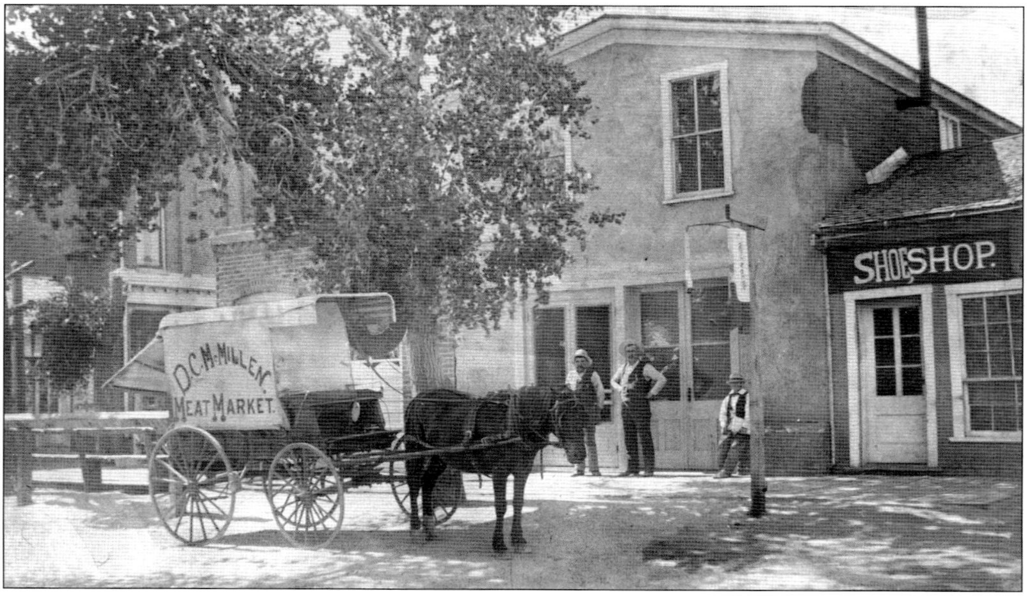

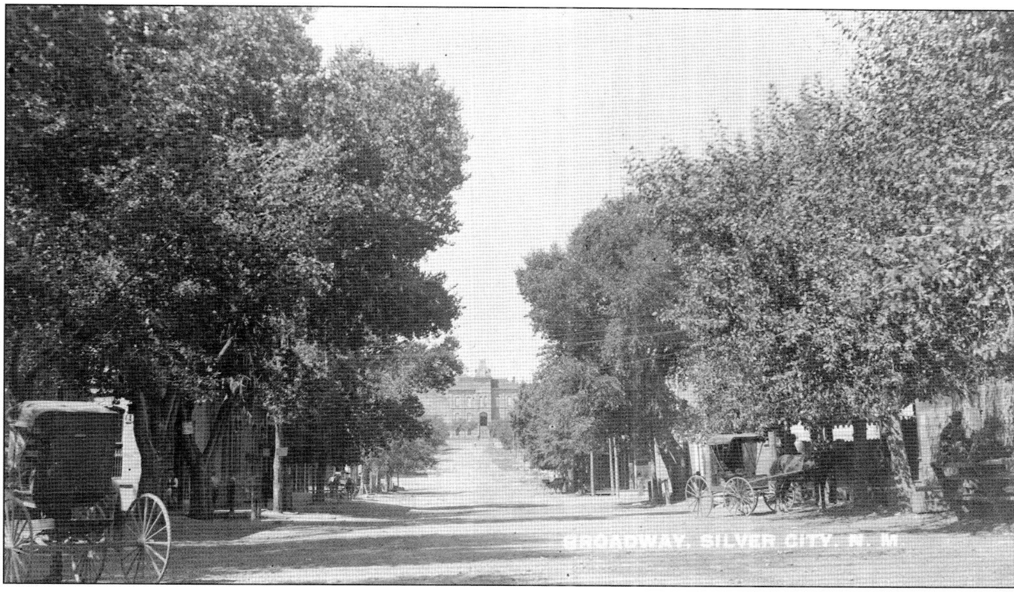

Above, a c. 1900 view up Broadway shows Silver City's first courthouse at the top of the street. Below is the view from behind the courthouse, looking to the northeast. Broadway runs along the right side of the courthouse. In the center of the image is O.C. Hinman's furniture store with its six white-framed windows. (Both, courtesy of Jean Uhli.)

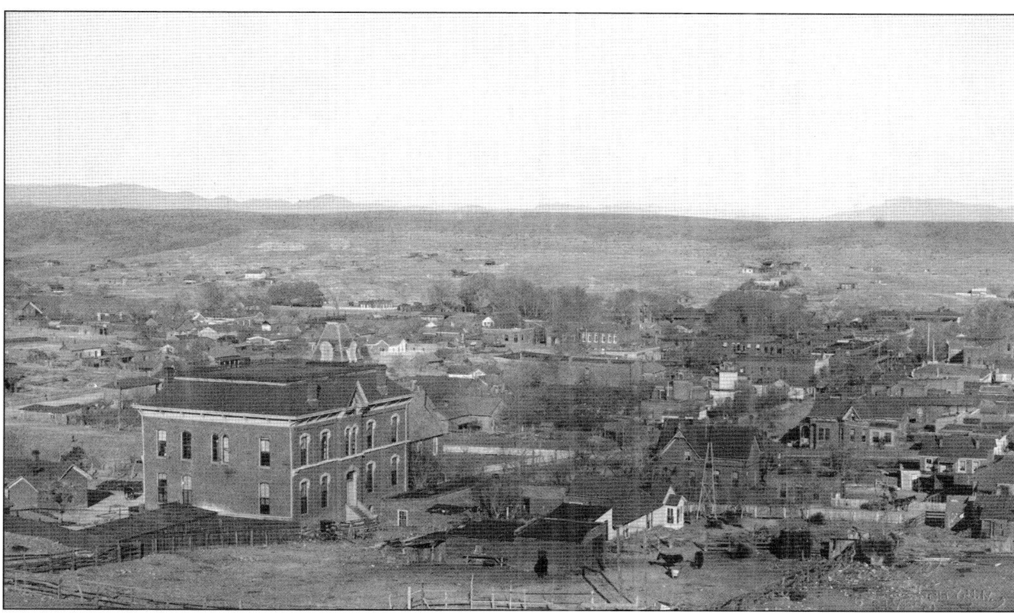

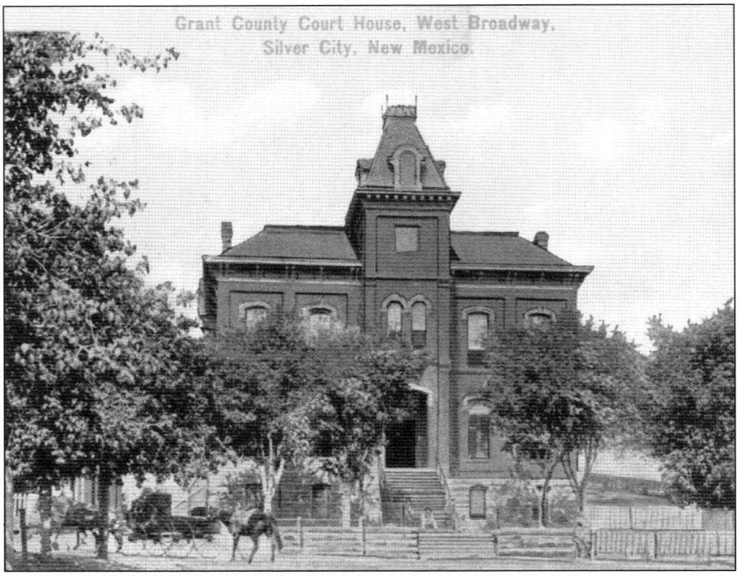

The first Grant County Courthouse was built in 1883 at the west end of Broadway. Several modest structures in Central, Pinos Altos, and Silver City had previously housed county functions. Steps led up to the main entrance of the building, which also had a jail in the basement. This building stood until 1930, when it was demolished and replaced with a new courthouse. (Courtesy of Don Turner.)

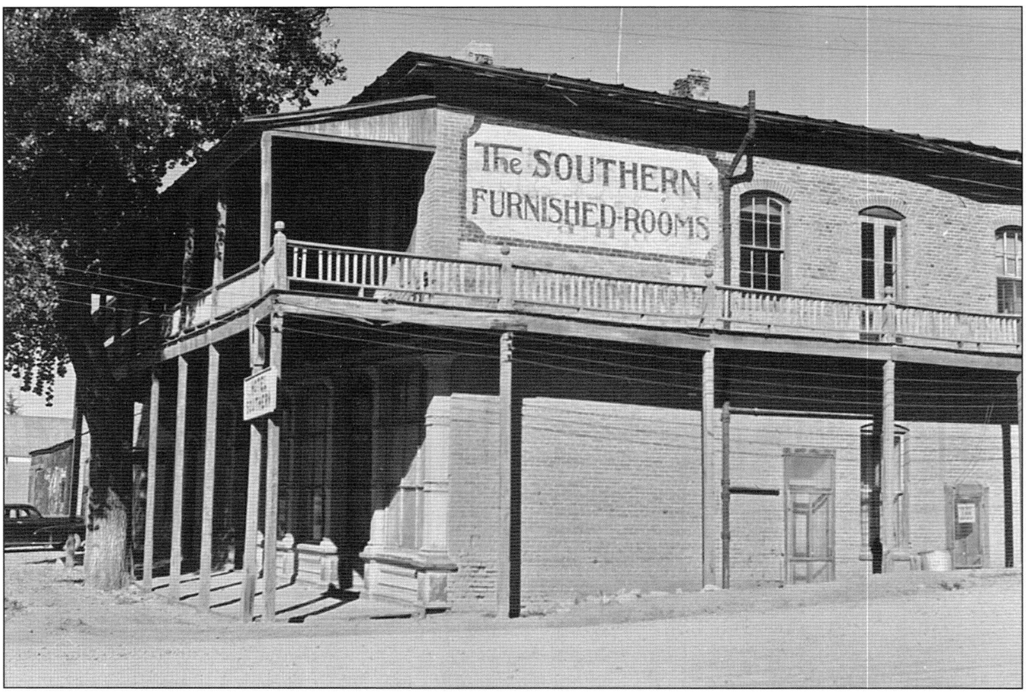

The two-story Southern Hotel was the third brick building constructed in Silver City. Built in 1872 to house the Bennett Brothers Mercantile, it was located on the northeast corner of Hudson Street and Broadway. In the 1880s, it was considered a first-class hotel and restaurant. In the early 1960s, Hudson Street was widened and paved, and the historic structure was demolished in 1962.

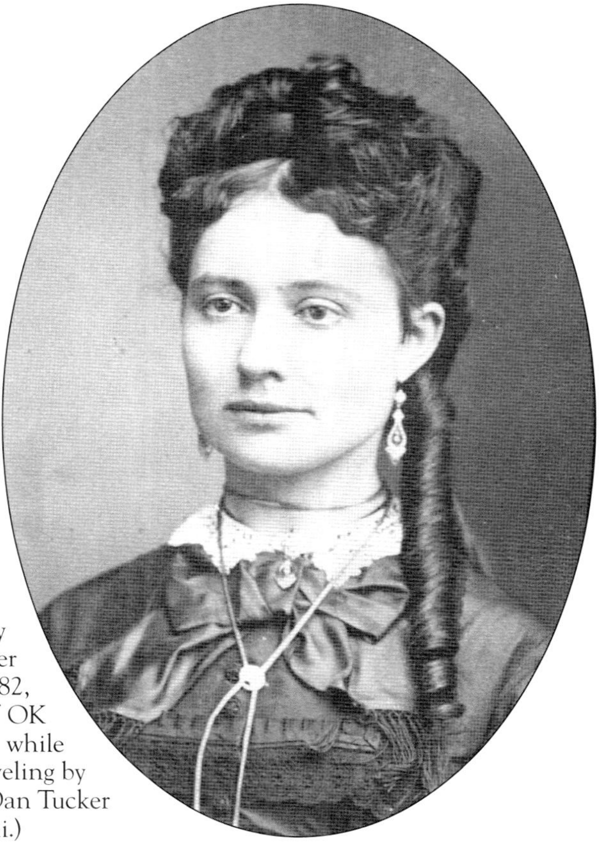

Levi D. Miller was a soldier who came to Silver City in 1870 and helped lay out the town. His wife, Margaret Keays (right), was a mail-order bride from Canada. After an exchange of letters, Miller sent her $500 to travel to Silver City, with a promise to pay for her return if she did not want to stay. Levi and Margaret were married within an hour of her arrival. Their home, located on the south end of Bullard Street in the middle of the block, had a passageway to the interior of the block, where Miller operated the Tenderfoot Corral. In 1882, Doc Holiday and the Earp brothers of OK Corral fame sold their horses to Miller while making their getaway from the law, traveling by stagecoach to Rincon to avoid Sheriff Dan Tucker in Deming. (Both, courtesy of Jean Uhli.)

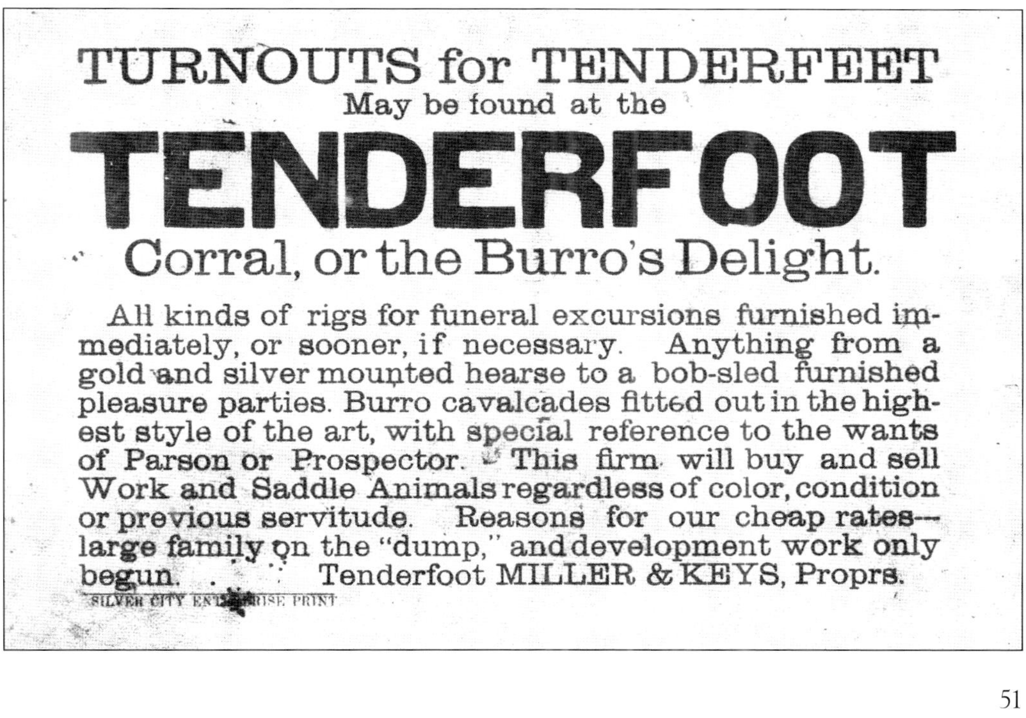

TURNOUTS for TENDERFEET
May be found at the
TENDERFOOT
Corral, or the Burro's Delight.

All kinds of rigs for funeral excursions furnished immediately, or sooner, if necessary. Anything from a gold and silver mounted hearse to a bob-sled furnished pleasure parties. Burro cavalcades fitted out in the highest style of the art, with special reference to the wants of Parson or Prospector. This firm will buy and sell Work and Saddle Animals regardless of color, condition or previous servitude. Reasons for our cheap rates—large family on the "dump," and development work only begun. Tenderfoot MILLER & KEYS, Proprs.

SILVER CITY ENTERPRISE PRINT

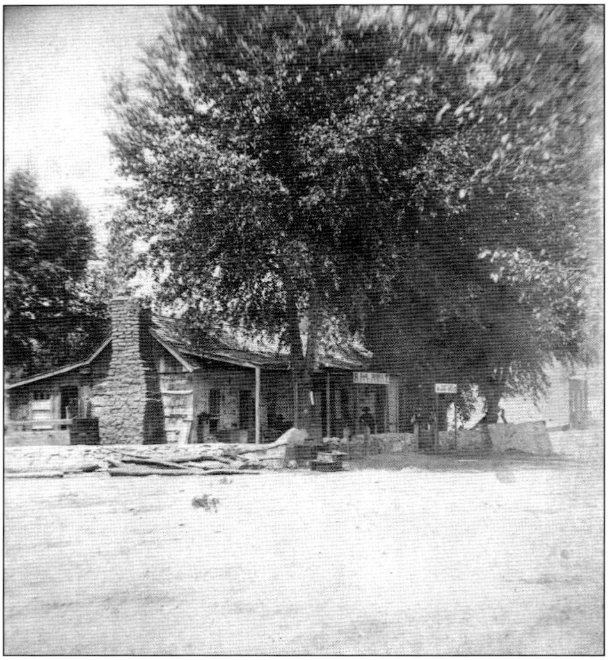

Henry McCarty, the future Billy the Kid, came to Silver City in 1873 with his mother, Catherine McCarty; stepfather, William Antrim; and brother Joseph in a vain effort to cure Catherine's tuberculosis. The family lived in a log house on Main Street, north of Broadway. The cabin, which later became a shoe-repair shop, was demolished about 1894. (Courtesy of the New Mexico History Museum, photograph by Alfred S. Addis, negative 99054.)

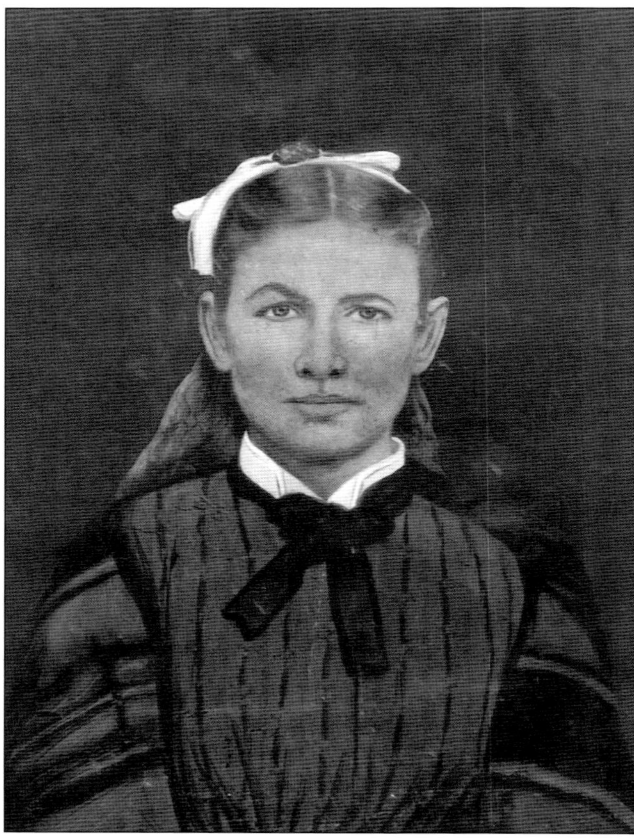

This photograph is thought to be of Catherine McCarty, Billy the Kid's mother. Catherine, who traveled to Silver City with her sons and second husband in 1873, died of tuberculosis a year after arriving in New Mexico Territory. On her deathbed, she confided to a friend that she was sad about leaving her boys in a wild country. She was buried in the first Silver City cemetery. (Courtesy of Leon C. Metz.)

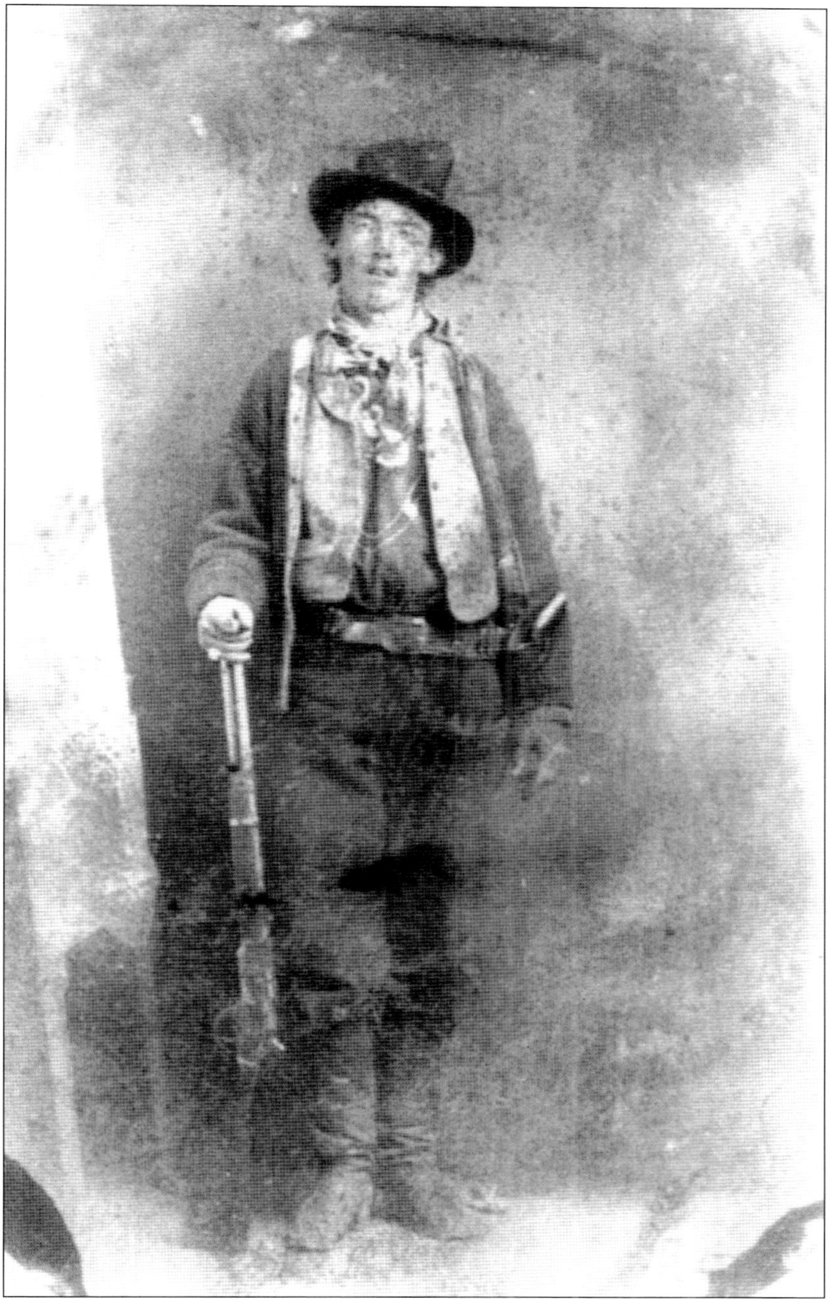

Henry McCarty, alias Billy the Kid, began his life of crime in Silver City in 1875 at age 15. After his mother's death, his stepfather, William Antrim, abandoned Henry and Joseph and left town to work at a gold mine. Billy found work at a hotel, but when he stole clothes from the Chinese laundry, Sheriff Harvey Whitehill locked the boy in the local jail, hoping to teach him a lesson. Two days later, Billy escaped through the chimney and fled to Arizona. He shot a man in a barroom brawl and then moved on to stealing horses, cattle rustling, and more killings. Billy's short life of crime ended in a shootout in Fort Sumner, New Mexico, in 1881. (Courtesy of Bob Alexander.)

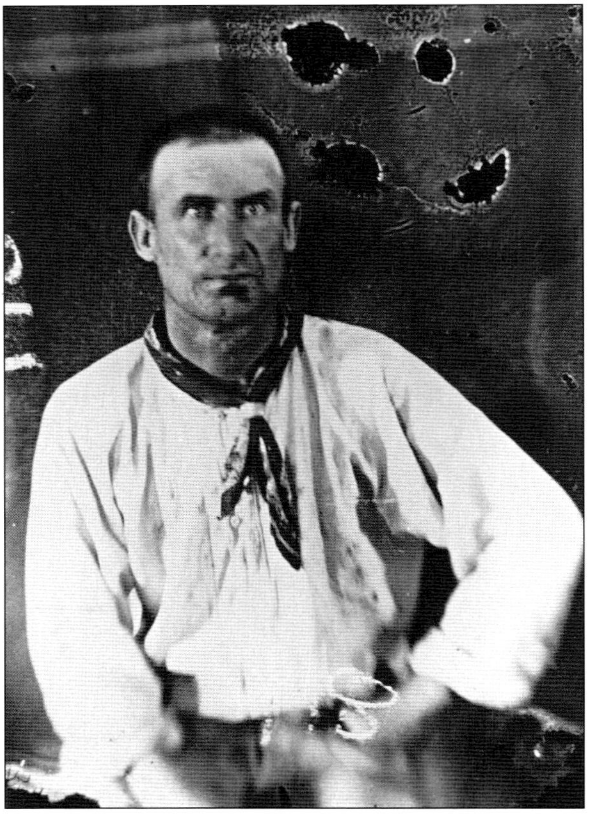

John W. Gilmo arrived in Silver City in 1880 and went on to become town marshal and a Grant County deputy sheriff. As a bounty hunter, he captured fugitive train robber Frank Taggart. Gilmo lost his job for killing the Southern Hotel cook and later spent three years in Yuma Territorial Prison for killing a man in Arizona Territory during an attempted robbery. (Courtesy of Bob Alexander.)

Joel Fowler had a "wicked fondness for gratuitous violence," according to historian Bob Alexander. The convicted murderer was hung in Socorro in 1883 by a lynch mob. The rope proved to be too long, allowing his feet to touch the ground, so several men promptly grabbed his legs and pulled, choking him to death with their weight. (Courtesy of Holm O. Bursom III.)

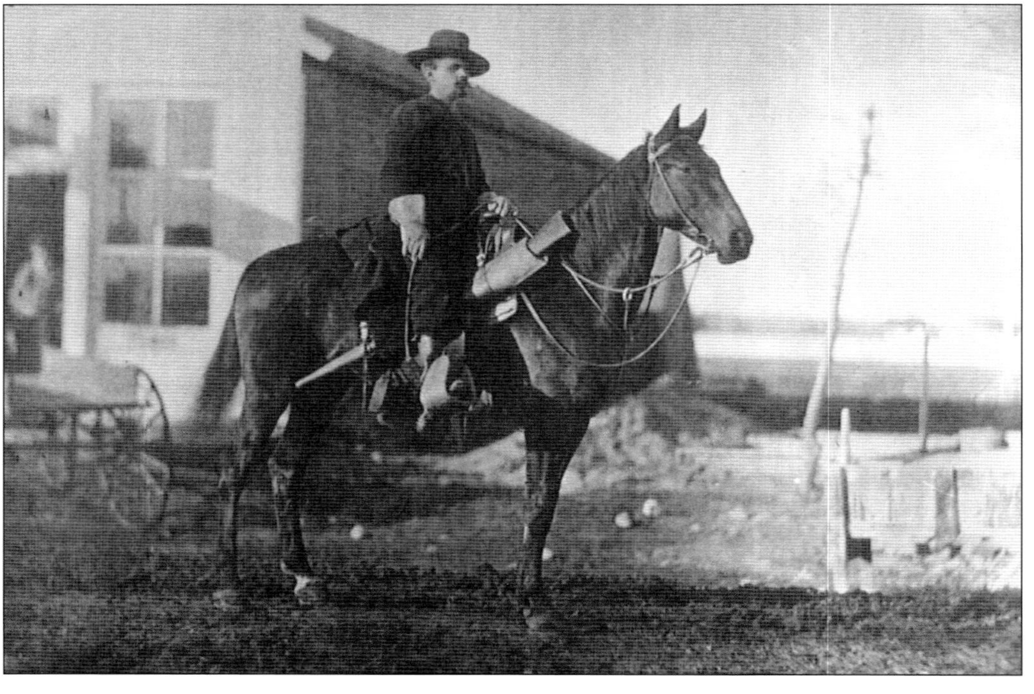

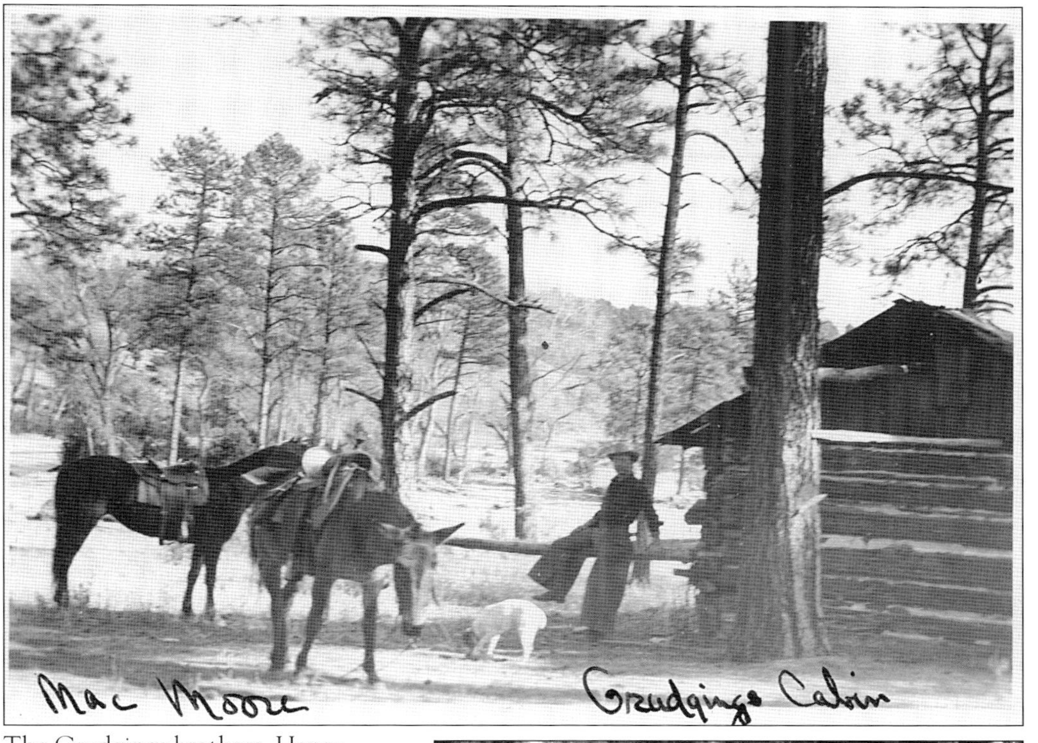

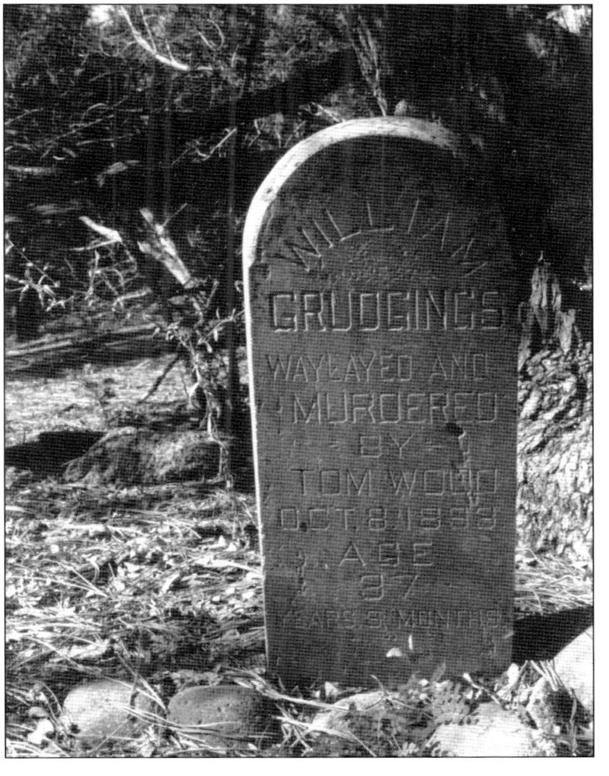

The Grudgings brothers, Henry, William, and Charley, built a cabin on the West Fork of the Gila River in 1885. They were known to be cattle rustlers, although they made similar claims against the Wood family, who had a homestead over the mountain on Iron Creek. In 1893, William allegedly ambushed and killed 15-year-old Charley Wood and Francisco Diaz, who were bringing in supplies from Mogollon. In retaliation, Tom Wood killed William Grudgings, but was found not guilty upon surrendering to Silver City authorities in 1896. William was buried by his brothers near the Grudgings cabin, which stood for many years. His headstone inscription, which reads "William Grudgings, Waylaid and Murdered By Tom Wood, October 8, 1893, Age 37 Years 8 Months," is all that remains of the legendary feud. (Both, courtesy of Ida Campbell.)

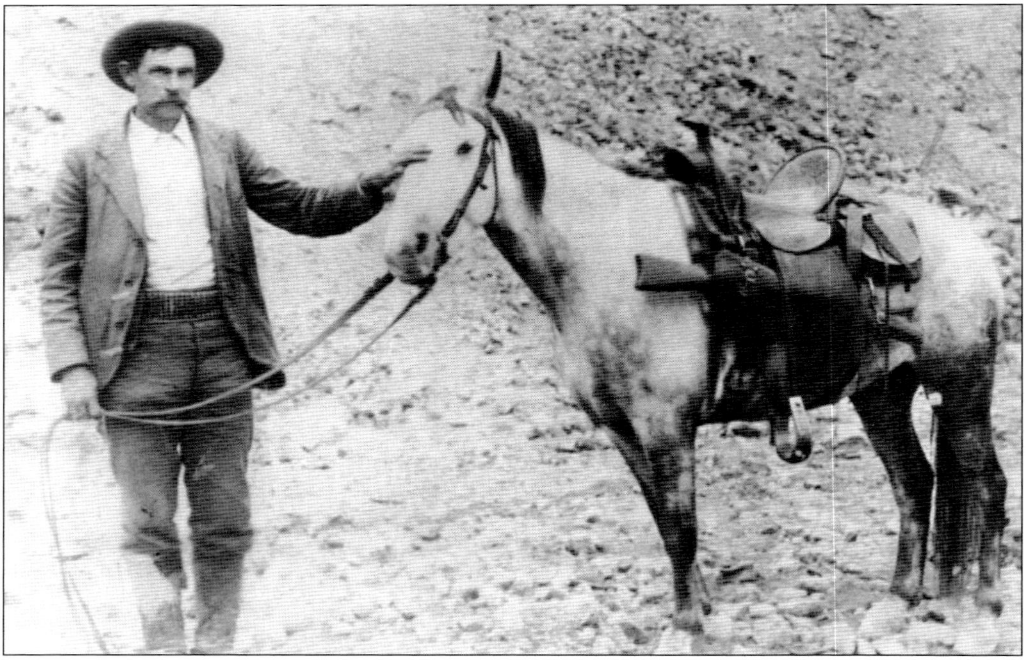

In 1900, deputy sheriffs William D. "Keechi" Johnson, above, and Miles Marshall trailed two murderers into Mexico. Upon capturing them, however, they had to hold them in leg irons for weeks until authorities allowed the prisoners to be extradited back into the United States. The *Silver City Independent* described the three-month trip as "one of the longest pursuits ever made by a local officer." Later that year, Johnson arrested cattle rustler Ralph Jenks. While bringing in his prisoner, Johnson was shot twice, supposedly by a pair of outlaws. Jenks went for help, but it arrived too late to save Johnson, who was buried on the spot. Suspicious of Jenks's story, Sheriff Scarborough went to bring in the cattle rustler, but when Jenks allegedly tried to take his rifle, the sheriff shot him three times, killing him instantly. Jenks's cabin is pictured below. (Above, courtesy of Roy and Gary Sinclair; below, courtesy of Ida Campbell.)

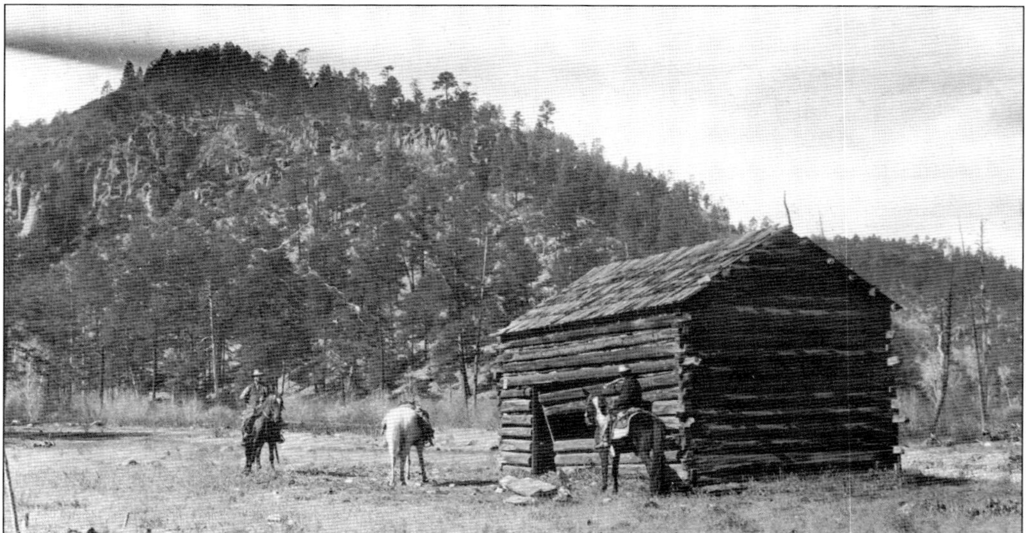

Diamond A cowboy Howard Chenowth killed Silver City marshals Perfecto Rodriquez and William Kilburn in a shootout at the Club House Saloon in 1904. After a jury found him guilty and sentenced him to 50 years, Chenowth escaped to Brazil. In 1927, he returned to New Mexico and was granted a pardon. Chenowth became an honorable citizen, cowboying until his death in 1947. (Courtesy of Retta Smith.)

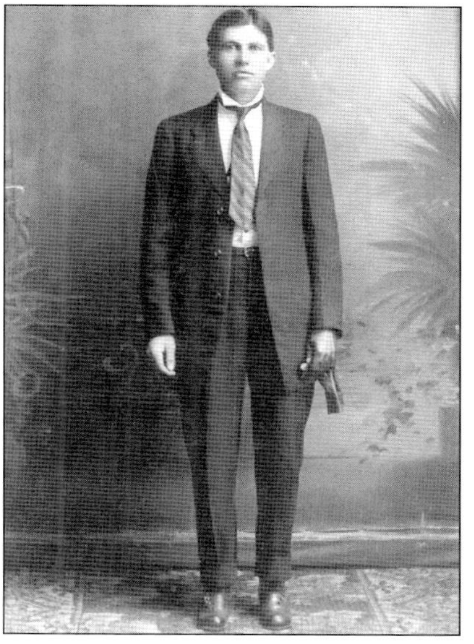

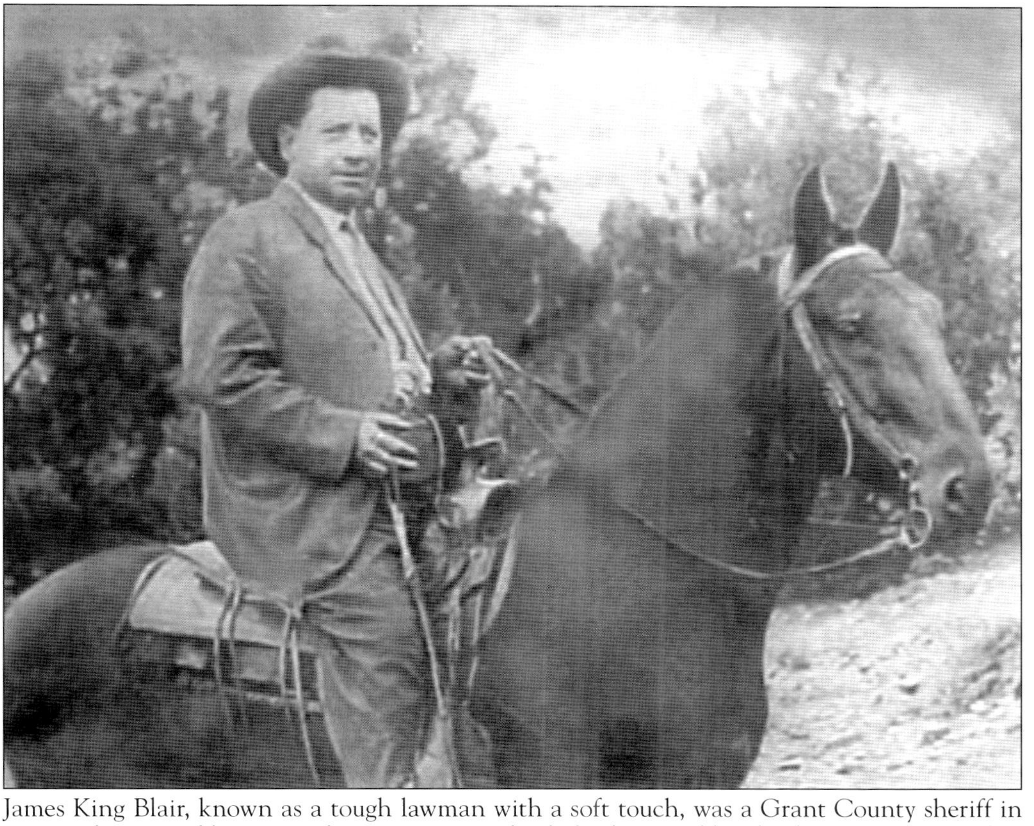

James King Blair, known as a tough lawman with a soft touch, was a Grant County sheriff in 1899 and 1903 and later served as Santa Rita's chief of police until his death in 1941. Here, Blair is mounted on his horse Carrie, named after his friend Dr. Frank Carrier. Blair married Inez Diaz about 1912, and the couple and their five children lived on what became known as "Blair Hill" in the Hispanic section of Santa Rita.

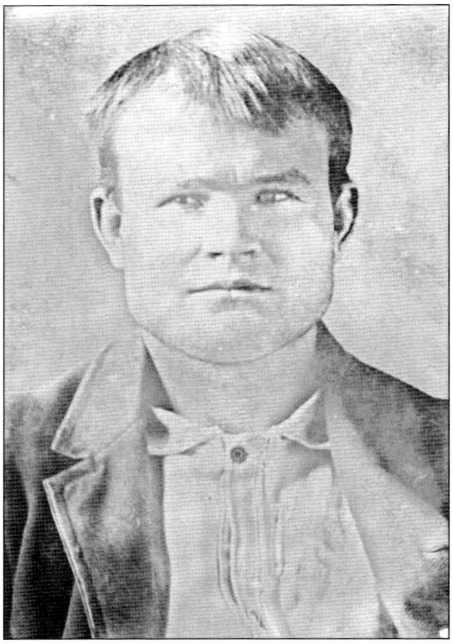

Butch Cassidy and some of his Wild Bunch gang took a break from robbing trains in the 1890s, hiding out at the WS Ranch northwest of Silver City, working as ranch hands under assumed names. Ranch manager Capt. William French remembered them as good cowboys, noting that Butch led a 200-mile cattle drive to Magdalena, New Mexico, and never lost a cow. (Courtesy of the Library of Congress.)

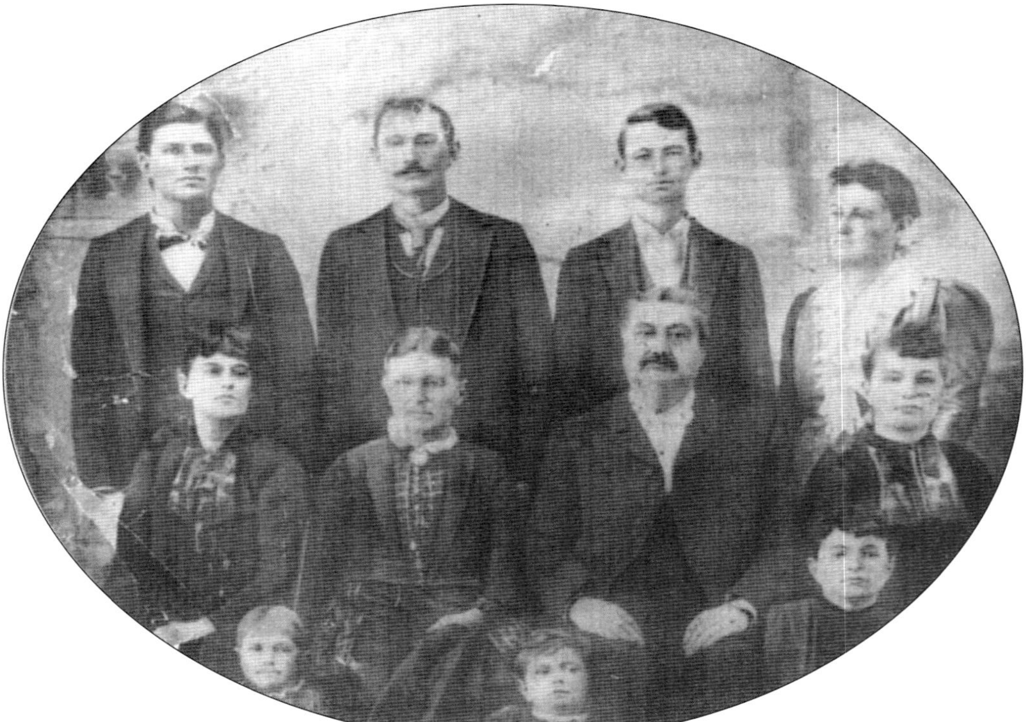

Harvey Howard Whitehill came to Silver City as a prospector and became a Grant County sheriff. He was the first lawman to arrest Billy the Kid. His family, pictured here in 1891, includes, from left to right, (first row) Carolyn Clayton, Mary Hudson, and Olive Priscilla; (second row) Josephine Stevens, Harriet Margaret, Harvey Whitehill, and Harriet Jeanette; (third row) Wayne Washington, Harry Vance, Cornelius Cosgrove, and Emma Smith. (Courtesy of William Bishop.)

Carlotta Thompkins was a gifted card player, and, as "Lottie Deno," is said to have beaten Doc Holliday at poker. After hours, Lottie also worked the back rooms. Her biographer, Jan Devereaux, wrote that Lottie's sleight of hand could lay out an ace just as easily as she could lay down for a dollar. Later, in Deming, Lottie reinvented herself when she became Mrs. Frank Thurmond. She is seen in the center of this photograph during an outing in the mountains. (Courtesy of Jan Devereaux.)

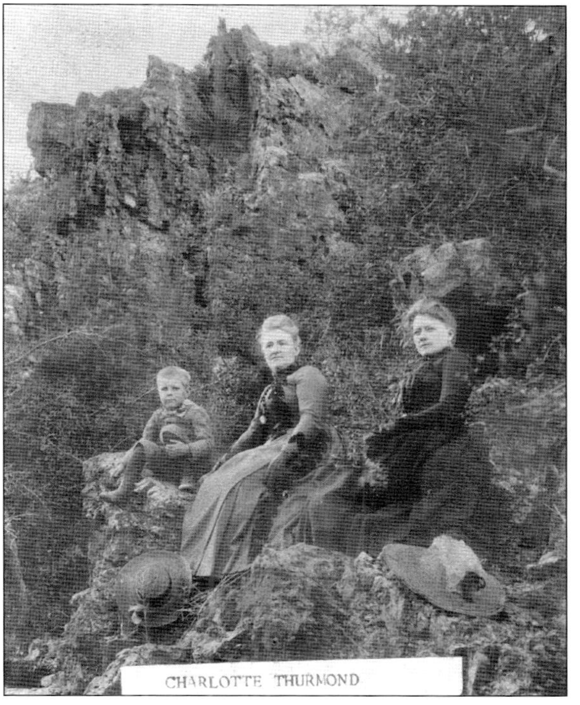

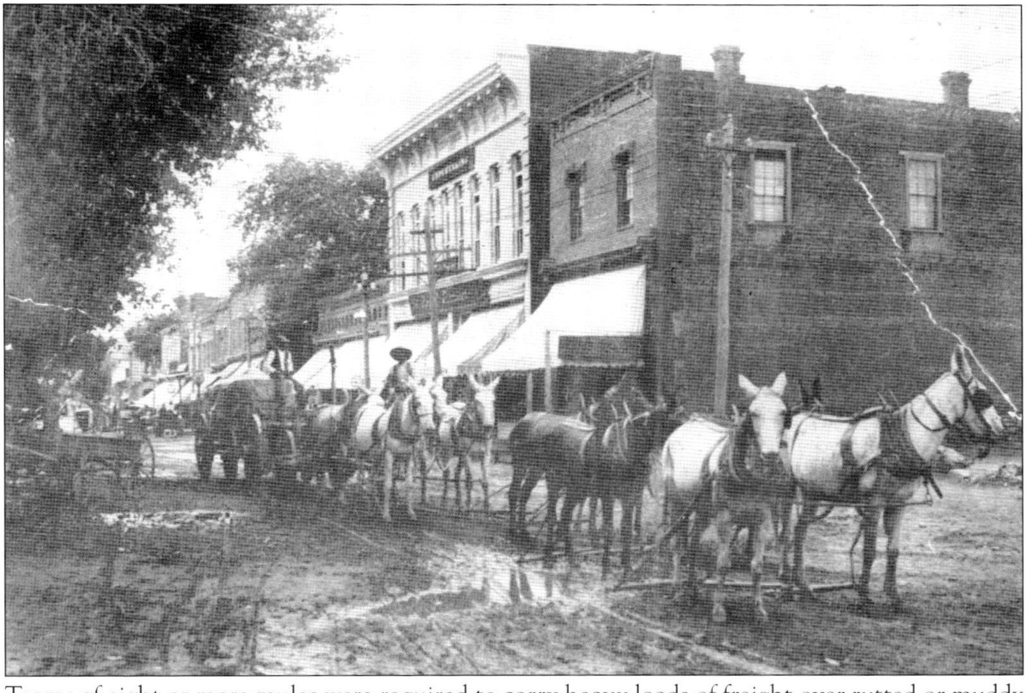

Teams of eight or more mules were required to carry heavy loads of freight over rutted or muddy dirt roads, and Silver City's unpaved streets made heavy work even of town travel. In this 1905 photograph, a W.A. Tenney freighting team at Bullard and Market Streets is likely heading north to Mogollon. (Courtesy of Don Turner.)

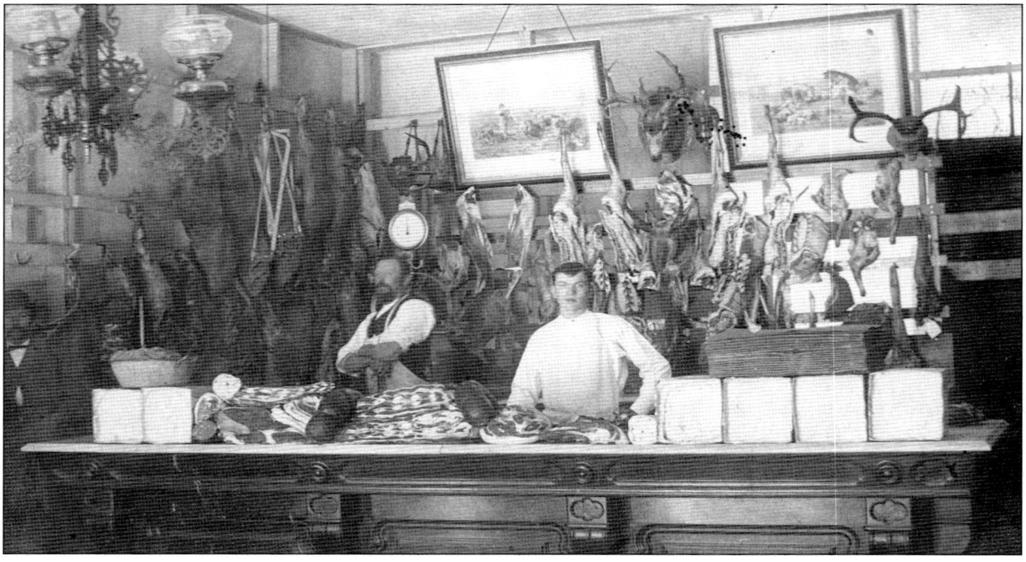

Born in Germany in 1863, Stephan Uhli came to Silver City in the early 1880s and worked at McMillen's meat market. In the photograph above, Uhli is on the right, and Henry Geitz is to the left. In 1885, Uhli started a saloon business, and in 1897, when he was in his early 30s, he built the Uhli Block. Below, he stands in front of his Cave Saloon at the southwest corner of Broadway and Texas Streets. Uhli died in 1903, soon after this building was completed. He was only 40 years old. (Above, courtesy of Don Turner; below, courtesy of Jean Uhli.)

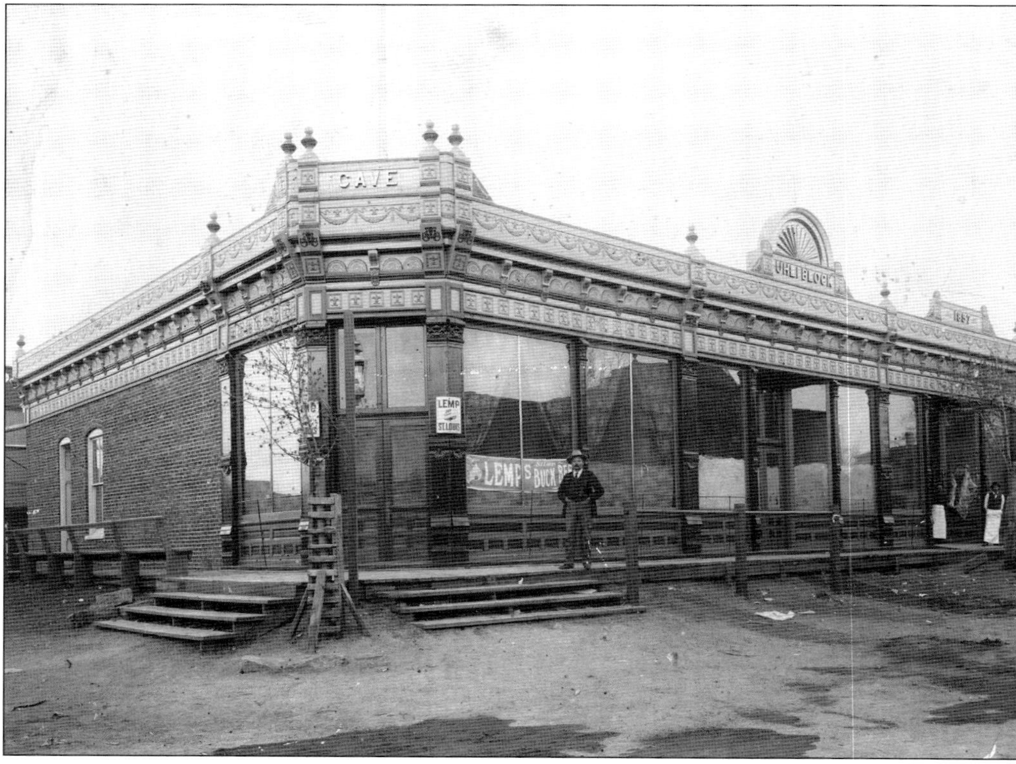

Fourth of July celebrations have always been very popular in Silver City. At right, townspeople are assembled in front of the Palace Hotel at the corner of Broadway and Bullard Street, apparently listening to speeches being given by dignitaries on a platform in front of the hotel. Below, a 1911 parade entry from the Texas Petroleum Company (an oil tank decorated with American flags) is being pulled by a team of horses. (Right, courtesy of Don Turner; below, courtesy of Anthony Romero.)

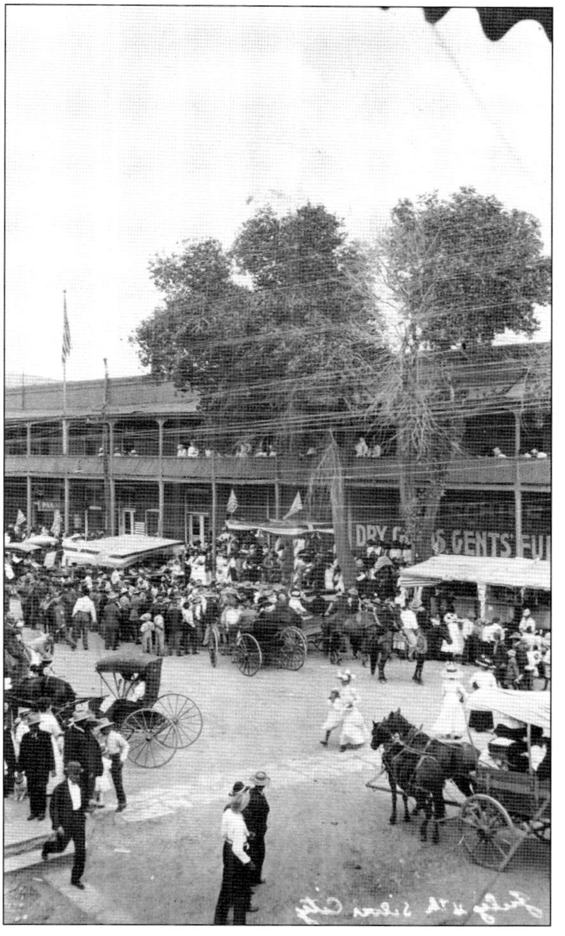

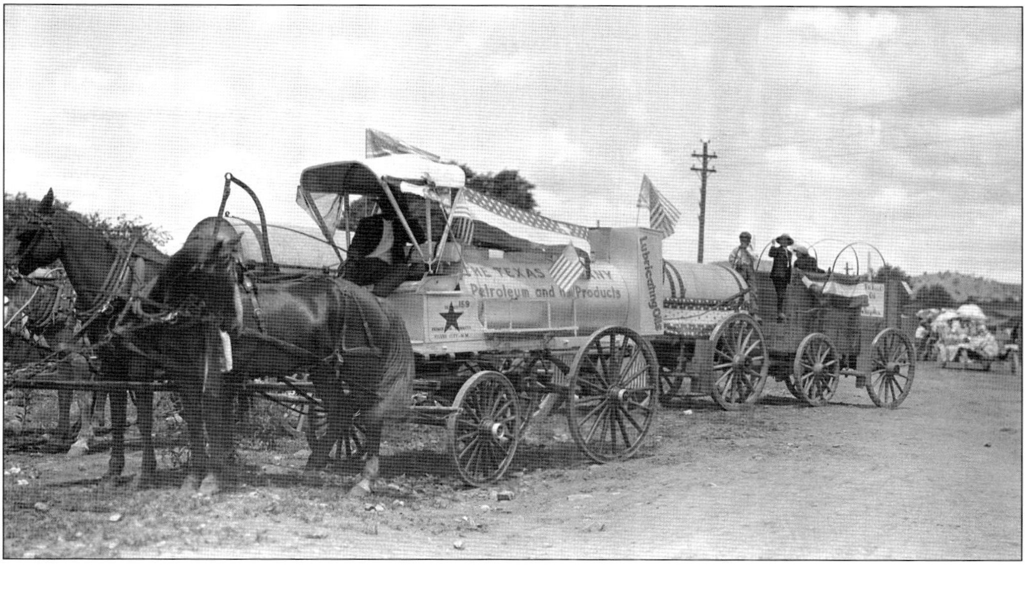

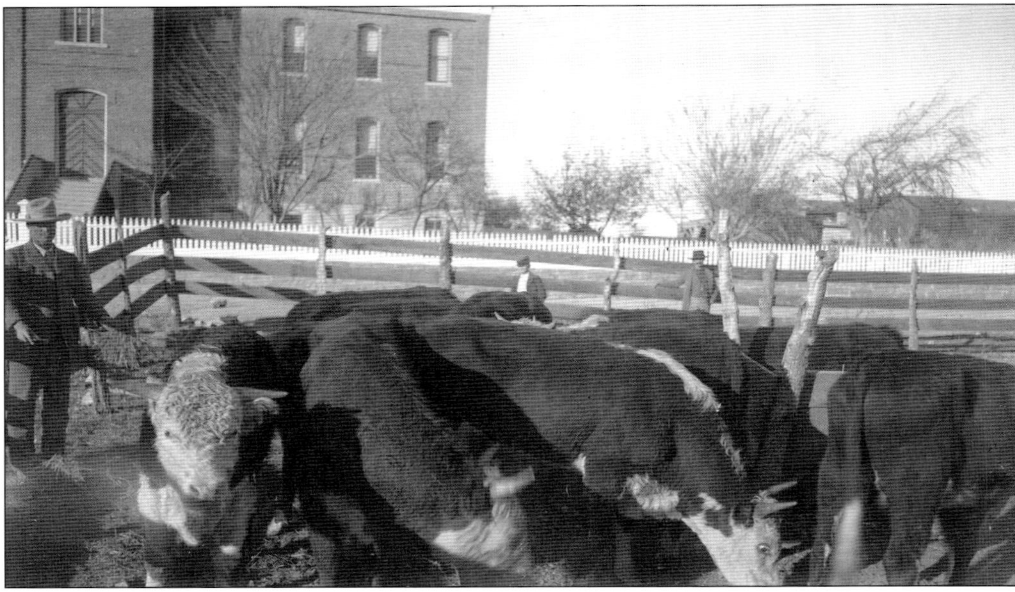

Daniel C. McMillen brought in some of the first registered bulls to his AT Cross Ranch. Initially, they were shipped to Silver City and held in the cattle pen in back of the Academy of Our Lady of Lourdes on Kelly and Cooper Streets. Later, the registered cattle were moved to the ranch. McMillen came to Silver City in 1876 and worked at the 76 Mine. Afterwards, he homesteaded northwest of town. Although he and his family lived on the ranch, they were never bothered by Apaches. McMillen also had a butcher shop in Silver City, but over time he bought up neighboring ranches, and his holdings grew to be some of the largest in the country. Below, McMillen Ranch cowboys move a herd of cattle. (Both, courtesy of Judy Billings.)

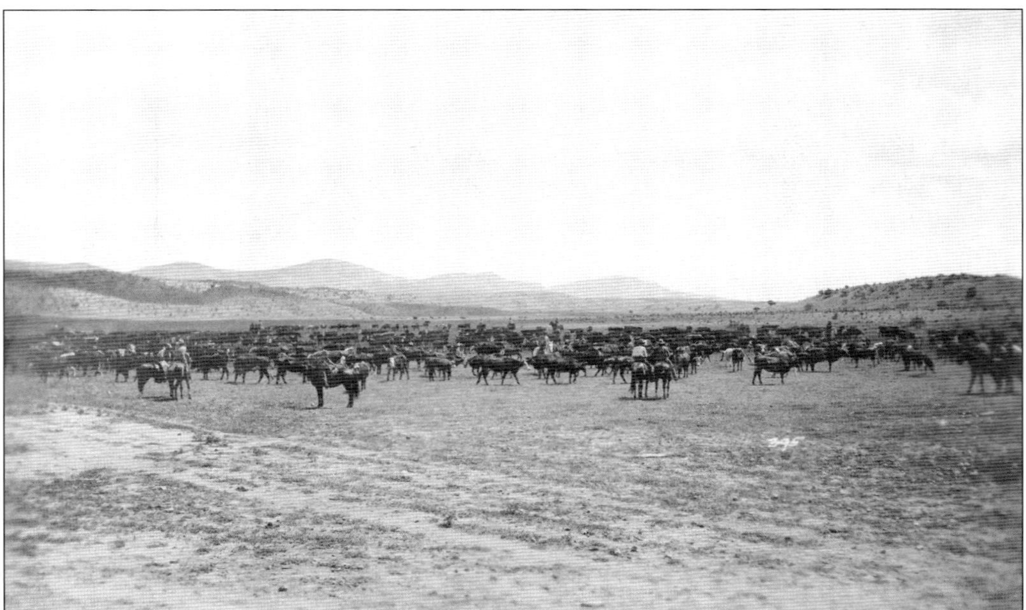

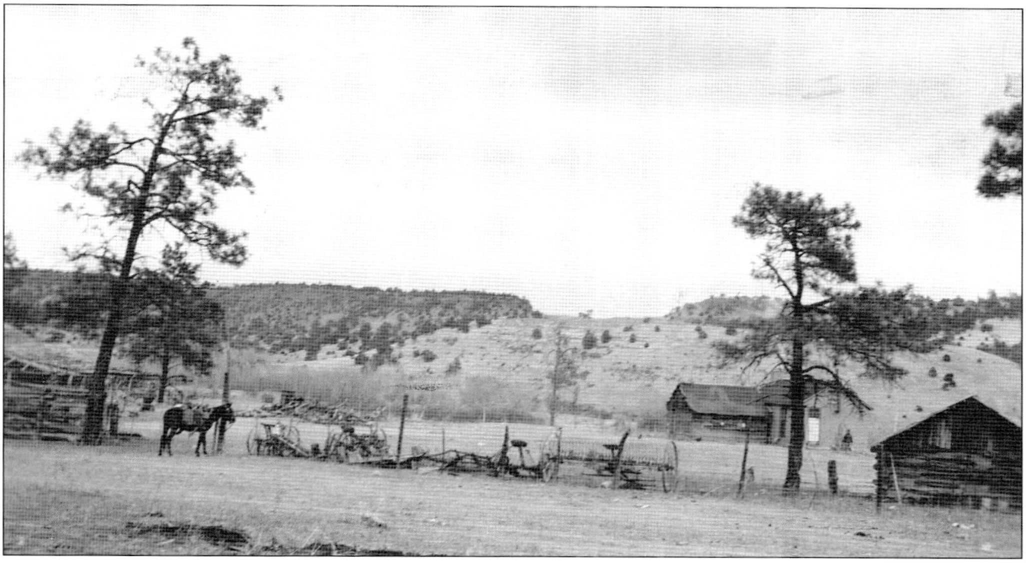

TJ Ranch, shown in this 1922 photograph, later became the Heart Bar Ranch owned by Johnny Converse, a Princeton man lured west with tales of cowboys and cattle. The Heart Bar is now managed through the Gila Cliff Dwellings National Monument. On the bench across the river are the ruins of a prehistoric Mimbres village. This flat was also the polo field for Converse's Princeton visitors. (Courtesy of Ida Campbell.)

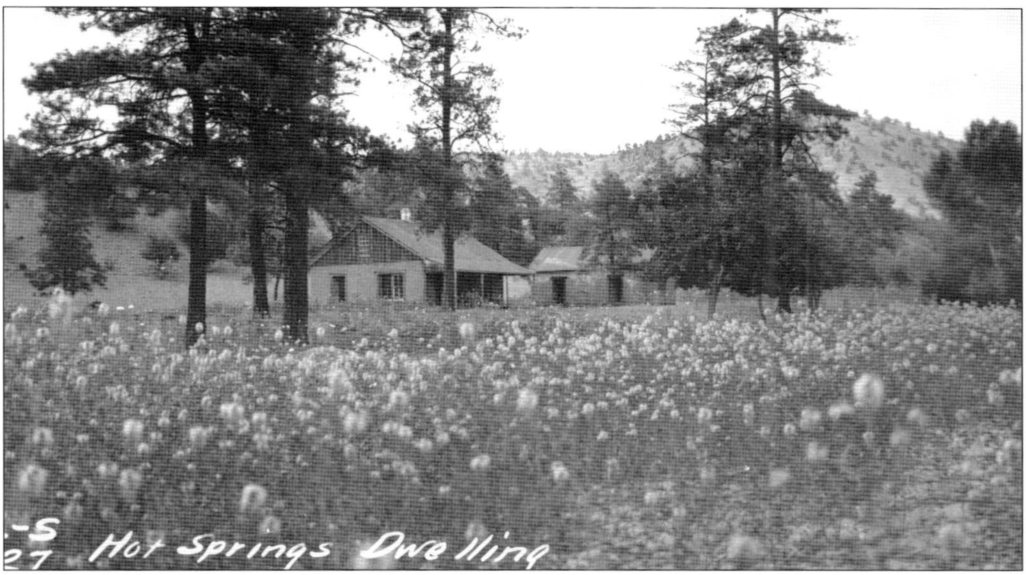

Brothers Spencer, James, and Samuel Hill moved to New Mexico in 1870 to raise horses for military use in the Indian Wars. The brothers homesteaded adjoining pieces of land at Gila Hot Springs, downstream from TJ Ranch, and built the two-story adobe house in the middle section in 1888. (Courtesy of Ida Campbell.)

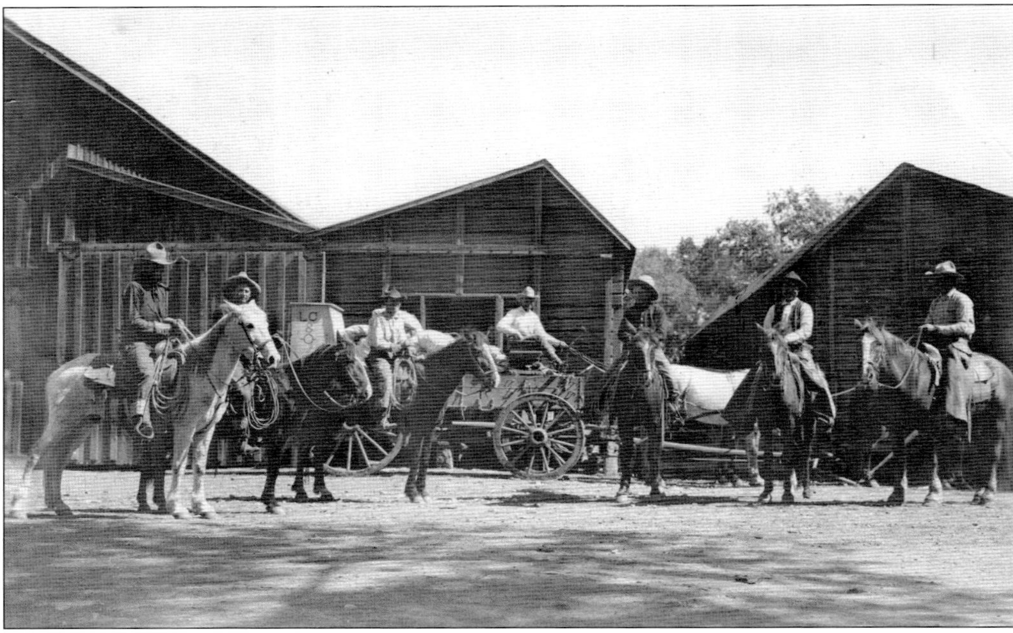

Angus Campbell discovered the Cosette Mine in the 1870s and built a foundry in Silver City. In 1880, he and Thomas Lyons each sold their mining interests and partnered in a new cattle-business venture called the LC. They established a ranch headquarters on Duck Creek, northwest of Silver City, and built a cattle empire that stretched from Silver City to the Arizona border and from Mule Creek south to Animas, New Mexico, controlling more than 1.5 million acres. The LC Ranch grazed 60,000 cattle, and was supported by 100 wagons, 750 horses, 400 workhorses, and 75 employed cowboys (including some hired gunmen) during roundup and branding seasons. Angus Campbell died in 1892, and the cattle empire came to an end in 1917 when Thomas Lyons was murdered by an unknown assailant. (Both, courtesy of Ida Campbell.)

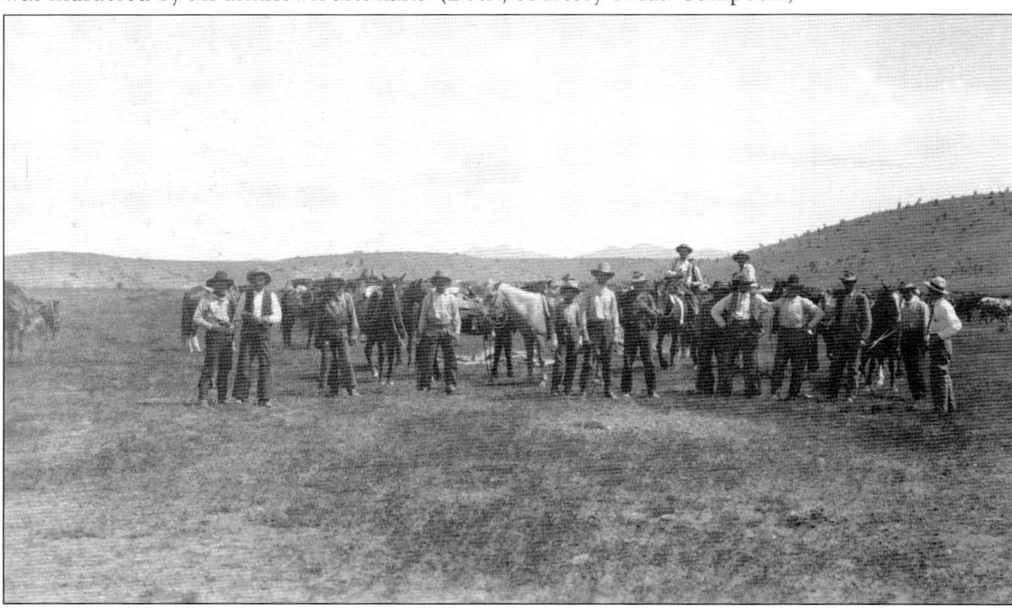

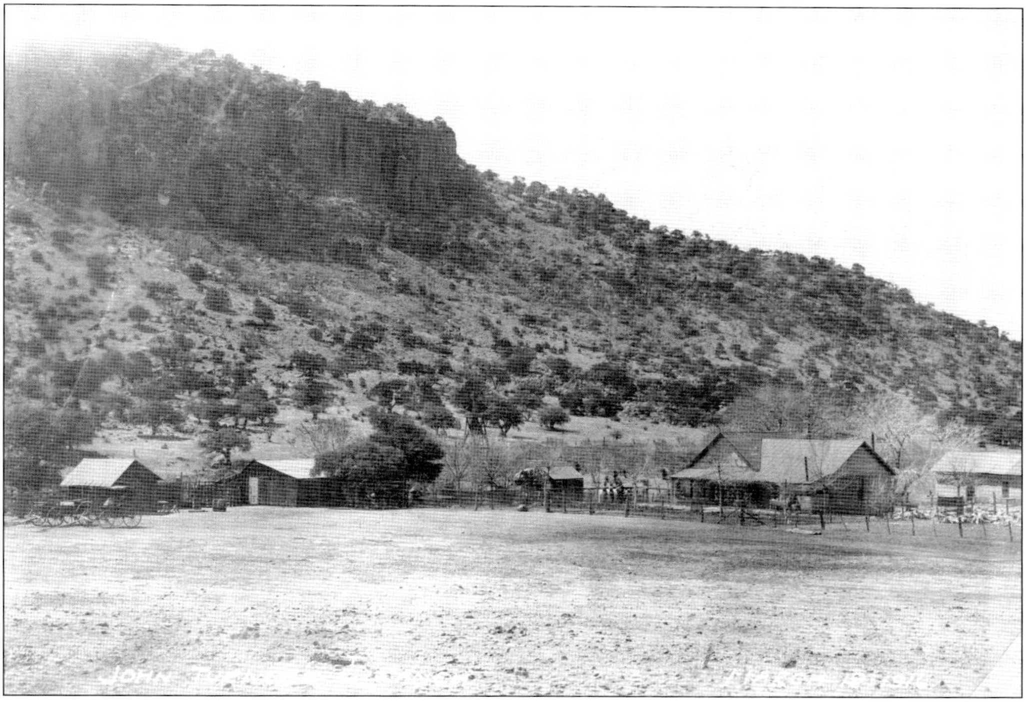

The beautiful T-Box Ranch is eight miles east of Santa Rita. Owned by Charles Hugo in the 1880s, the property consisted of almost 1,000 acres. George L. and John W. Turner purchased the ranch in 1908, and Tom Harrington bought it in 1917 from the GOS Cattle Company. The Turners and the Harringtons were prominent Grant County ranching families. Pictured below around 1910 are, from left to right, Tom, Ruth, and Flora Flury Harrington. The T-Box Ranch was a showplace, and was known for the popular swimming and dancing parties hosted by the family during the 1930s. (Both, courtesy of Don Turner.)

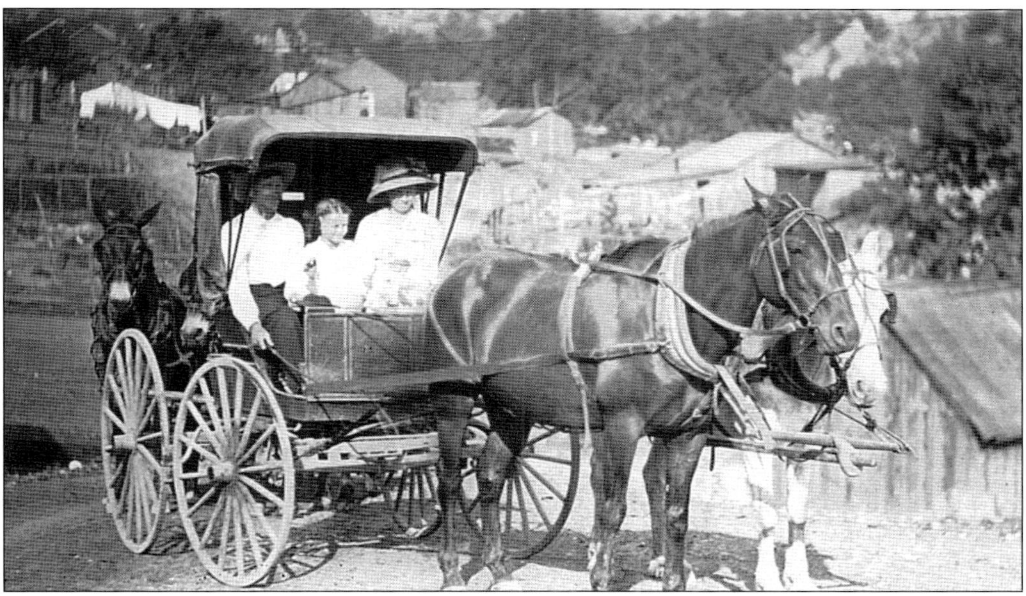

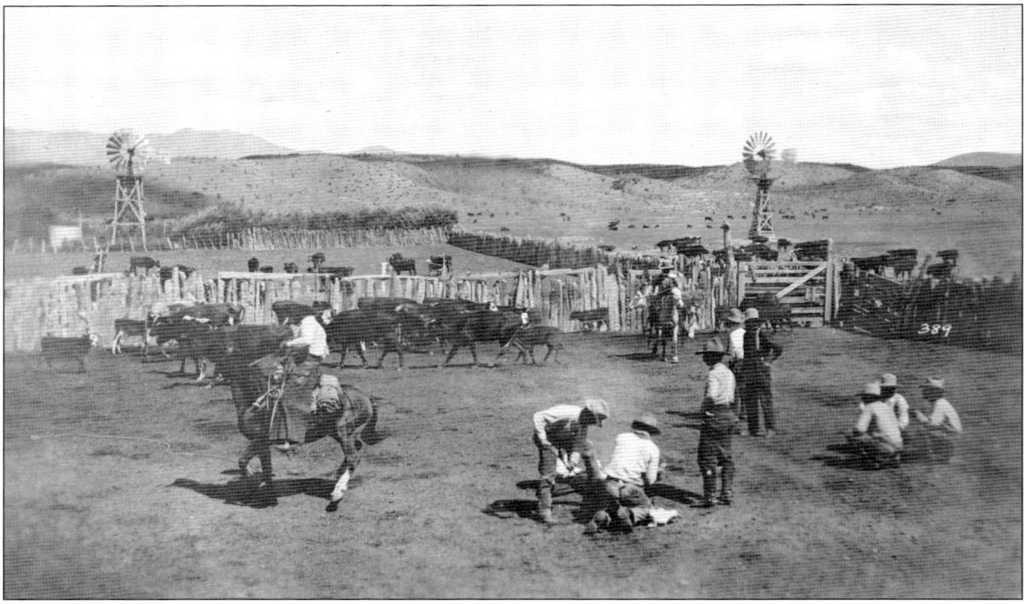

Roundups were annual events at the ranches surrounding Silver City. Cattle were gathered into pens for branding and the chuck wagon provided food and coffee for the hardworking cowboys. On Mangas Creek, 12 miles west of Silver City, McMillen Ranch cowboys branded the AT Cross in 1909. (Both, courtesy of Judy Billings.)

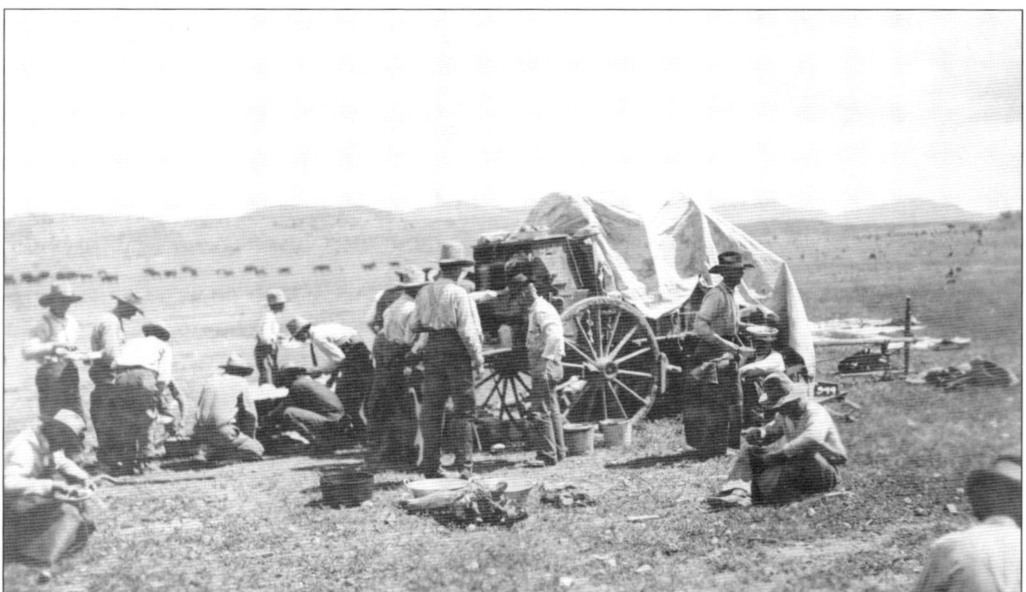

Brooks Lee was a real cowboy, working for the Diamond A Cattle Company. During World War I, he enlisted in the US Army and stayed on to fight with the White Armed Forces (White Russians), against the pro-Bolshevik Red Army. Lee was killed in action in Siberia on June 25, 1919. (Courtesy of Don Turner.)

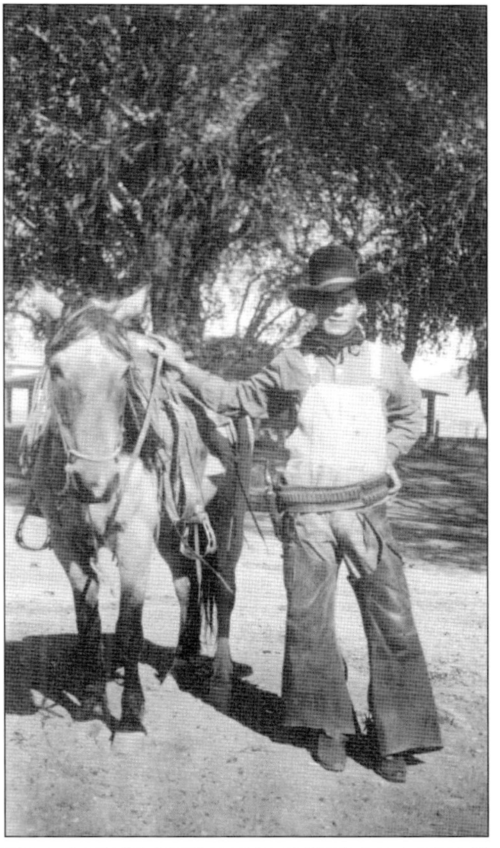

The Diamond A Cattle Company was a vast ranch in southwestern New Mexico, and the chuck wagon covered many miles traveling out into the range to keep the cowboys well fed. Note the Dutch ovens in front. Pictured in this c. 1895 photograph are, from left to right, Jim Reynolds, Richard Hudson (founder of Hudson's Hot Springs), Herbert Bishop, three unidentified men, Louis Bishop, and Charles Holson. (Courtesy of William Bishop.)

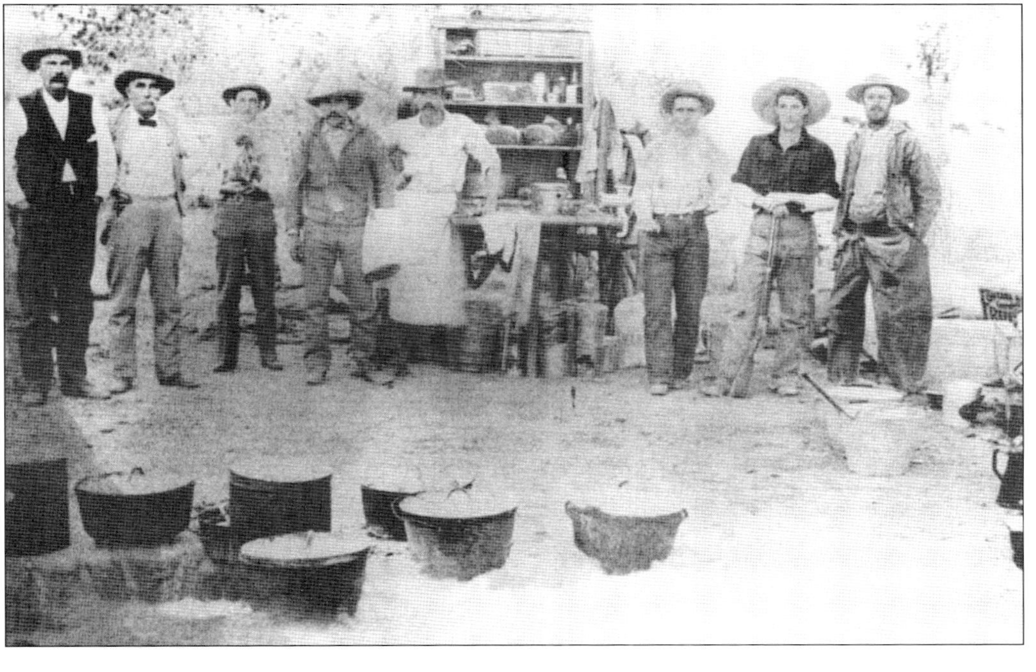

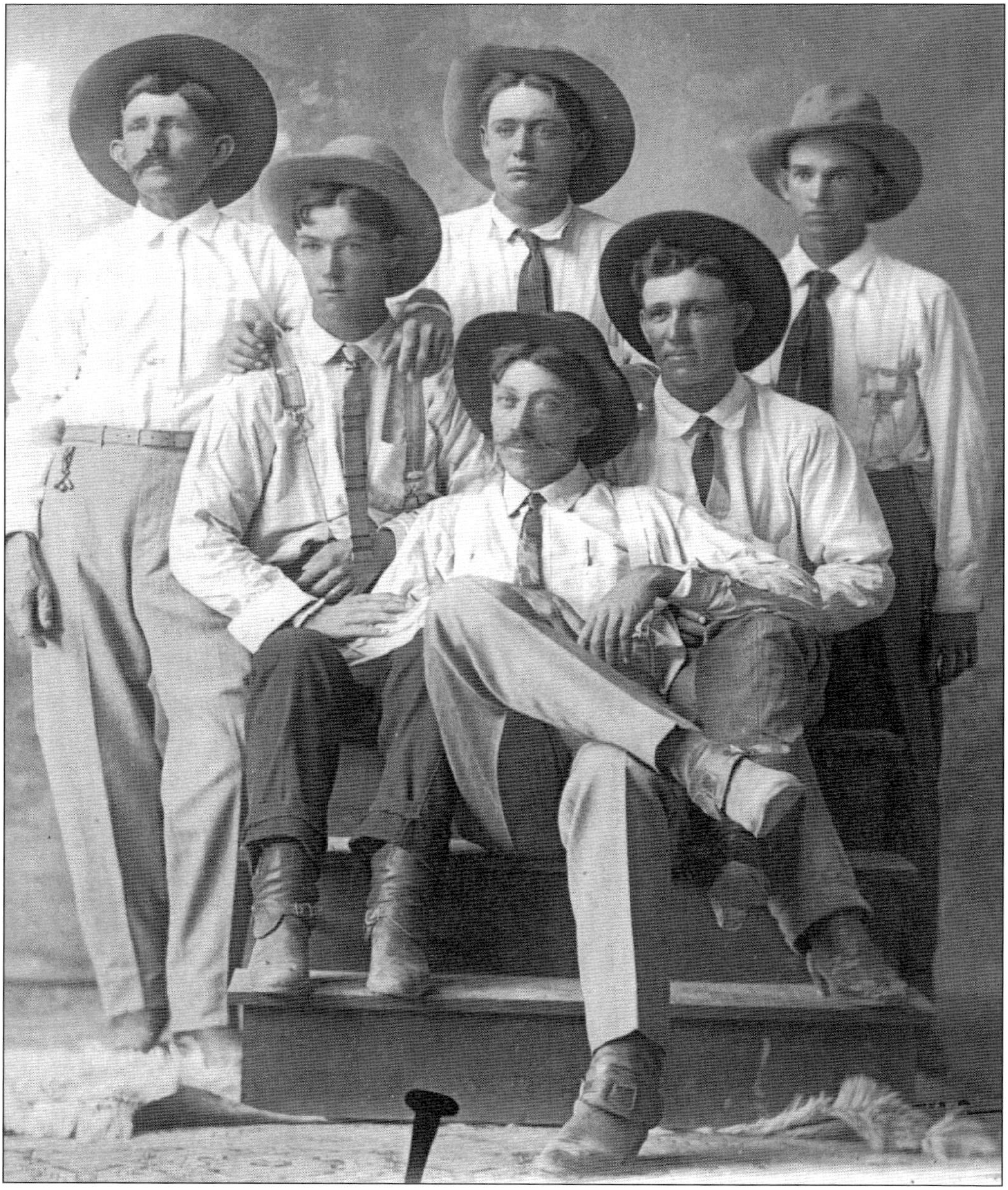

These NAN Ranch cowboys put on their town clothes and went to Deming, New Mexico, in 1911. They are, from left to right, (first row, seated) Dudley Lyons, Will Colson, and Will Bullard; (second row, standing) John B. Gibson, Bob Richardson, and Leslie K. Goforth. The ranch, which is also the location of a large, prehistoric Classic Mimbres village, was named by archaeologist Cornelius Burton Cosgrove in 1926 after its cattle brand, NAN. Beginning in the 1970s, the site was studied for 25 years by archaeologists from Texas A&M University. (Courtesy of Don Turner.)

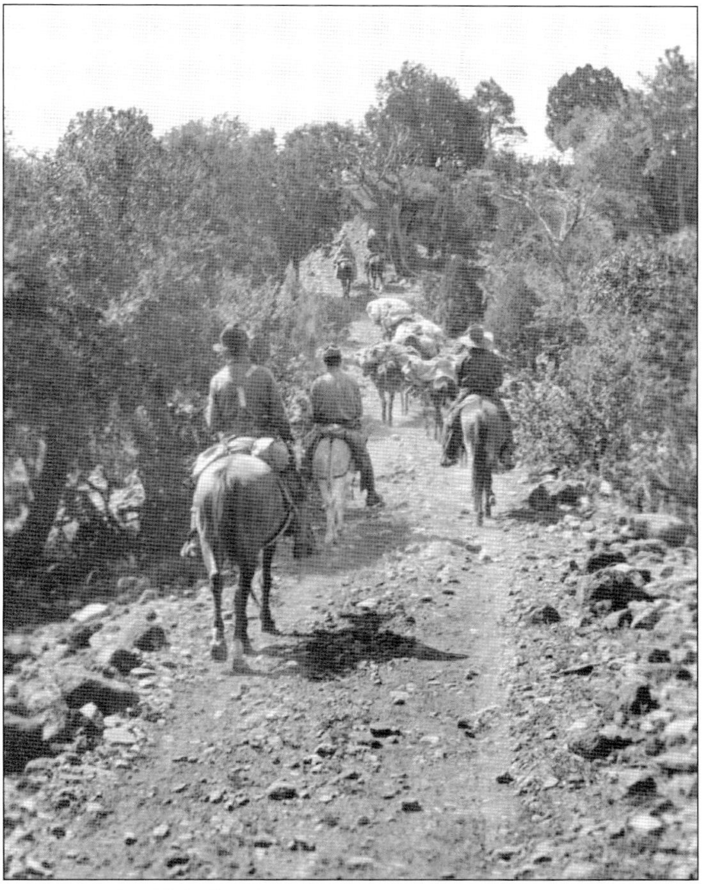

A group of young friends from Silver City made the long horse-packing trip to the Gila River in 1910, following the trail near Meadow Creek, then dropping into the Hot Springs, and following the Gila River to the Gila Cliff Dwellings for a few days of camping and exploring. They proudly show off their stringer of fish caught in the Gila River. (Both, courtesy of Jean Eckard.)

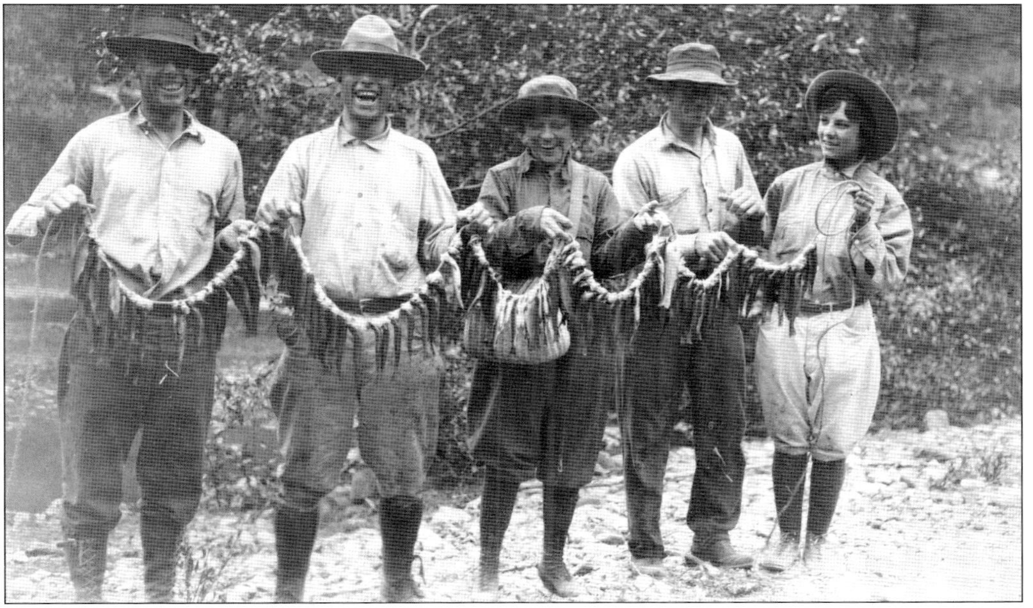

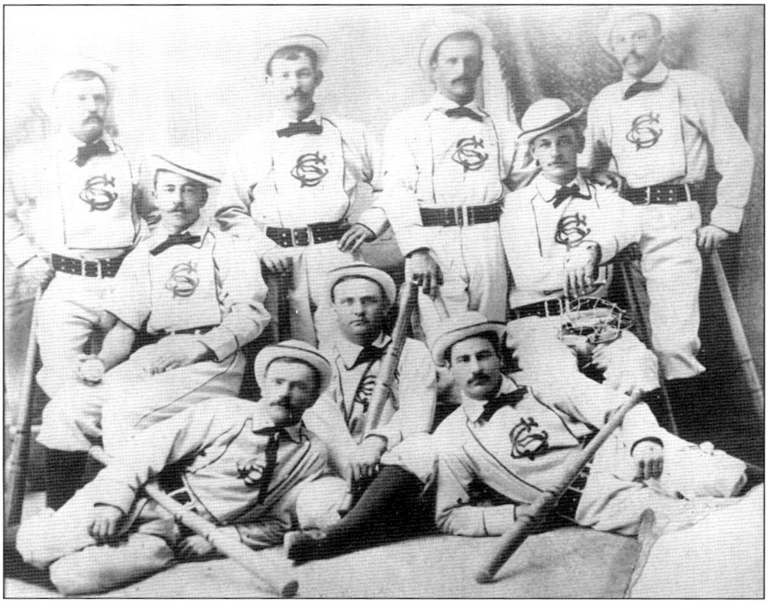

Silver City has long loved baseball. This early photograph shows 1882 Silver City baseball team members Jerry Hurley, short stop; Sam McAninch, third base; J.B. Risque, second base; Harry Booth, first base; W.E. Watson, pitcher; Andy Mills, catcher; Pat Rose, left field; George Huffaker, center field; and Jean Le Baux, right field. (Courtesy of Don Turner.)

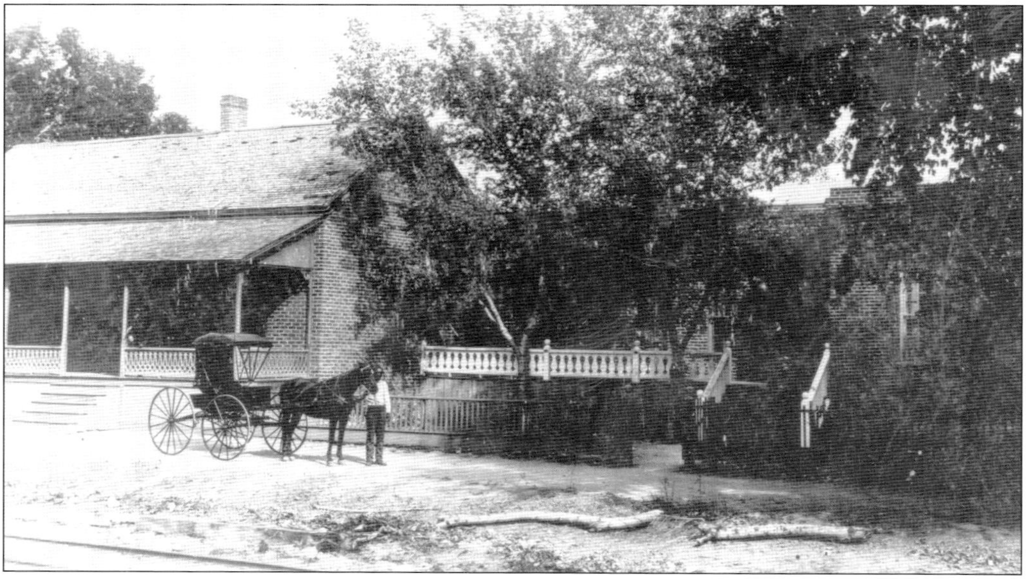

In 1883, when a women's sewing circle reorganized itself as the Grant County Charity Hospital Society, Silver City's only public health facility was a pest house for the isolation of smallpox patients. The first hospital soon opened in a donated cottage and, in 1884, moved to a building at Hudson and Market Streets. After several name changes and multiple locations, the hospital survives today as Gila Regional Medical Center. (Courtesy of Gila Regional Medical Center.)

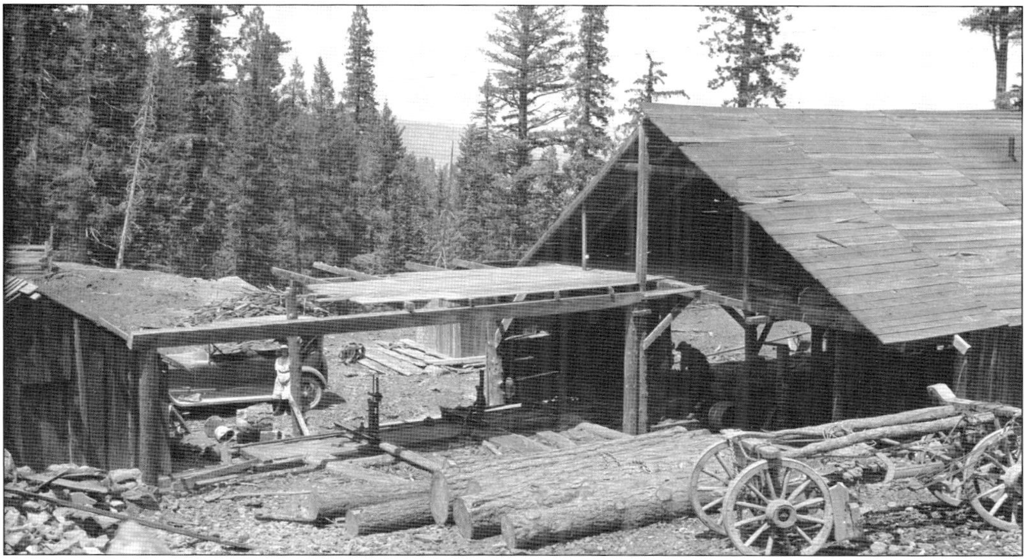

The government sawmill, above, was located in the hills eight miles above Fort Bayard. The forests were heavily logged for lumber for the fort and the town, as well as for mine timbers. Woodcutters harvested scrub growth as fuel for homes and businesses, and huge herds of horses, cattle, sheep, goats, and burros grazed the hillsides around Silver City. Without trees and vegetation to absorb the water, summer rains washed down the hillsides, and floodwaters filled Silver City streets every year. In the c. 1910 photograph below, a wagon is traveling against the current, going north on Bullard Street during one of the seasonal floods. (Both, courtesy of Anthony Romero.)

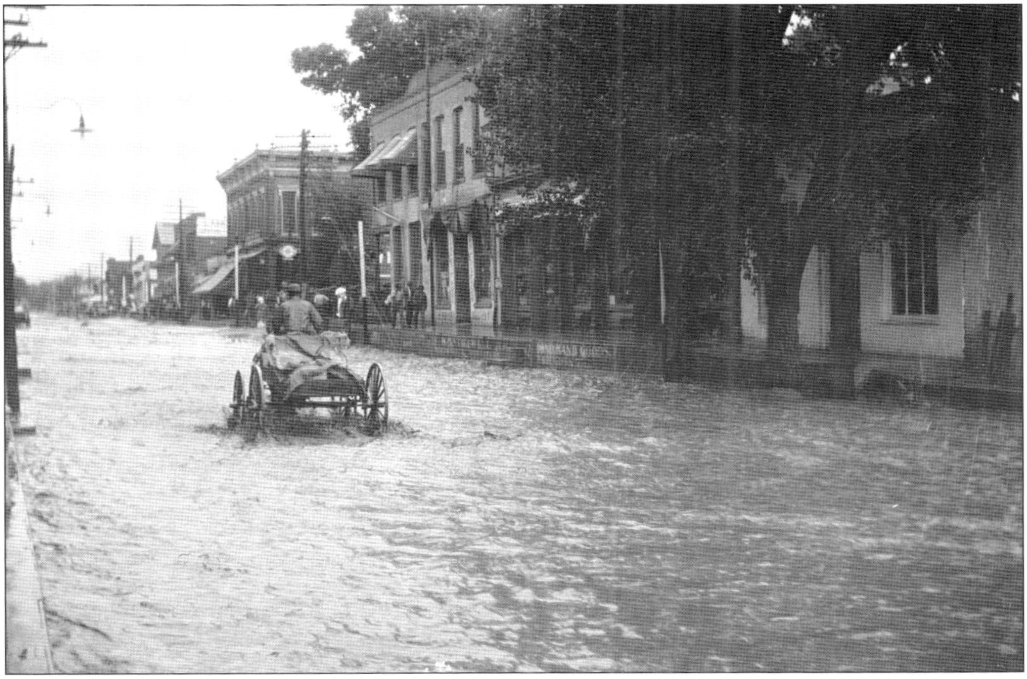

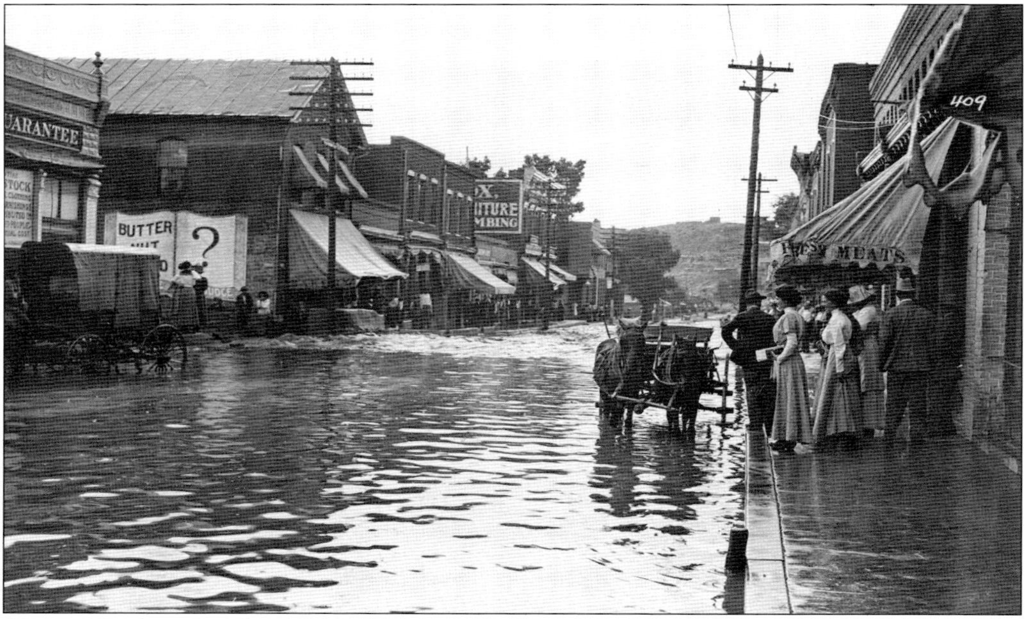

As more settlers moved to Silver City, the watershed above town was denuded, and by the 1890s, local newspapers spoke of an annual "flood season." The 1910 image above, looking south from Market Street, shows Bullard Street transformed into a wide, rushing stream. More water flowed down Main Street, one block to the east, and buildings were washed away when floods gouged an arroyo over 50 feet deep. Main Street moved one block west to Bullard, and the arroyo became a recessed downtown park known as the Big Ditch. Below, the *Silver City Enterprise* newspaper office on Main Street was undermined in the disastrous flood of August 1902. Bullard Street and Broadway became more important business venues after Main Street's demise. (Above, courtesy of Don Turner; below, courtesy of Jean Uhli.)

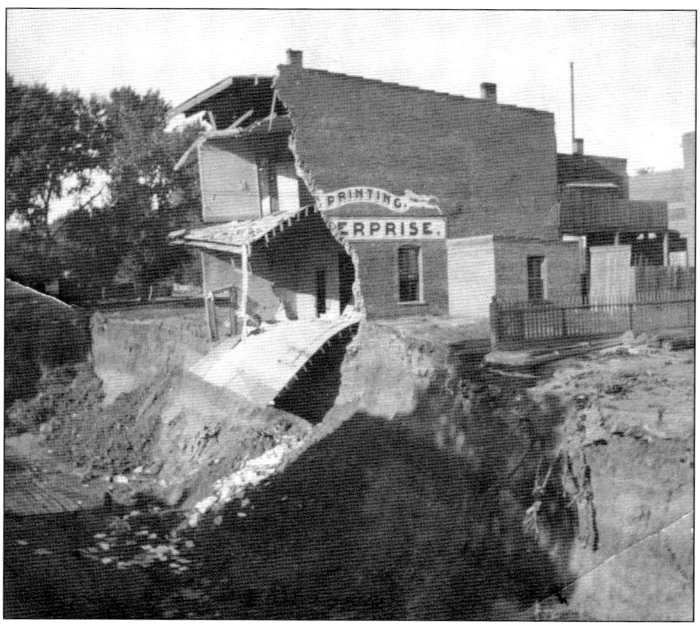

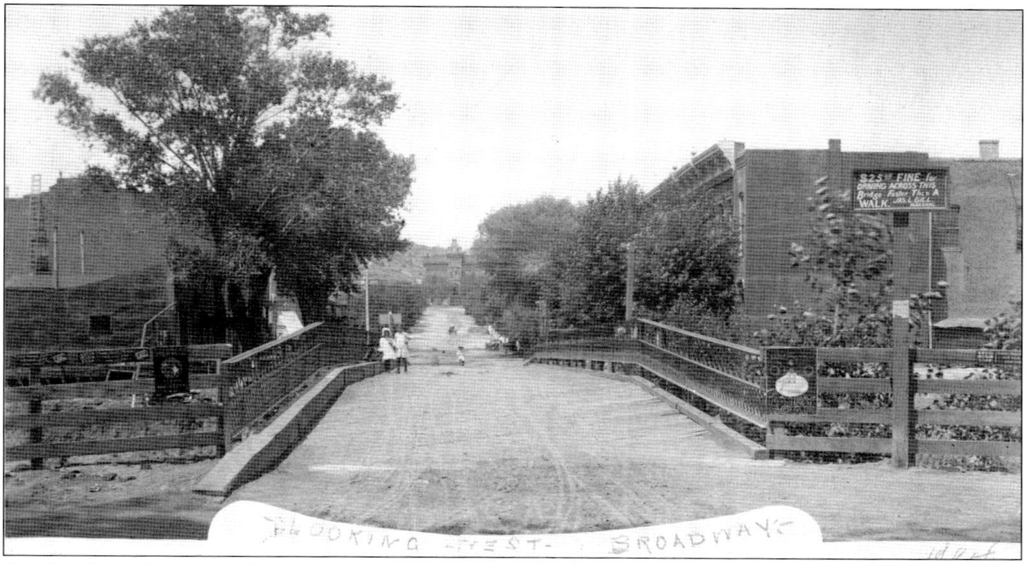

As floods washed out Main Street, a succession of bridges was built over the arroyo. In this early-20th-century view looking west on Broadway, the courthouse sits at the top end of the street. At left is the Exchange Saloon, and the Howell Drug Company building is on the right. The sign warns of a $25 fine for driving across the bridge any faster than a walk. (Courtesy of Lynn Geyer.)

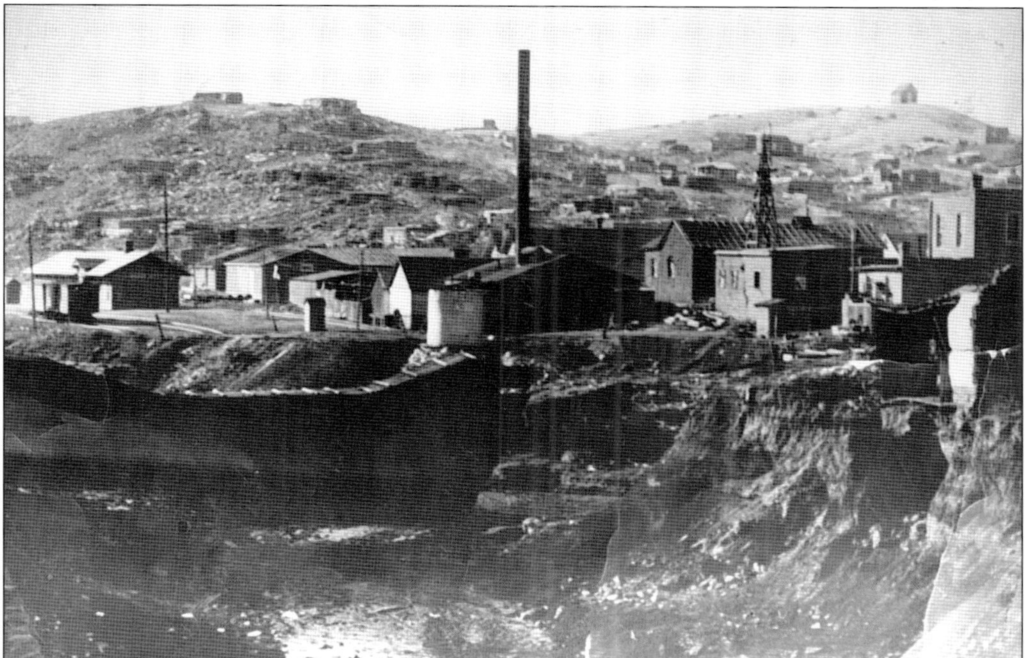

A dam was built across the Main Street arroyo at Spring Street early in 1903. The west half of the structure washed away that summer, leaving only the portion seen in this January 1904 view. The east half was destroyed by another flood the following August. Looking south, La Capilla perches on the skyline. The center building with the tall chimney is the electric power plant, and the railroad depot is at left. (Courtesy of Don Turner.)

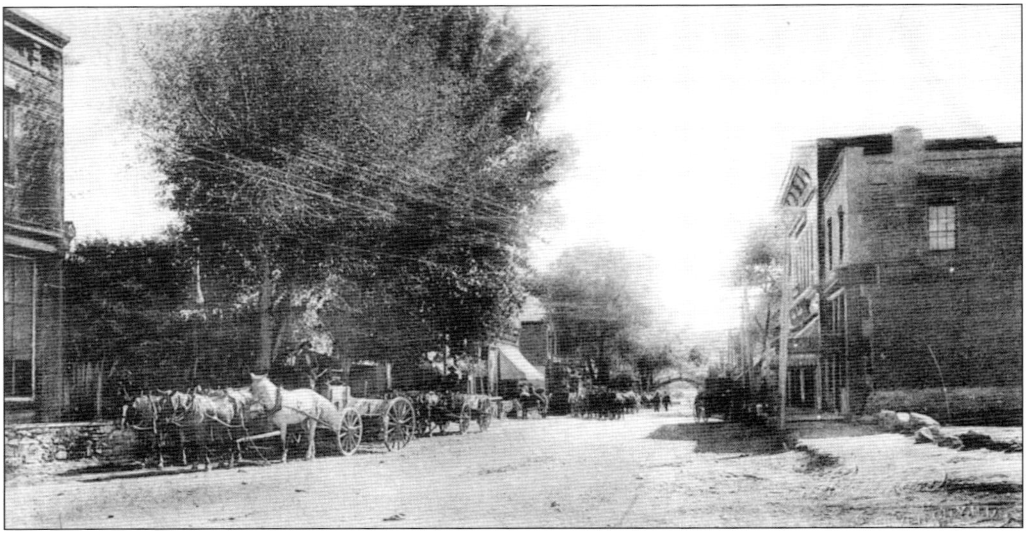

In the 1906 photograph above, looking south on Bullard Street, two freighters have their loads packed and ready to go. The front wagon is being pulled by a team of four horses, and to the right, a stagecoach is waiting for passengers. Chihuahua Hill is visible in the distance, and the arched rain bridge can be seen at the bottom of the street. The elevated walking bridge over Bullard Street at Broadway, pictured below, was constructed in the early 1900s to provide pedestrian access during the rainy season when floodwaters rushed south through the streets. The Silver City National Bank is on the right. (Above, courtesy of Jane Bardal; below, courtesy of Jan Blackwell.)

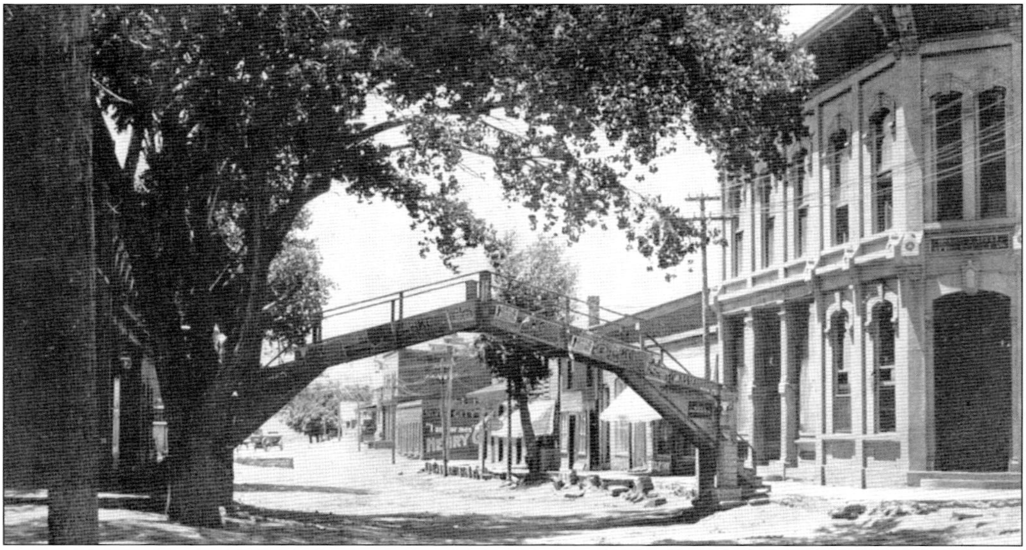

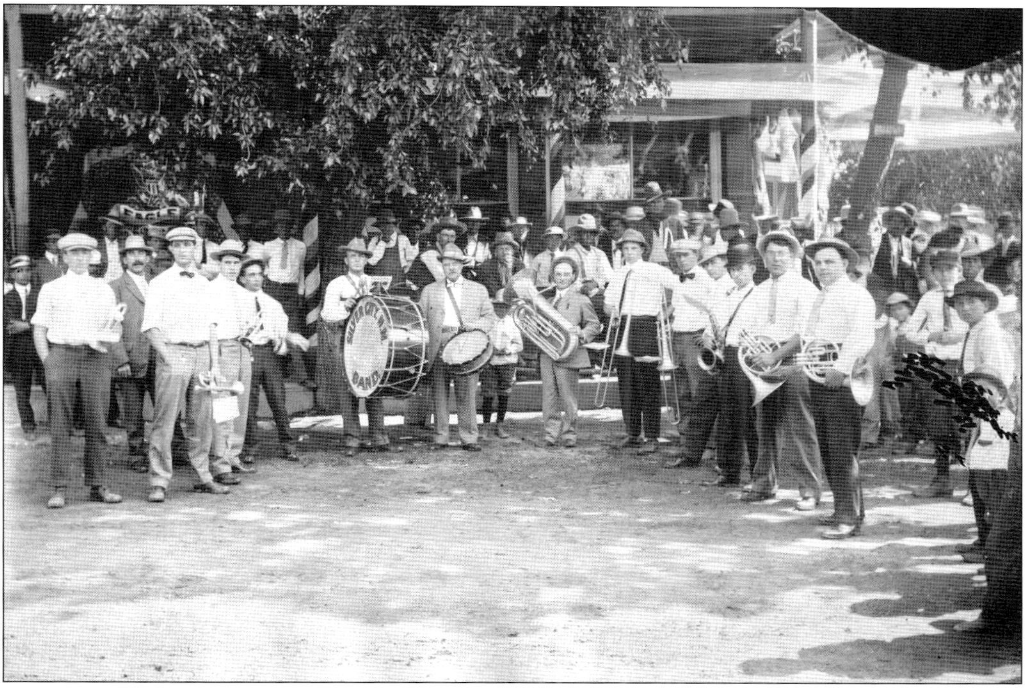

Brothers John and Walter Blackwell opened Blackwell's Bookstore at 300 North Bullard Street in Silver City. Later, they expanded the store to include musical instruments and sheet music. Above, Walter (second from left in a white shirt, holding a trumpet) was a member of the Silver City Band. There was always a Blackwell float or a decorated automobile in the Fourth of July celebrations, such as the entry from the 1911 parade seen below. The Blackwell business name continued in Silver City for years with Blackwell's Jewelers. (Above, courtesy of Jan Blackwell; below, courtesy of Anthony Romero.)

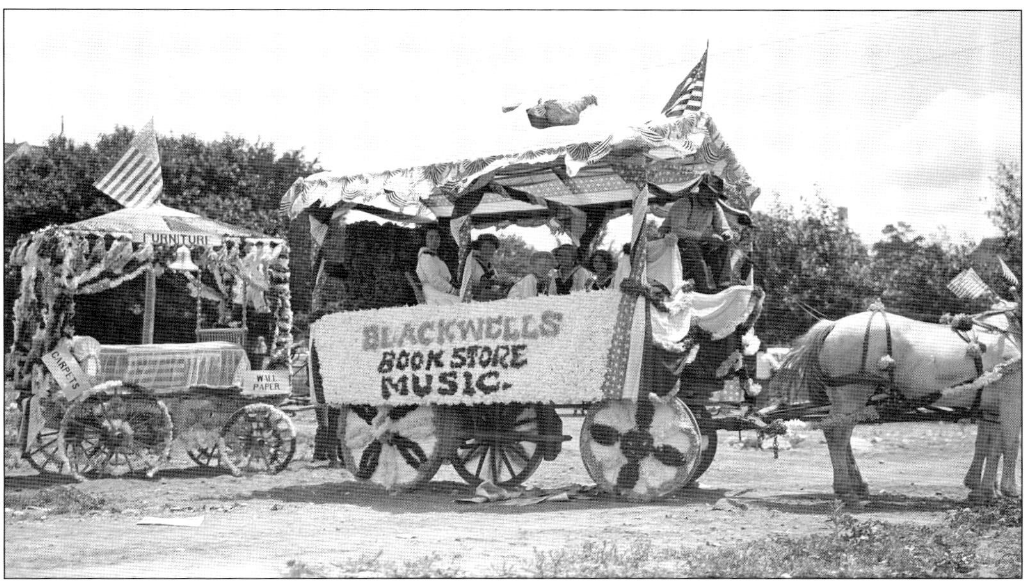

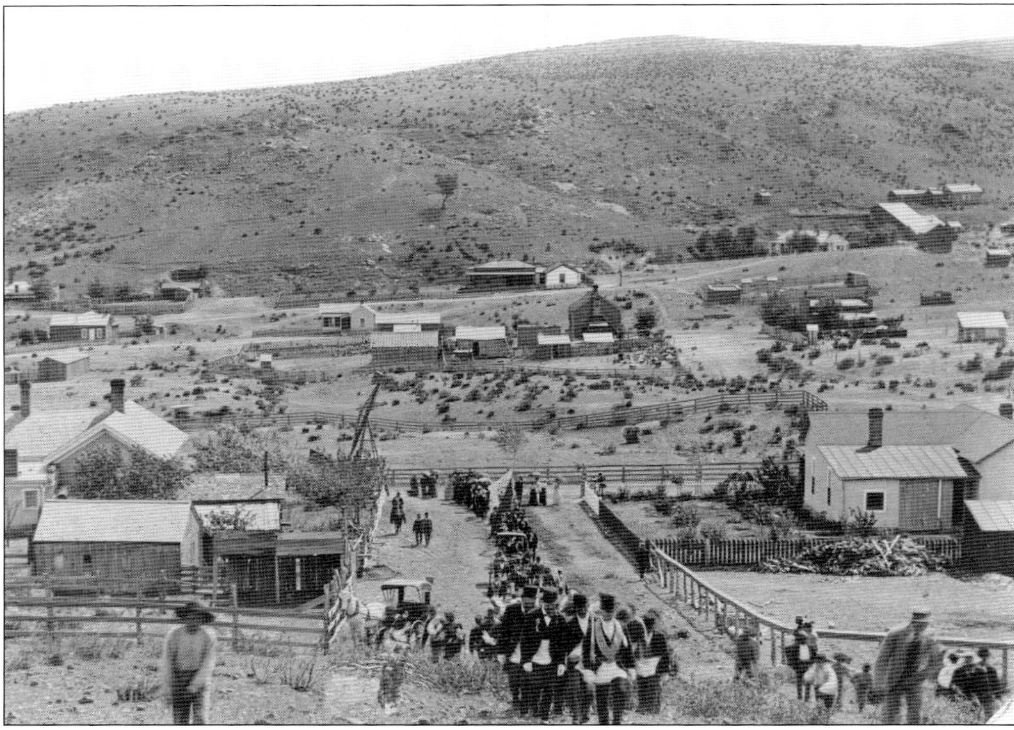

A grand procession in 1893, led by the Knights of Pythias, Masons, and Odd Fellows, drew Silver City townspeople to the cornerstone laying for Old Main, the first building of the New Mexico Territorial Normal School. The walk up the hill began at Ninth Street (now College Avenue), with Boston Hill in the background, and the remains of the old Boston Mill at top right. Old Main was completed in 1896 by local contractors Laizure & Grabe. In 1923, the Normal School became the New Mexico State Teachers College, expanding over the ensuing years to become New Mexico Western College and, finally, Western New Mexico University. Old Main was demolished in 1957 to make way for a new campus library. (Above, courtesy of Lynn Geyer; below, courtesy of Jane Bardal.)

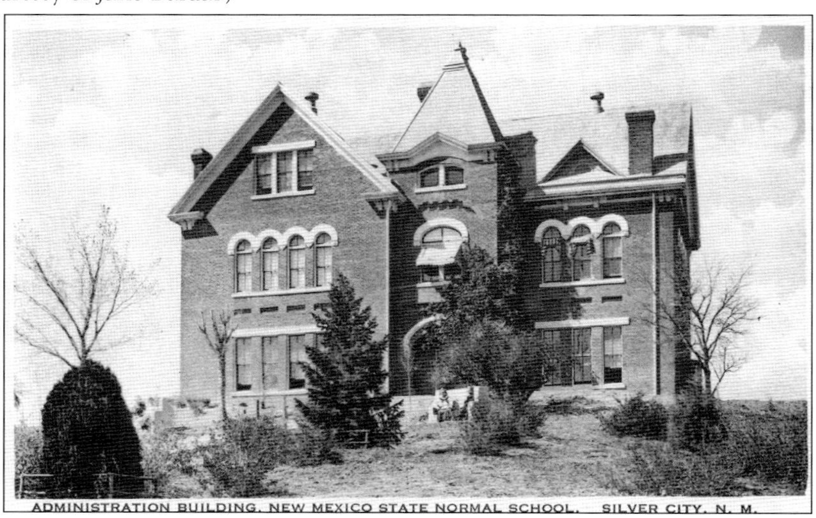

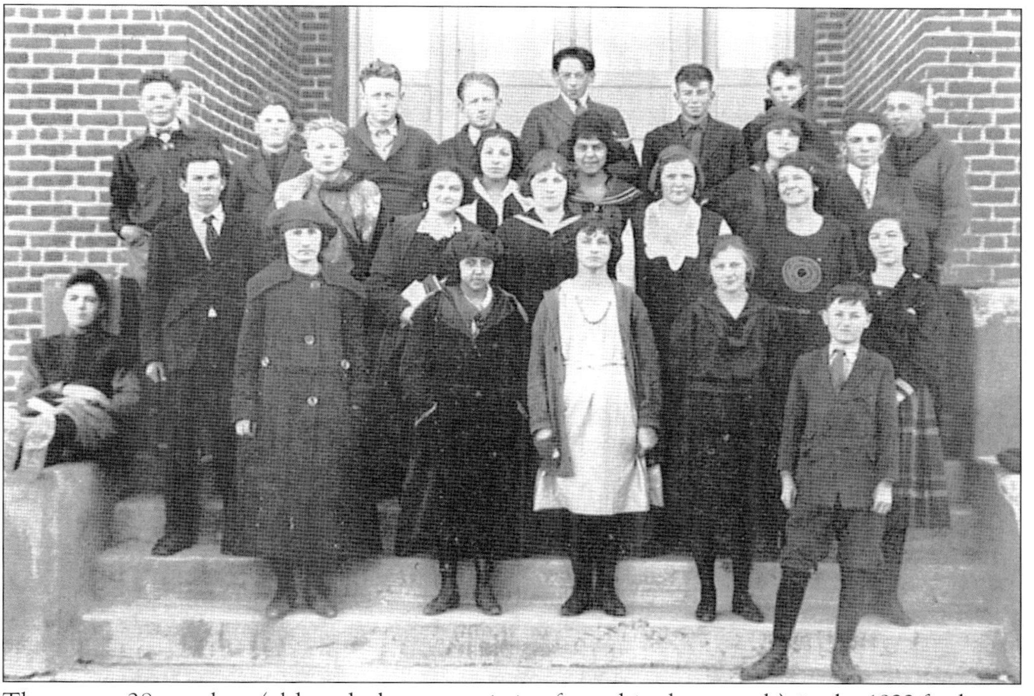

There were 28 members (although three are missing from this photograph), in the 1922 freshman class of the New Mexico State Normal School in Silver City. The New Mexico Territorial Normal School had become the New Mexico State Normal School after New Mexico became a state in 1912, and the school graduated many generations of fine teachers. (Courtesy of Don Turner.)

The New Mexico State Normal School's 1922 basketball team, pictured here, included, from left to right, Simon, forward; Wright, forward; McAlpine, guard; Boone, substitute; Franks, substitute; Woodward, guard; and Ely, center. (Courtesy of Don Turner.)

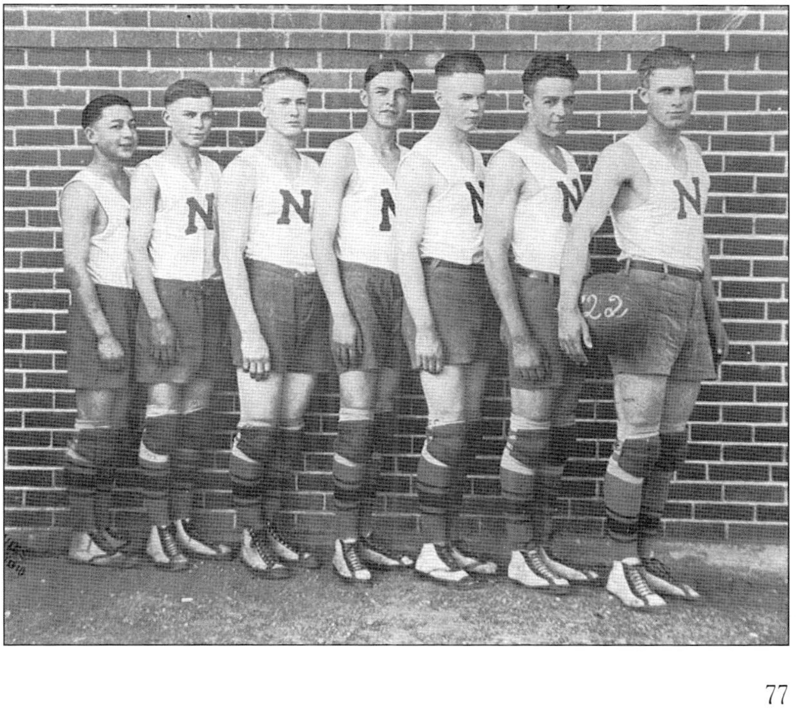

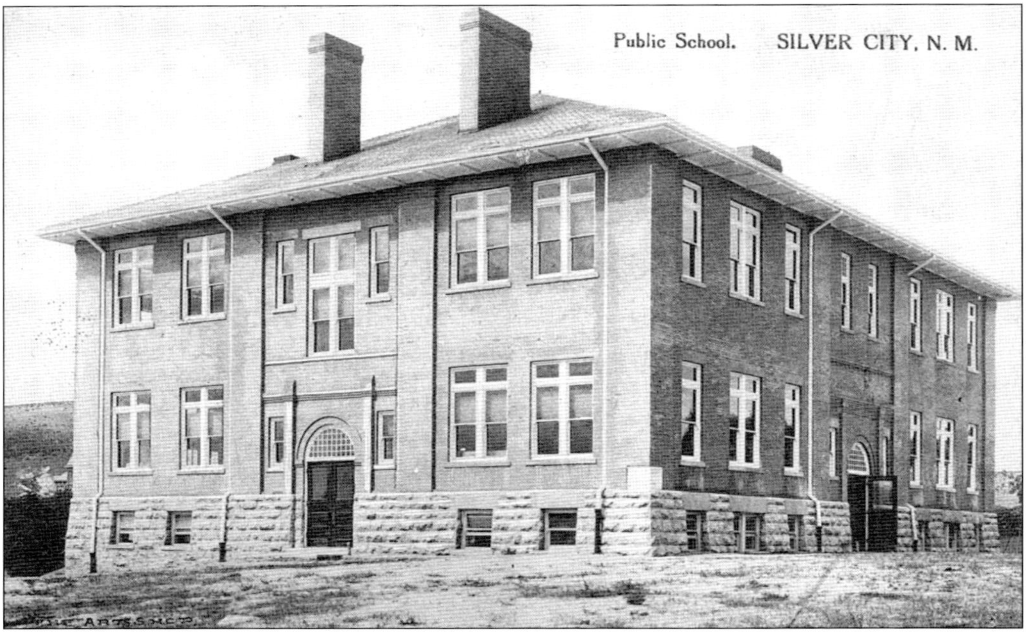

From Silver City's earliest years, residents supported public education. By 1874, public school classes were held in temporary quarters, and local women spearheaded a building fund through cake sales, dances, and subscriptions. Their efforts resulted in New Mexico's first brick public school building, completed in 1882. It was replaced in 1910 by the larger school pictured here, known as the Central Building. (Courtesy of Jane Bardal.)

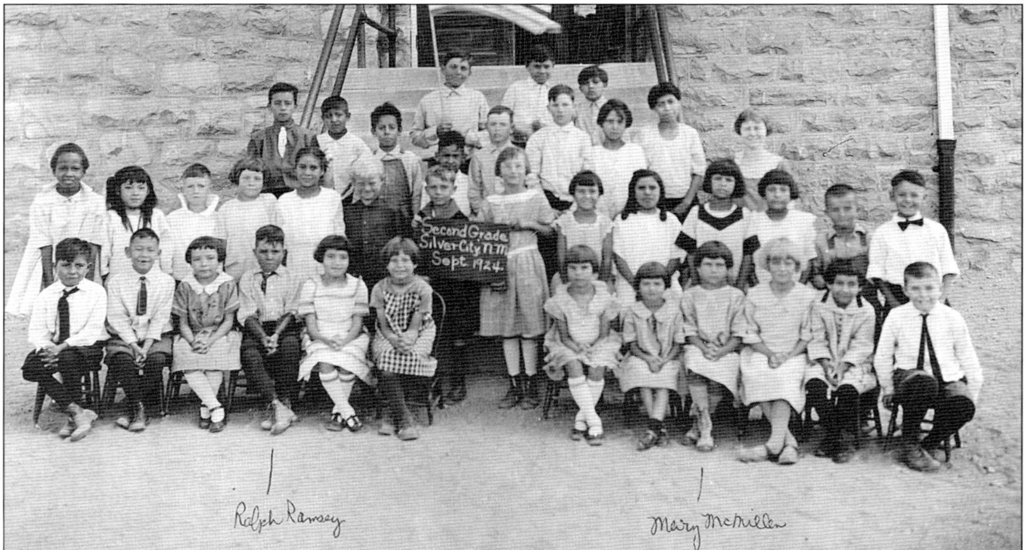

The 37 students of the school's second-grade class posed in 1924. Ralph Ramsey is in the front row, fourth from the left, and Mary McMillen, great-aunt of the photograph's donor, is fourth from the right in the same row. This group of students was not ethnically segregated, as many area classrooms would be in later years. (Courtesy of Judy Billings.)

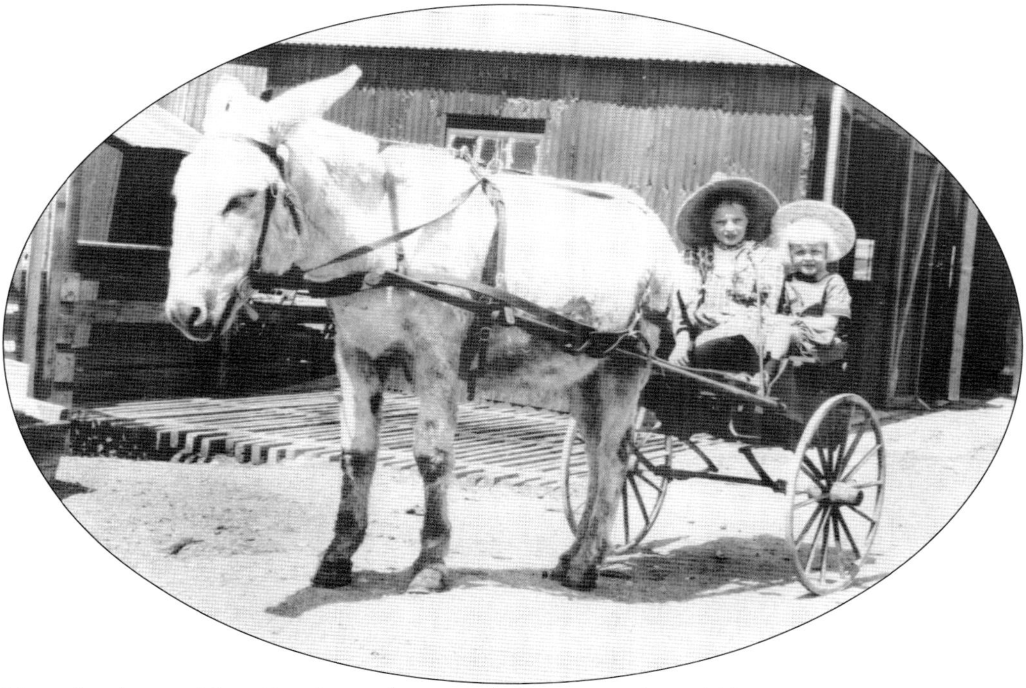

Many families in Silver City kept a burro, and there were also wild burros in the area that had been released after being used by miners and early settlers for packing loads. The Marriott children had a pet burro named Jack, seen in this 1905 photograph pulling Mary Florence and her friend Christopher Johnson. Jack was such a beloved pet that, when he died, his obituary was printed in the newspaper. (Courtesy of Jan Blackwell.)

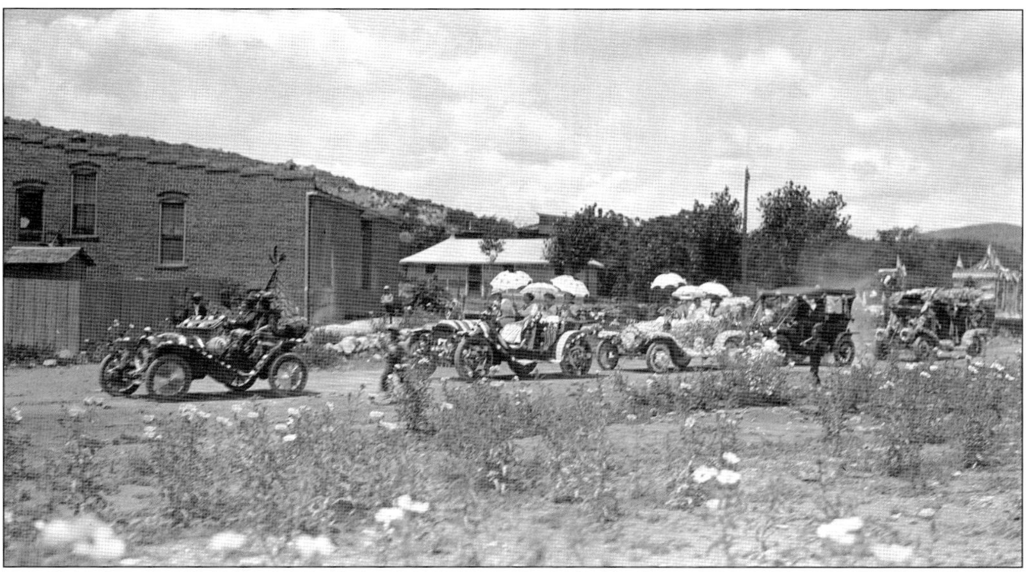

Families decorated their automobiles for the 1911 Fourth of July parade, adorning them with white tissue-paper flowers, and women wore white summer dresses and carried parasols. This photograph was taken looking west at Cooper and Yankie Street. (Courtesy of Anthony Romero.)

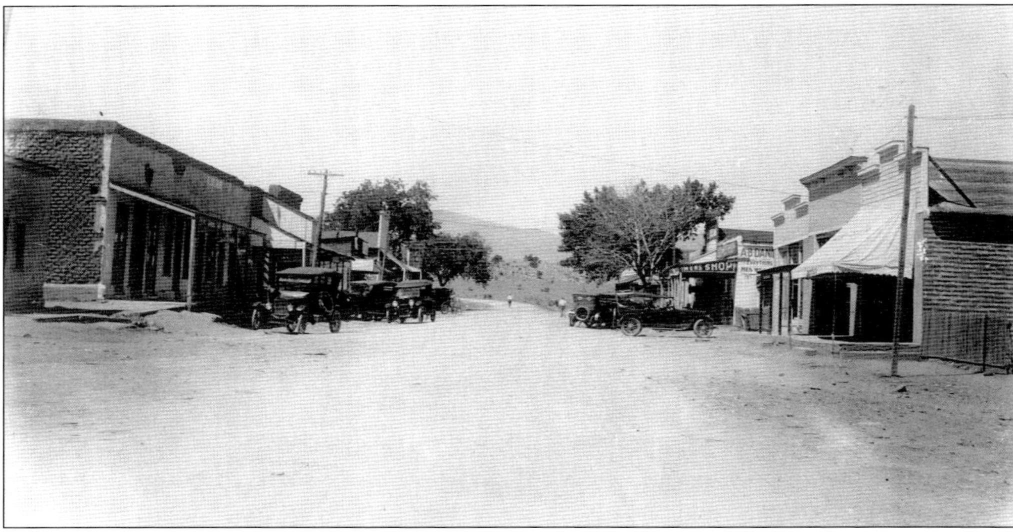

Central City, about nine miles east of Silver City, was founded in the 1860s. Located next to Fort Bayard, it was frequented by soldiers who most likely were visiting one of its many saloons. The village was named as the first Grant County seat from 1868 to 1869. In 1996, after a popular vote, the name of the town was reverted to Santa Clara, its original name from the 1860s. (Courtesy of Dillon Stone.)

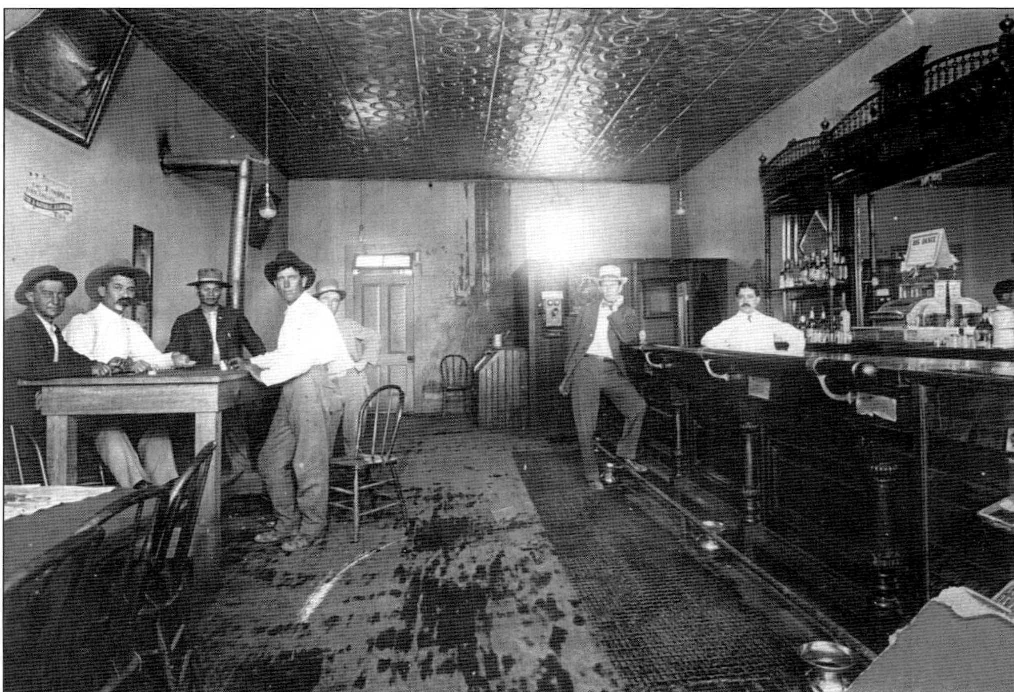

At the turn of the 20th century, James A. Wiley was a Central City businessman who owned several saloons. When he was in partnership with Matthew S. Cleveland, who died in 1904, one of his saloons was located on the southeast corner of Bayard and Maple Streets. Wiley shot and killed at least two people in Central City in the early 1900s. (Courtesy of Dillon Stone.)

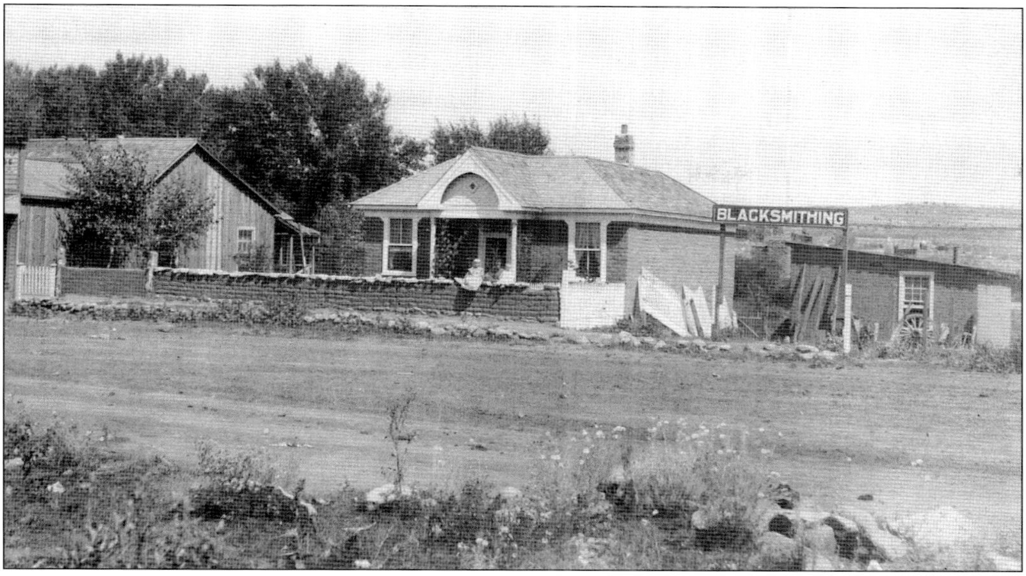

Above, two children sit on an adobe wall in front of the Emma Wiley home on north Bayard Street in Central. The house appears to also be constructed of adobe bricks. Below, the children of Central School pose for a photograph in 1912. There are several African American children in the photograph, possibly children of buffalo soldiers from nearby Fort Bayard, many of whom stayed on in the Silver City area after their service in the Army. There are also many Hispanic children in the photograph. Schools were integrated in the early years, but segregation became the norm as the area grew, with separate schools for Hispanics and Anglos, as well as separate areas for housing, restaurants, and social halls. (Both, courtesy of Dillon Stone.)

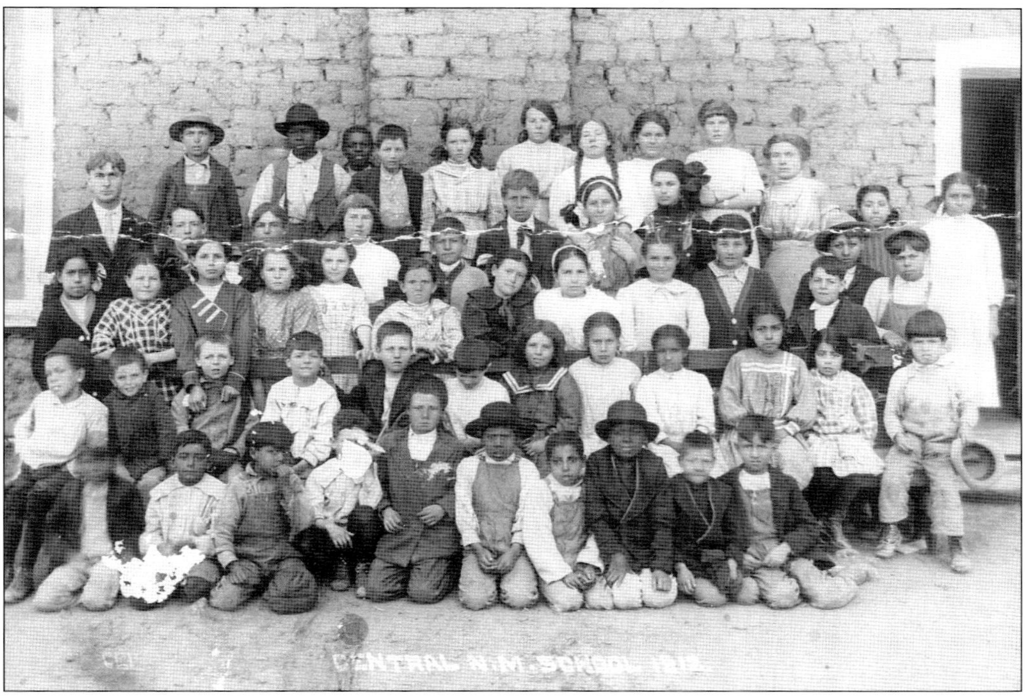

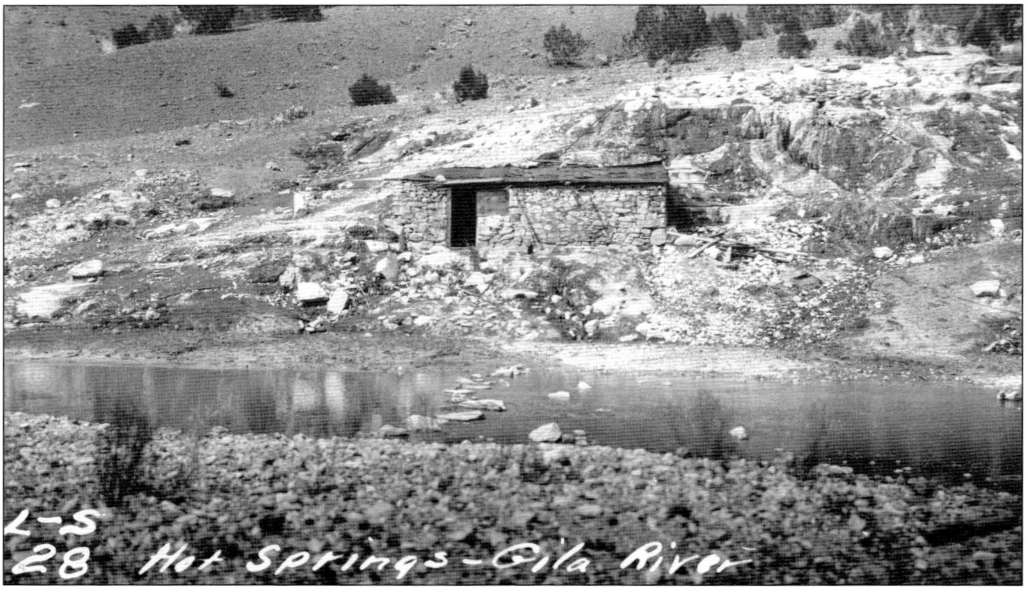

The hot springs along the Gila River have long been used for medicinal purposes. Apaches built wickiup sweat lodges, and mountain men and ranchers visited the springs to ease aching joints. In 1906, rancher Ben Kemp had a paralyzing arthritis attack and was taken in a wagon to the hot springs, where he "boiled out" (bathed) every day. Within a few weeks, he was walking again. (Courtesy of Ida Campbell.)

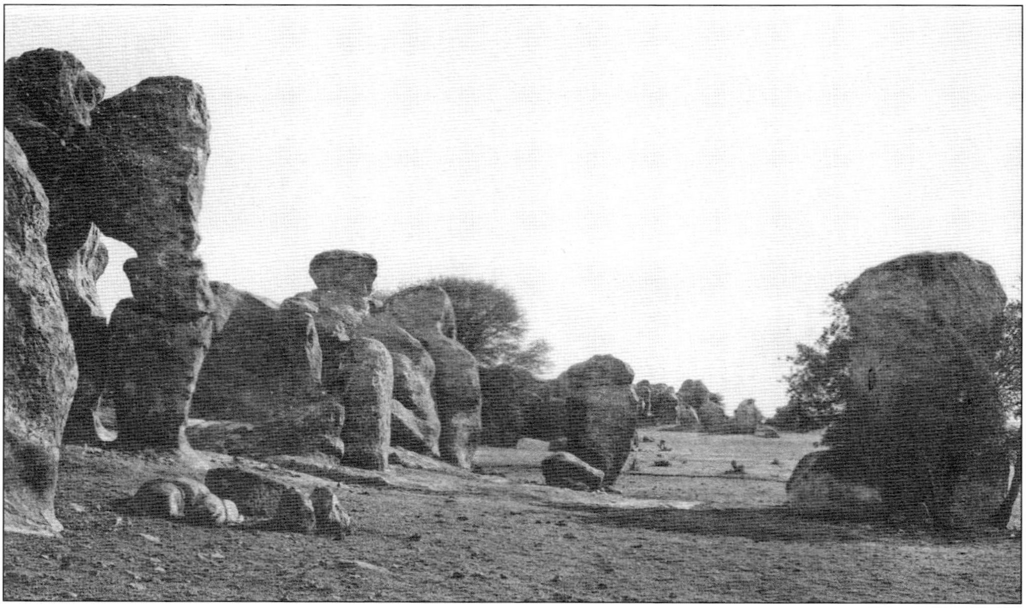

The City of Rocks, adjacent to Faywood Hot Springs, is a wonderland of stone monoliths formed 30 million years ago. Over time, the volcanic ash has eroded into a sea of boulders covering one square mile. The ancient Mimbreños lived in this area, and their grinding holes can still be found among the rocks. Stonecutter C.S. Couch used the rock to create headstones in the Silver City Cemetery. (Courtesy of Jane Bardal.)

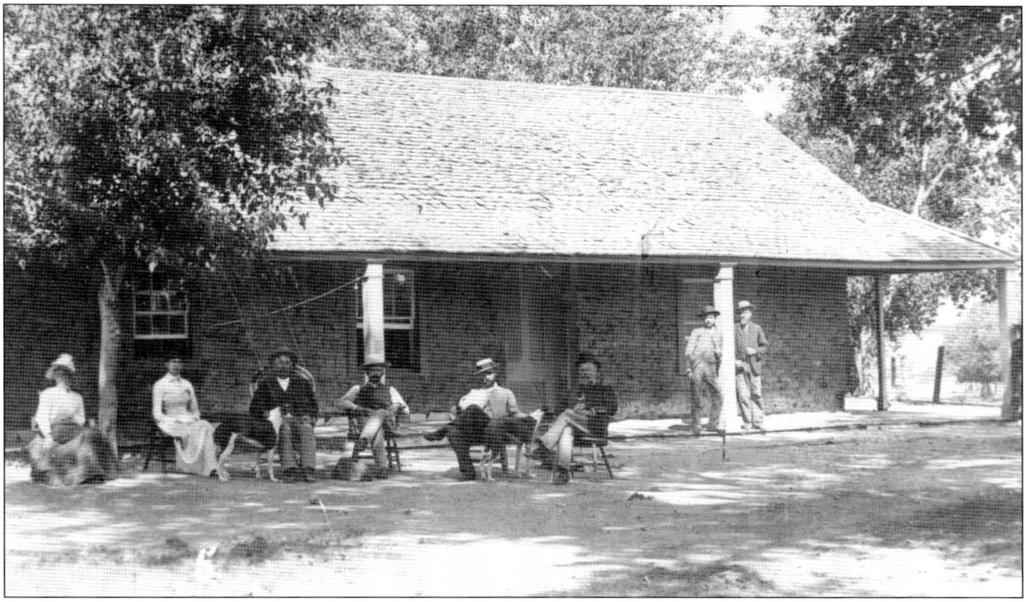

Above, Richard Hudson visited the hot springs southeast of Silver City in 1870. Finding relief from his gout after soaking in the mineral springs, he purchased the property with his father-in-law, Isaac Stevens, and built a 50-room hotel that became a stop on the stagecoach route between Mesilla and Silver City. The hotel was destroyed in an 1892 fire, but was rebuilt (below) as Casa de Consuelo (House of Comfort), by A.R. Graham. At the turn of the century, J.C. Fay and William Lockwood purchased the property, renaming it Faywood. The hotel, along with the hot springs, was a popular social spot for Silver City and Deming residents. Visitors to Faywood Hot Springs still enjoy bathing in the geothermal waters. (Above, courtesy of Ida Campbell; below, courtesy of Jane Bardal.)

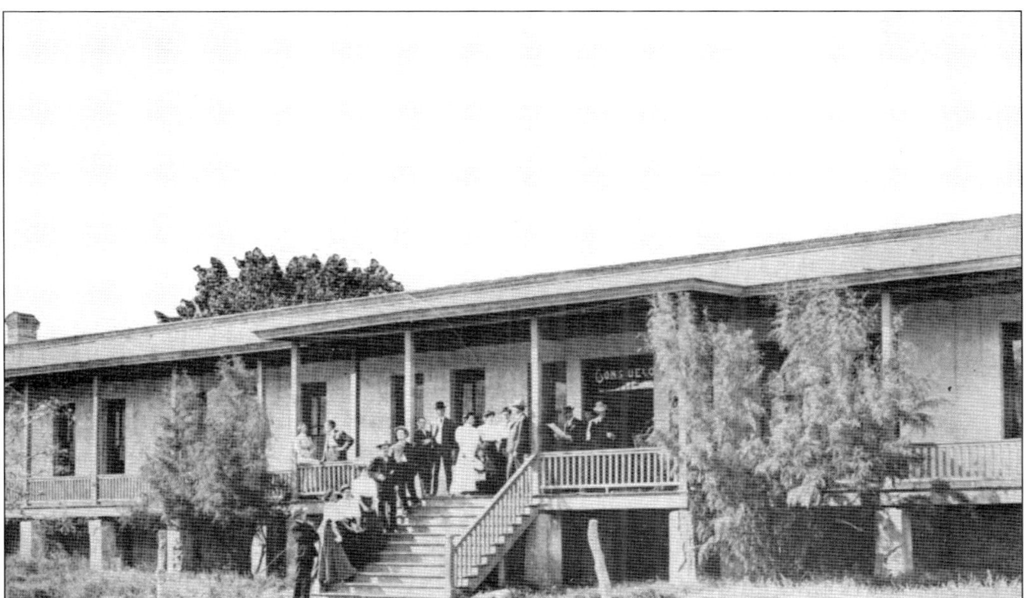

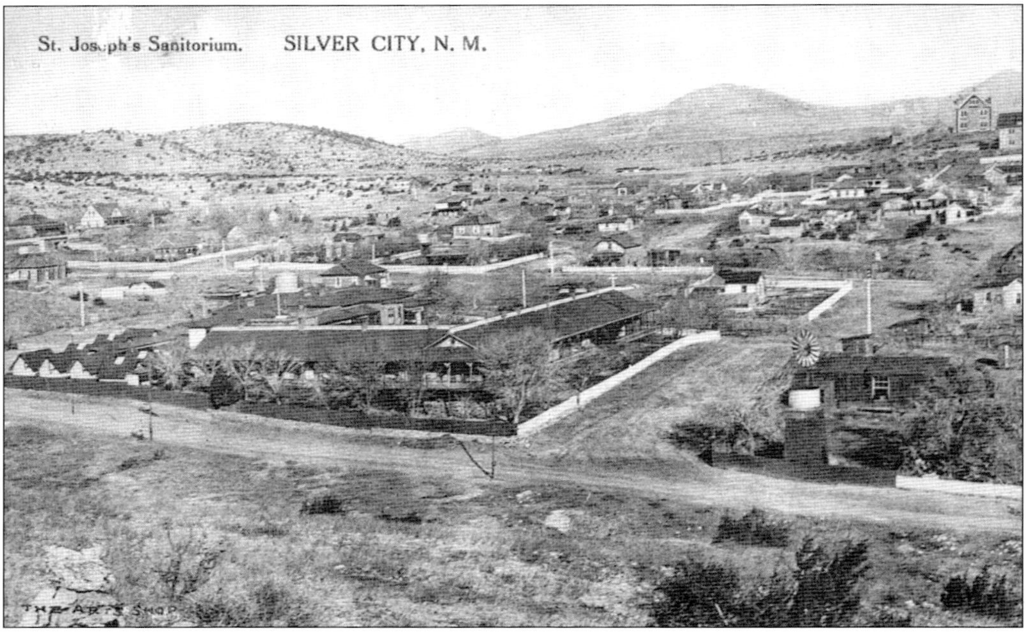

St. Joseph's Hospital, operated by the Sisters of Mercy, moved to the western edge of Silver City in 1888. It was reorganized as a sanatorium in 1902. The L-shaped building on the corner of Market and B Streets featured long, covered porches and an interior courtyard. In a 1902 lecture, local physician Dr. E.L. Woods promoted "plain living, pure thoughts, and good digestion" as safeguards against contraction of tuberculosis.

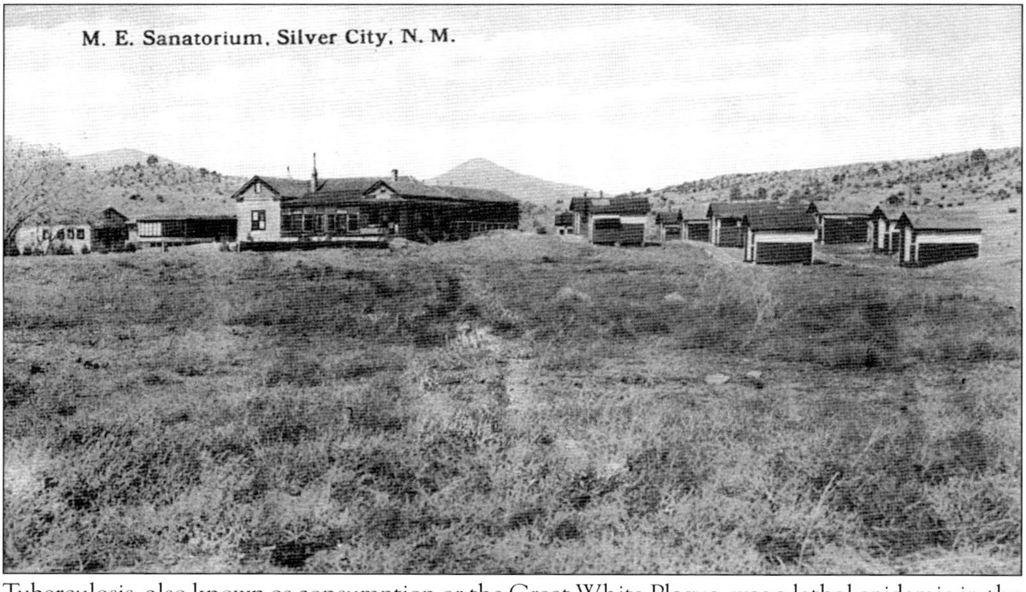

Tuberculosis, also known as consumption or the Great White Plague, was a lethal epidemic in the early 20th century. There were no drugs to treat the contagious disease, but Silver City capitalized on the theory that its high altitude, sunshine, and fresh air would offer a cure for "lungers" who traveled west to sanatoriums. The Methodist Episcopal, or Sunnyside, Sanatorium was located on Cottage San Road. (Courtesy of Jane Bardal.)

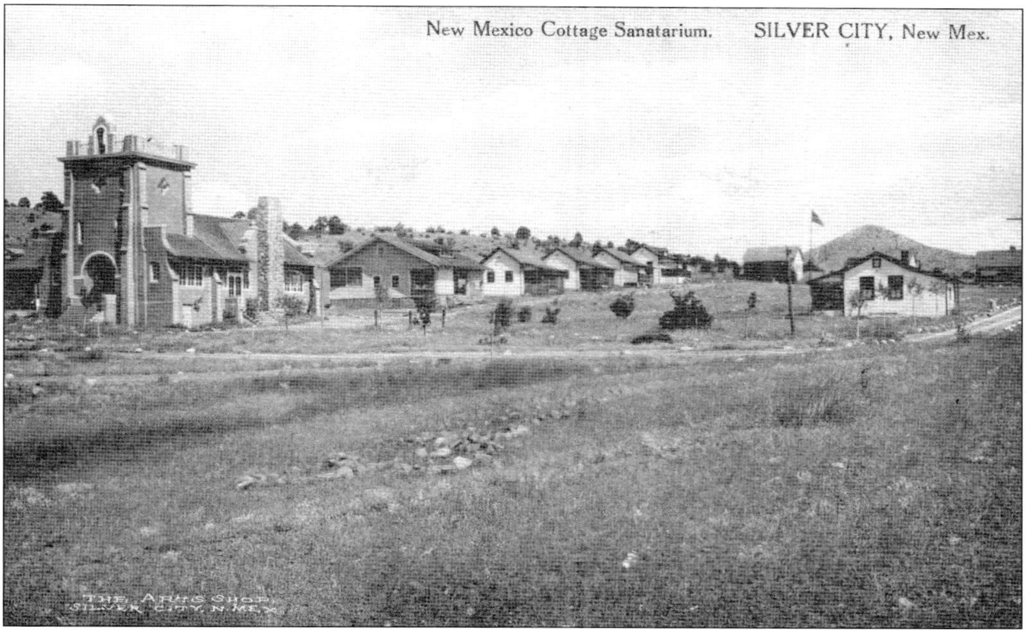

The Mission-style New Mexico Cottage Sanatorium was built by Dr. Earl Bullock and Wayne Wilson in 1905, two miles north of town. Silver City residents helped to raise the money for construction, and donor's names were on each cottage. There was a large administration building, a library, a pavilion for plays, the Anne Thompson Infirmary for very ill patients, and a chapel. At one time, there were 50 cottages, and many patients slept outside in sun or snow, believing that fresh air, especially the cool night air, killed tuberculosis bacteria. With modern treatment and a perfect locale, Silver City was known as the World's Health Resort. Patients in New Mexico did have a fairly high cure rate, but their poignant letters home express loneliness. As one woman dryly wrote, "Oh, I could pine and balsam." (Both, courtesy of Jane Bardal.)

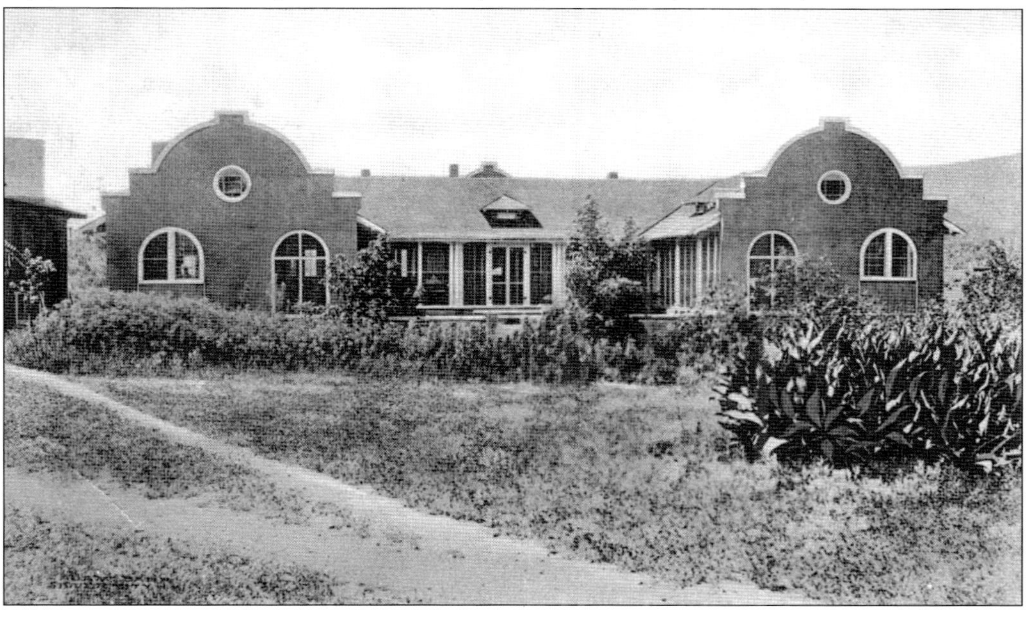

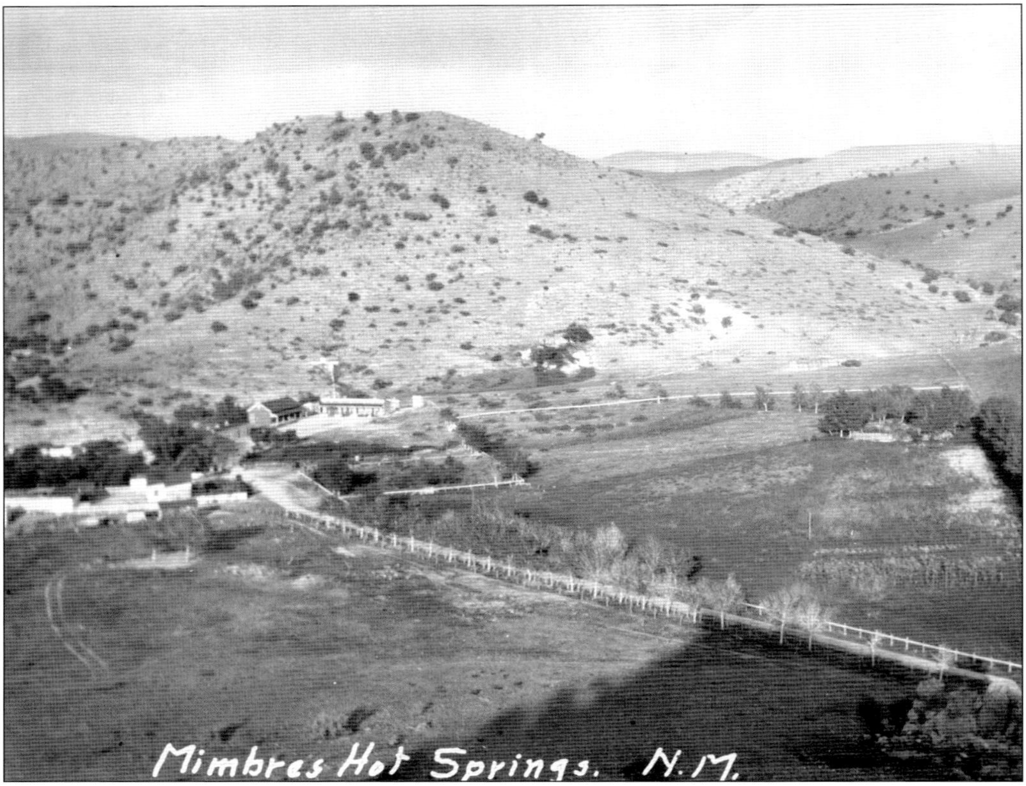

Dr. Richard Stovall owned the Mimbres Hot Springs Ranch. Many people came west seeking a cure for tuberculosis, while others just soaked in the hot springs along the Mimbres River, enjoying the benefits of the rejuvenating mineral waters and believing them to be a cure for many ailments. Below, Doctor Stovall stands at the top right on the porch of the ranch house, while his wife (and nurse), Maude, sits on a step at lower right. (Above, courtesy of Don Turner; below, courtesy of Anthony Romero.)

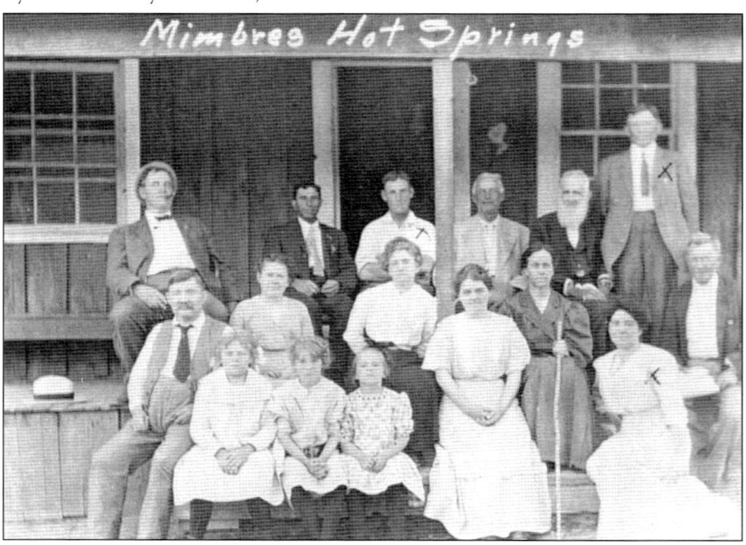

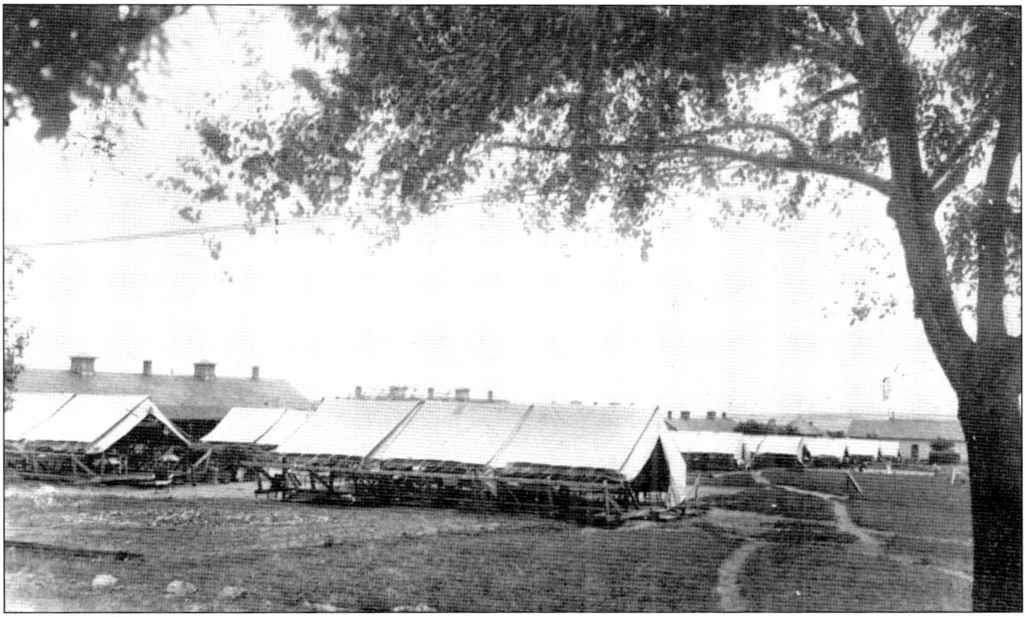

After Geronimo's surrender ended the Apache Wars in 1886, the need for military protection in the Southwest diminished. In 1899, Fort Bayard became a sanatorium operated by the US Army for the treatment of tuberculosis and other lung diseases. As at many of the early sanatoria, patients were housed in tents in the belief that the fresh air would cure the disease. Below is the ambulant ward housing. (Both, courtesy of Jane Bardal.)

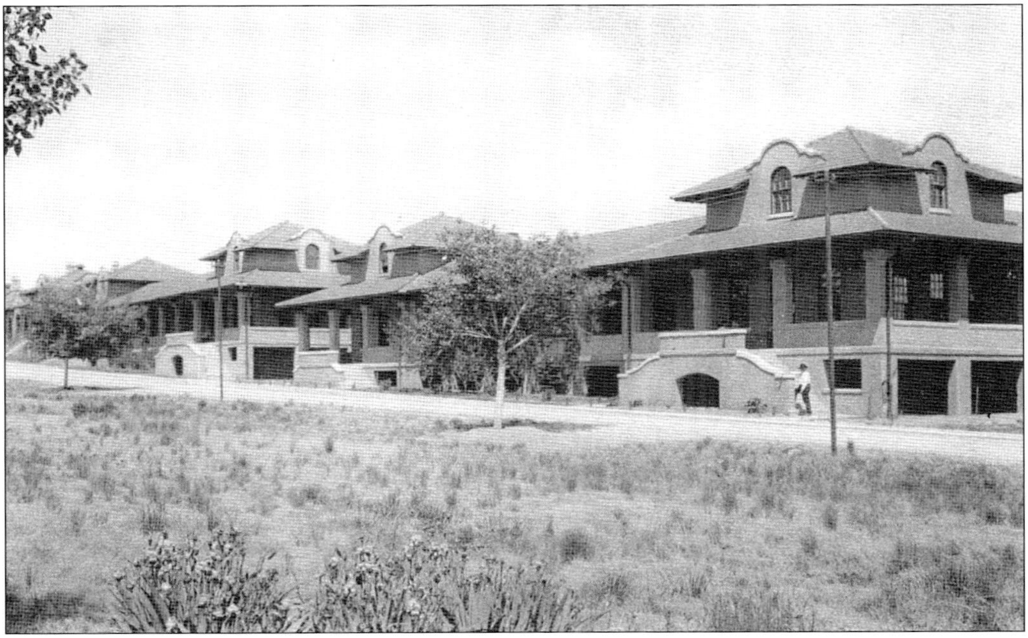

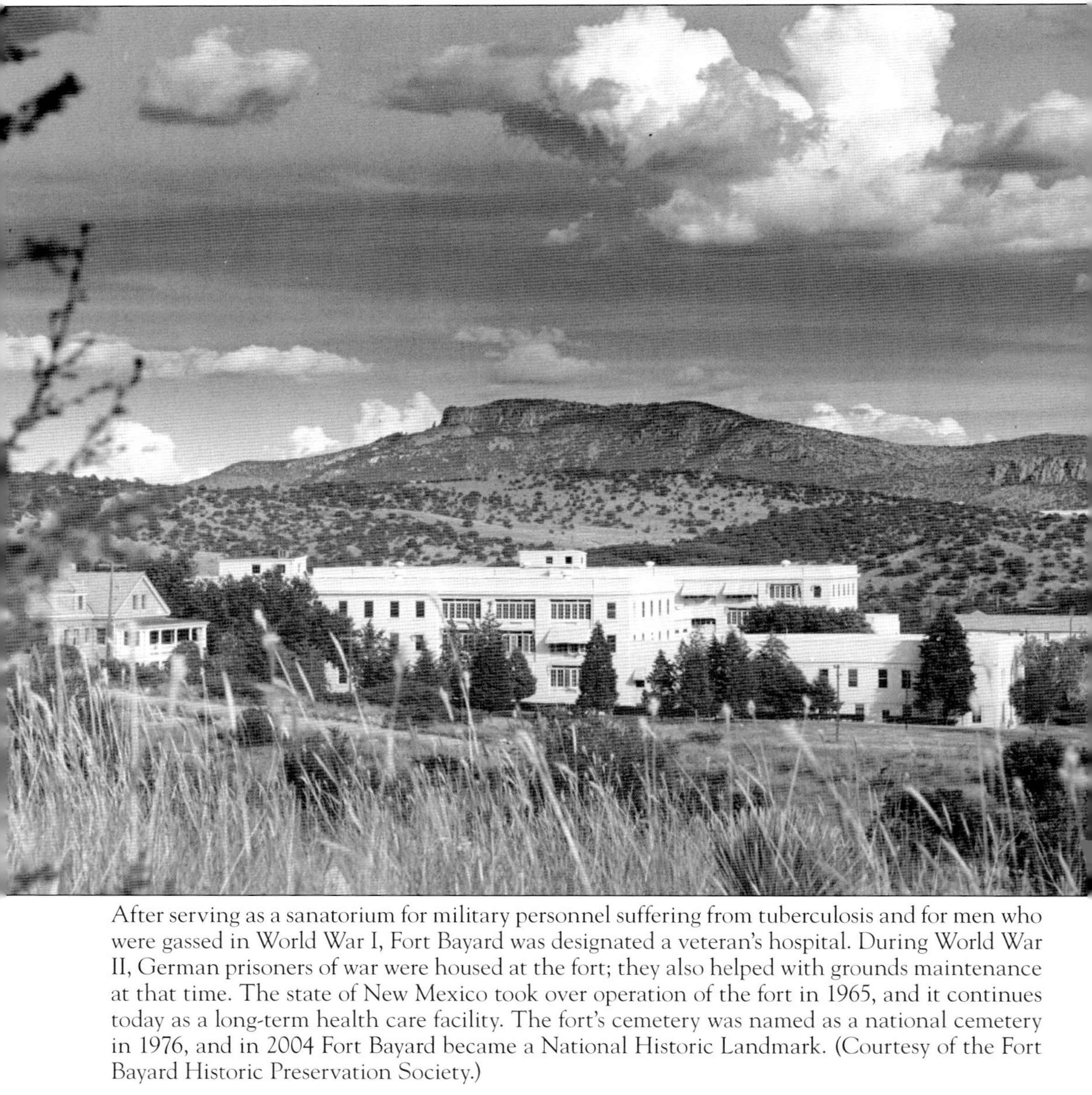

After serving as a sanatorium for military personnel suffering from tuberculosis and for men who were gassed in World War I, Fort Bayard was designated a veteran's hospital. During World War II, German prisoners of war were housed at the fort; they also helped with grounds maintenance at that time. The state of New Mexico took over operation of the fort in 1965, and it continues today as a long-term health care facility. The fort's cemetery was named as a national cemetery in 1976, and in 2004 Fort Bayard became a National Historic Landmark. (Courtesy of the Fort Bayard Historic Preservation Society.)

Five

A Lively Town

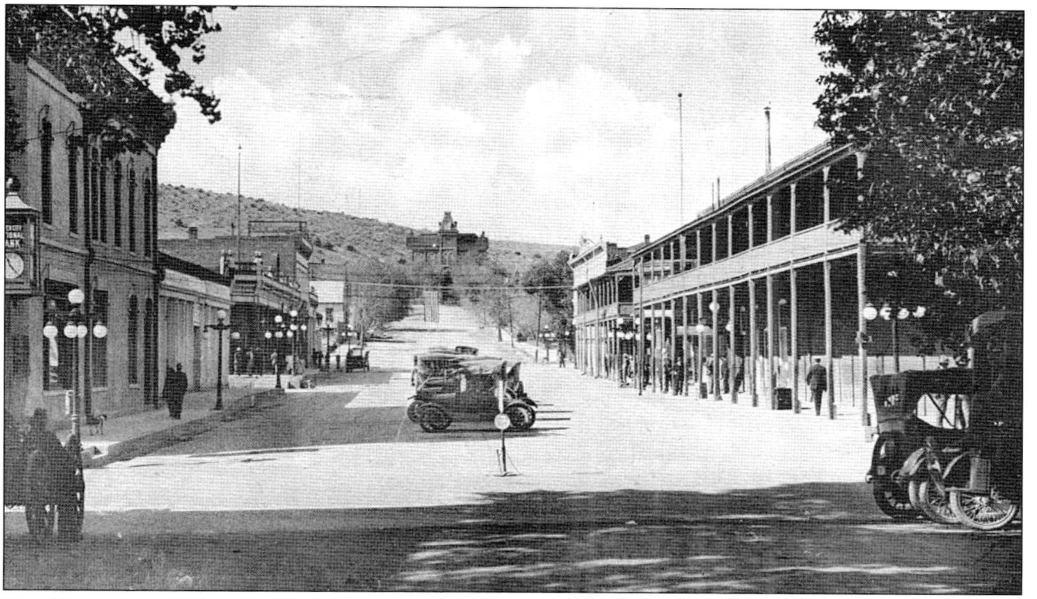

By 1920, automobiles replaced horses and buggies as the most efficient means of transportation, and downtown Silver City streets were paved. In this view, looking west up Broadway to the early courthouse, only one wagon can be seen at the lower left, and a row of automobiles is parked in the center of the street. The Silver City National Bank is on the left, on the southwest corner of Broadway and Bullard Street. Electric lamps line the concrete sidewalks. (Courtesy of Jane Bardal.)

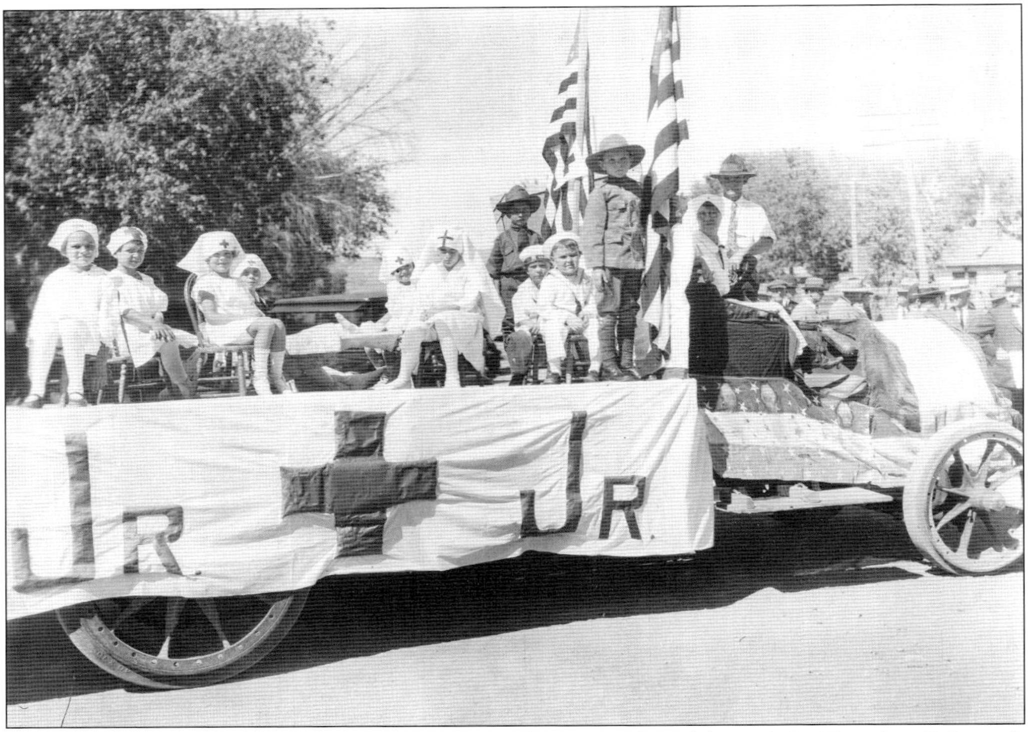

Like most American small towns, Silver City enthusiastically celebrated the Fourth of July with a parade. The photograph above shows a 1923 fundraising float with Junior Red Cross girls. Pictured are, from left to right, Leah Reese, Virginia Wright (in the back), Ida Foster (with her knees showing), and Bobby Hopkins seated in front in a white coat. Below is the 1919 Red Cross parade going south on Bullard Street. (Above, courtesy of Ida Campbell; below, courtesy of Jane Bardal.)

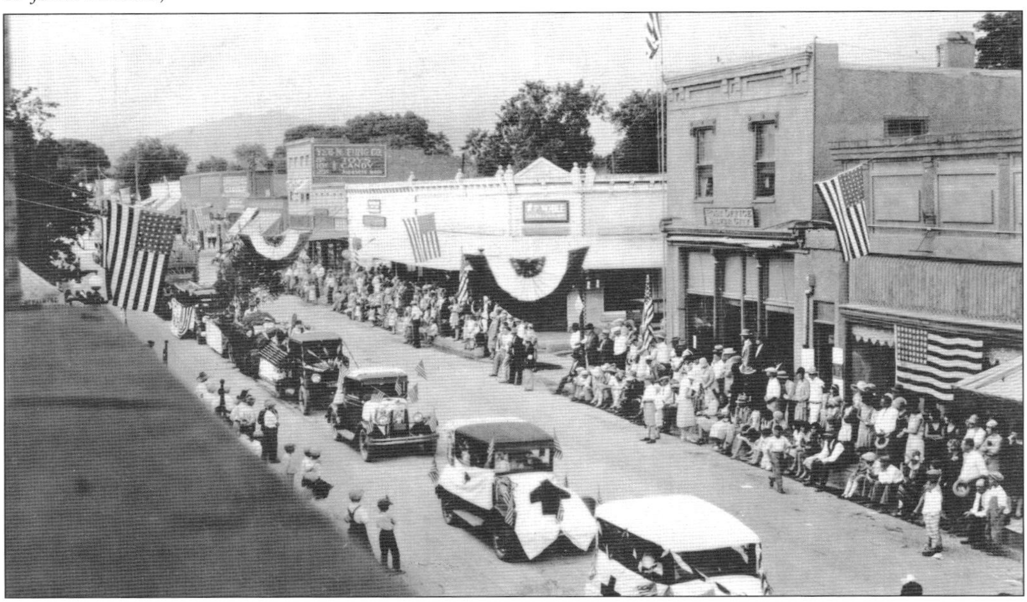

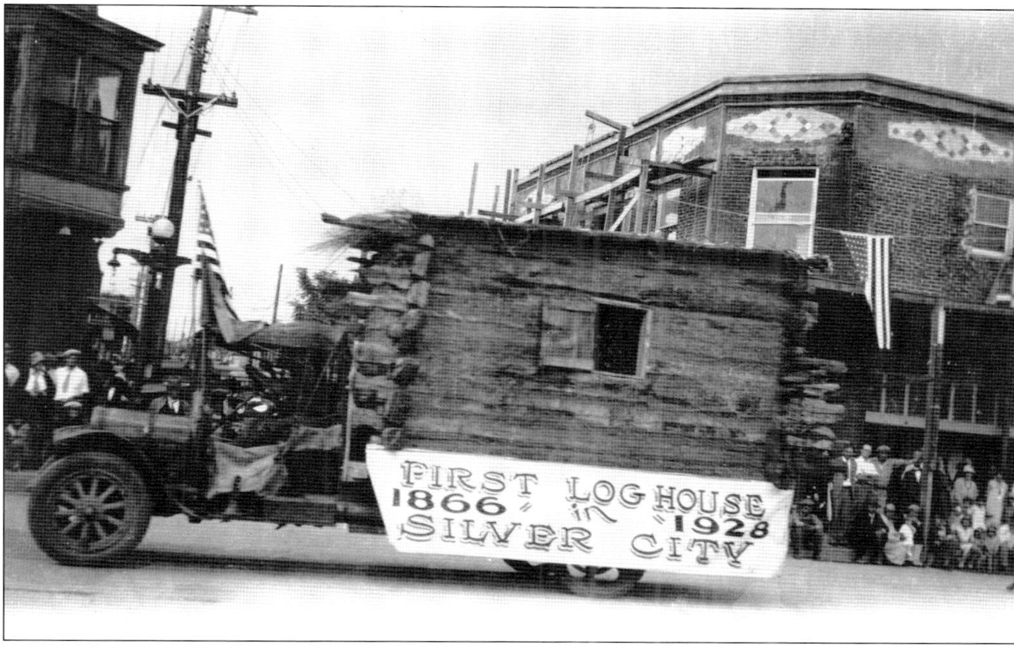

A Daughters of the American Revolution float in the 1928 Fourth of July parade featured the first log house built in Silver City. The 1866 structure was lifted onto the bed of a truck for the festivities. In this photograph, taken by Leslie K. Goforth, the truck is traveling west on Broadway, passing the Palace Hotel. (Courtesy of Don Turner.)

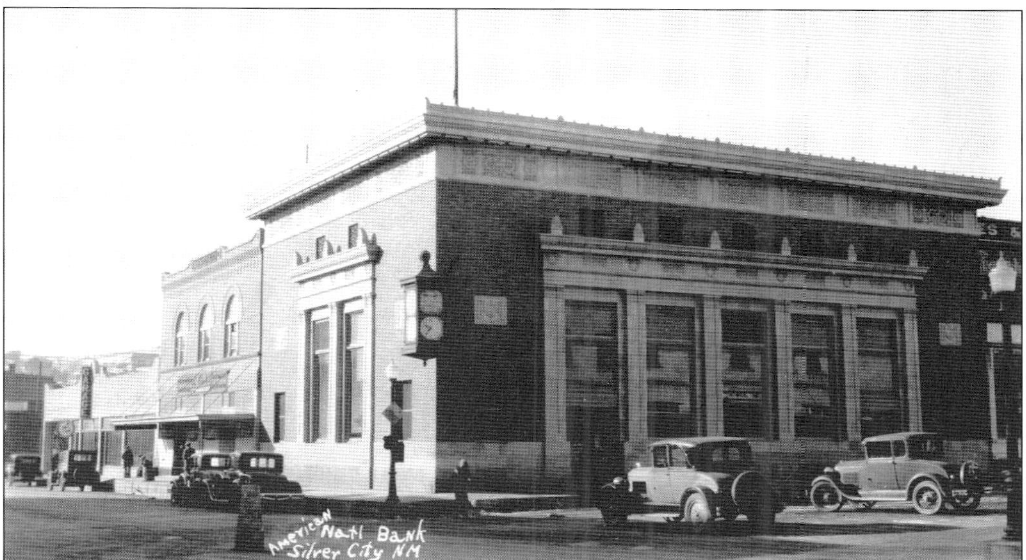

The 1923 Silver City National Bank Building, located on the southwest corner of Bullard Street and Broadway, was the masterpiece of El Paso architect Henry Trost and was called an "architectural triumph" in the *Silver City Enterprise*. It became home to the American National Bank in 1930. Purchased by the town of Silver City in 1984, the building served as city hall, continuing in that capacity today. (Courtesy of Don Turner.)

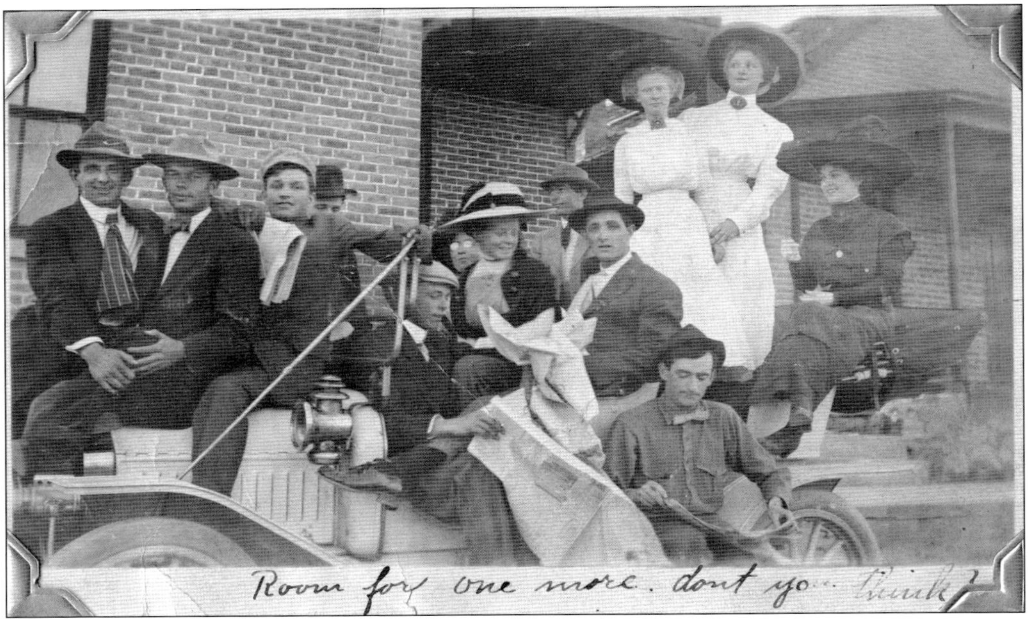

Members of the Blackwell family and friends piled into their new 1910 Buick with a four-cylinder overhead-valve engine, purchased for $1,050. Ralph Kiner (later the father of Baseball Hall of Famer Ralph Kiner) is at left; Beth Sturdivant and Ina Marriott stand to the right, wearing white dresses; and Walter Blackwell is seated in front of them. A handwritten caption under the photograph reads, "Room for one more, don't you think?" Below, Agnes Marriott (right) and friends pose in their white summer dresses in front of the C.W. Marriott home. Their hats, along with the automobile, are most likely decorated for a Fourth of July celebration. (Both, courtesy of Jan Blackwell.)

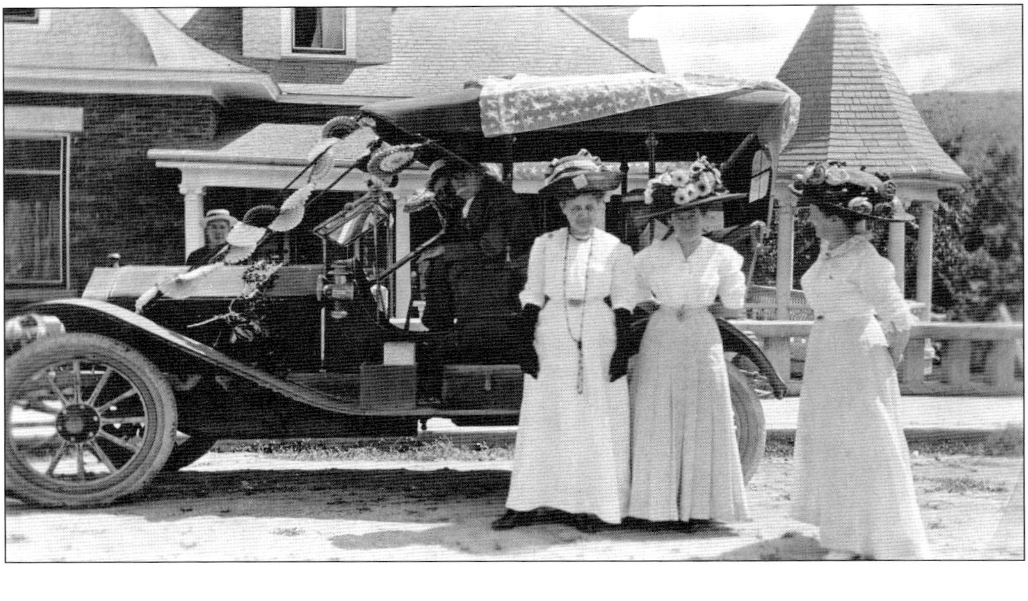

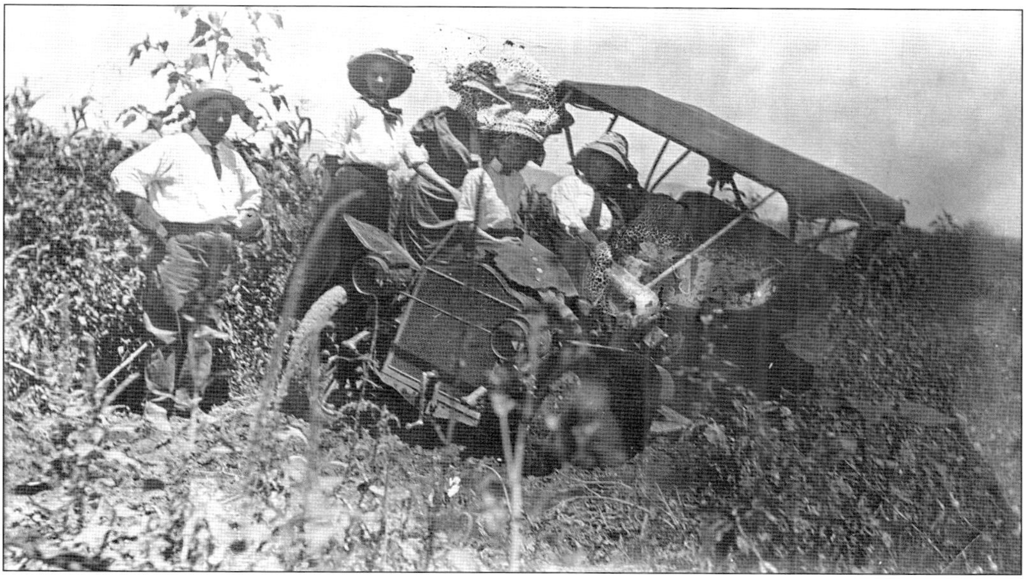

As automobiles became more popular, it became obvious that only the adventurous should venture out into the countryside, as most roads around Silver City remained unpaved and unimproved for many years. Above, C.W. Marriott and his five female companions wait for a team of horses to pull them out of the mud. One young lady has found a comfortable, but tilted, seat on the hood of the automobile. Below, a small landslide has blocked a group traveling into the mountains. It is very probable that anyone venturing outside of the city would have taken ropes and shovels to clear a road or tow an automobile. (Above, courtesy of Jan Blackwell; below, courtesy of Anthony Romero.)

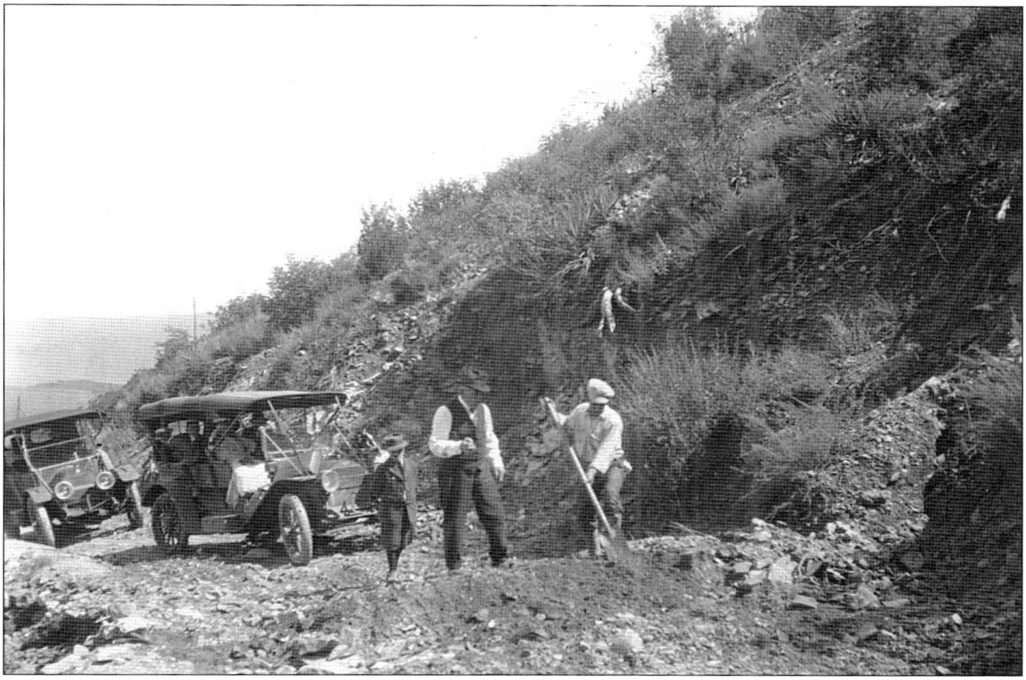

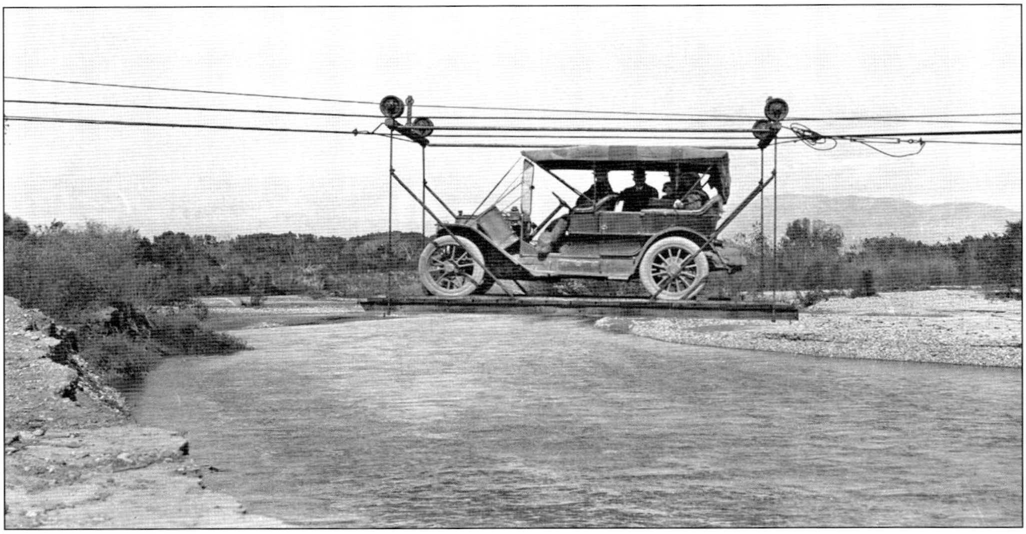

As manager for the local branch of Wells, Fargo & Company, C.W. Marriott provided transportation between Silver City and Mogollon. In addition to the threat of robbers in the early years (freight from Mogollon often consisted of gold and silver bullion), crossing the Gila River presented another danger. Marriott recalled that one time, when the river was high, a team of horses was used to help pull the car through the water. However, when a terrified female passenger began to scream, the frightened horses refused to move. As they sat immobile, the car began to sink into the sand, and the driver had to help the hysterical passenger walk to shore. A pulley system later carried cars and trucks across the river, although heavily loaded vehicles had to be unloaded and then reloaded at each side of the river crossing. (Both, courtesy of Anthony Romero.)

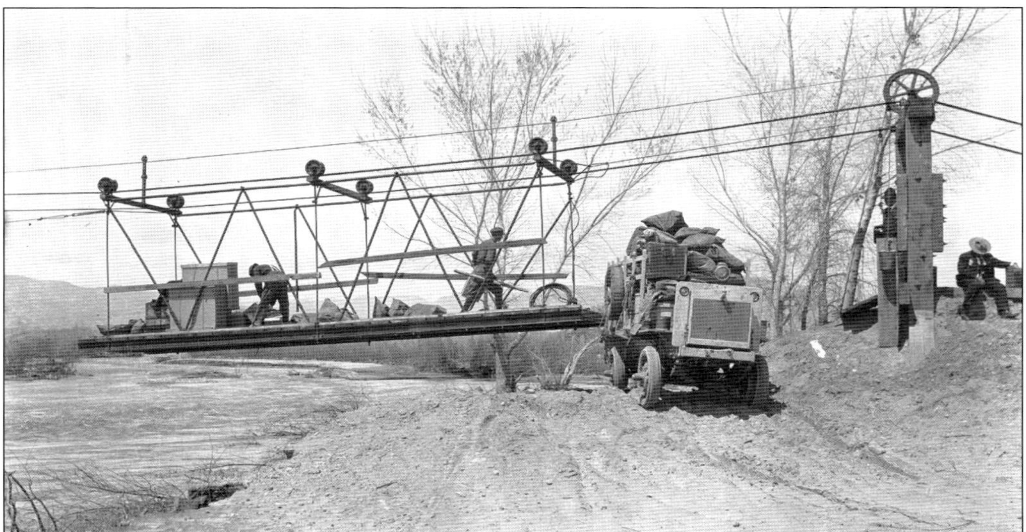

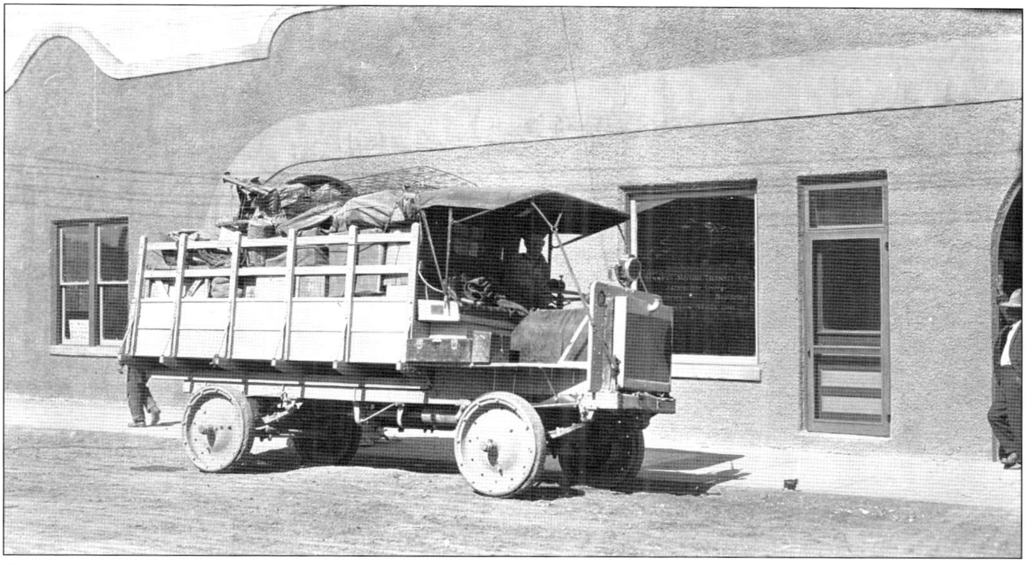

Bennett Motors carried freight between Silver City, Mogollon, and other mining camps and settlements in the area. (Courtesy of Anthony Romero.)

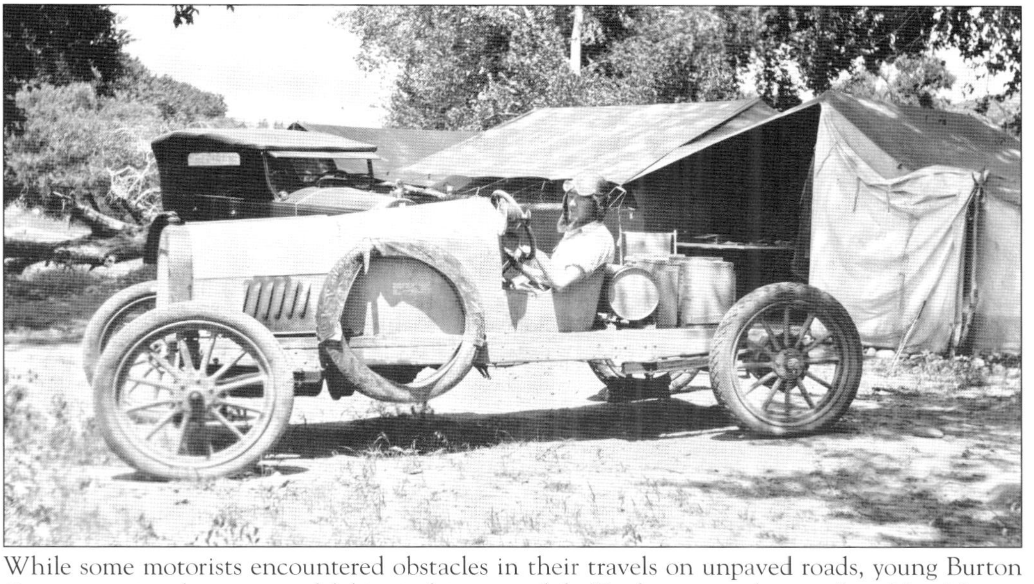

While some motorists encountered obstacles in their travels on unpaved roads, young Burton Cosgrove enjoyed an uneventful drive in his automobile, *Desdemona*, on his way from New Mexico Military Institute in Roswell, New Mexico, where he attended school, to visit his parents. Harriet and C.B. Cosgrove were camped along the Mimbres River, where they excavated Swarts Ruin for the Peabody Museum in 1925. (Courtesy of Burton Cosgrove.)

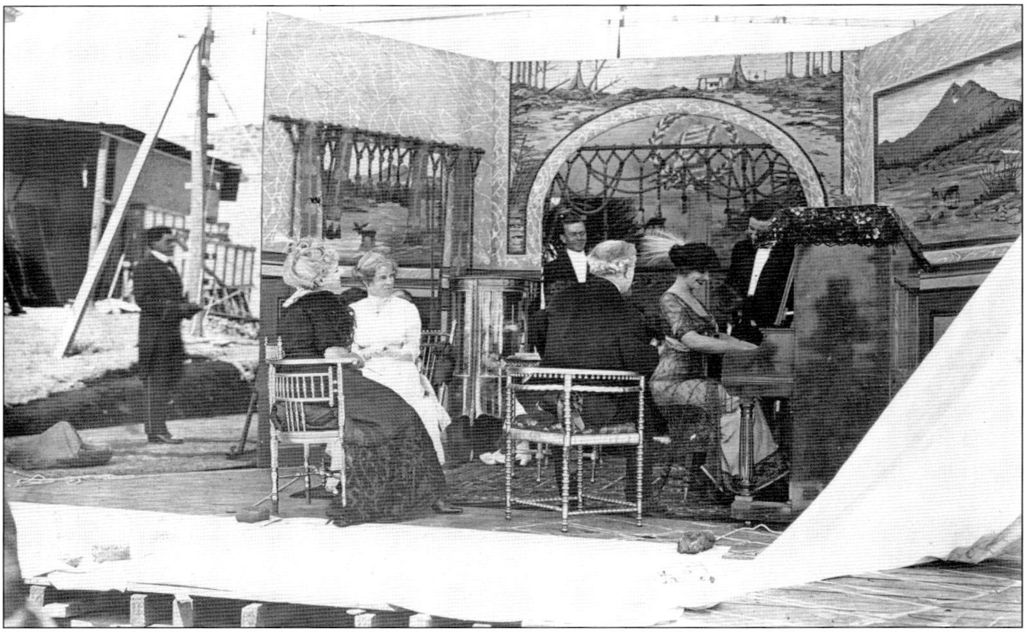

Motion picture actor, screenwriter, and director Romaine Fielding, representing Lubin Studios from Philadelphia, came to Silver City in the summer of 1913. Silver City residents, including siblings Mary Florence, Ina, and Charles Marriott, became extras, providing local color. Seven silent movies were filmed in the area, and several buildings were dynamited for special effects. Unfortunately, all the films were lost in a 1915 studio fire. (Both, courtesy of Jan Blackwell.)

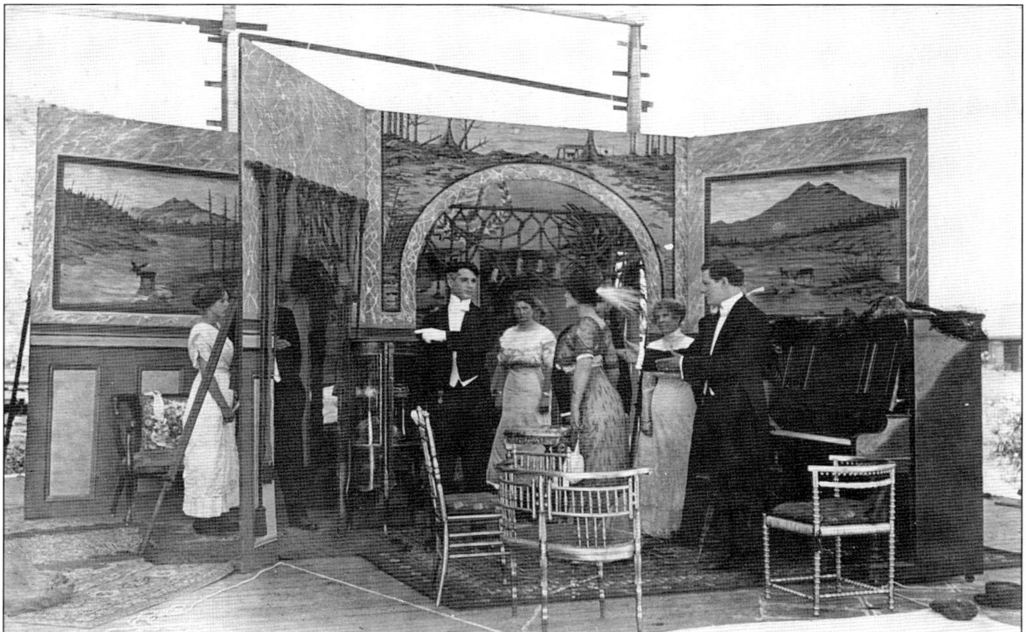

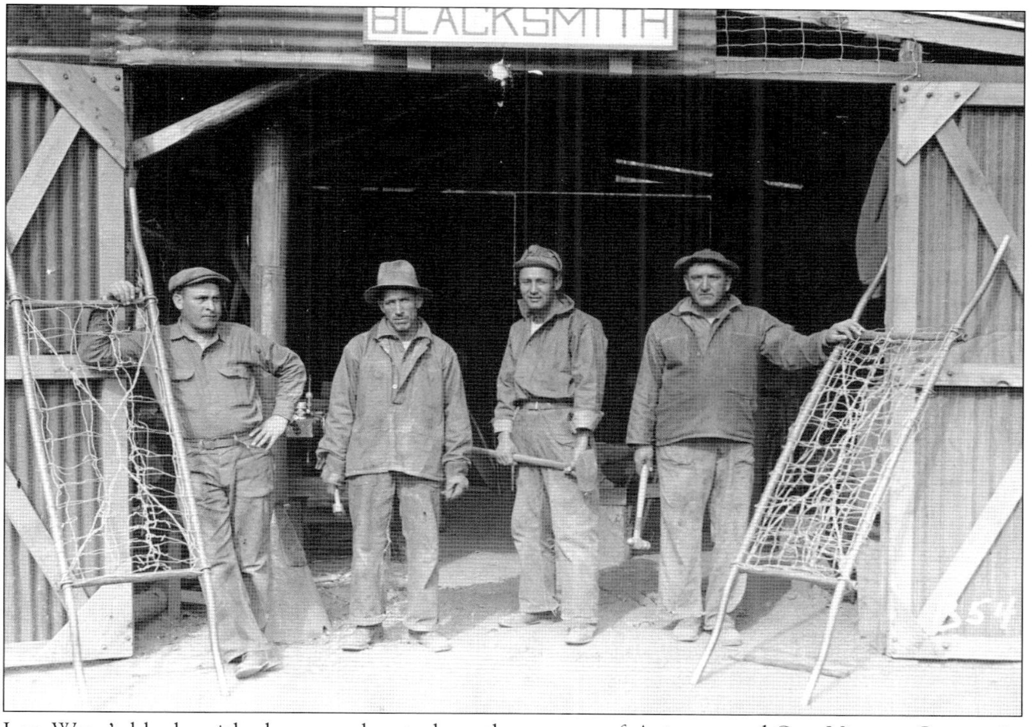

Leo Wray's blacksmith shop was located on the corner of Arizona and San Vicente Streets in Silver City. This 1930 photograph shows the crew with their hammers, ready for work. They are, from left to right, Leo Wray, unidentified, Juan Morales, and Max Madrid. The shop was the place to go to have the spokes on an automobile tightened. (Courtesy of Genevieve Johnston.)

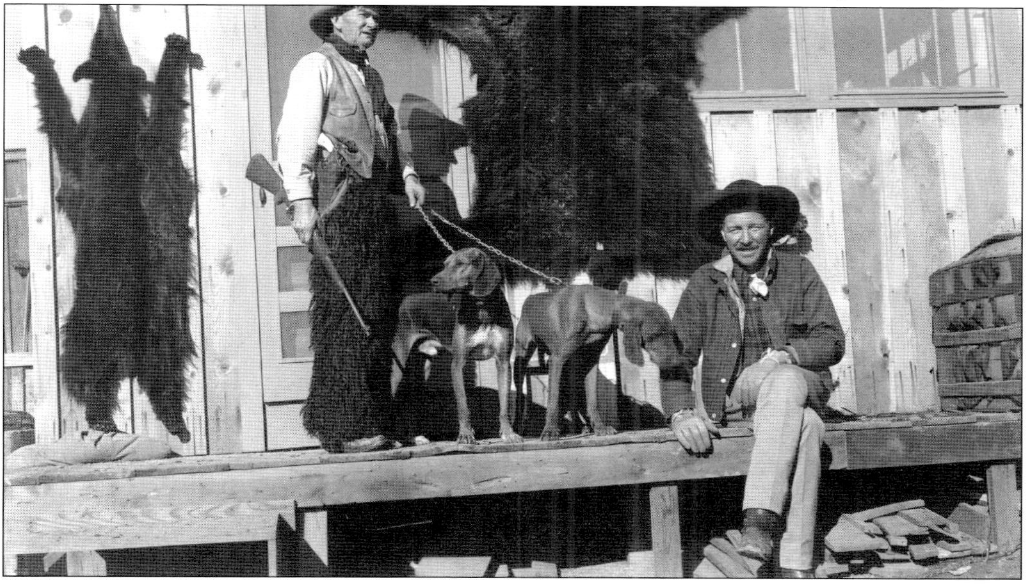

A.D. "Doc" Seitzler came to Silver City from Texas in 1907 and opened his harness shop on Bullard Street. Doc, pictured here in 1937 with his rifle and hunting hounds, was a famous saddle maker. Bob Chilton is seated on the porch step. (Courtesy of Don Turner.)

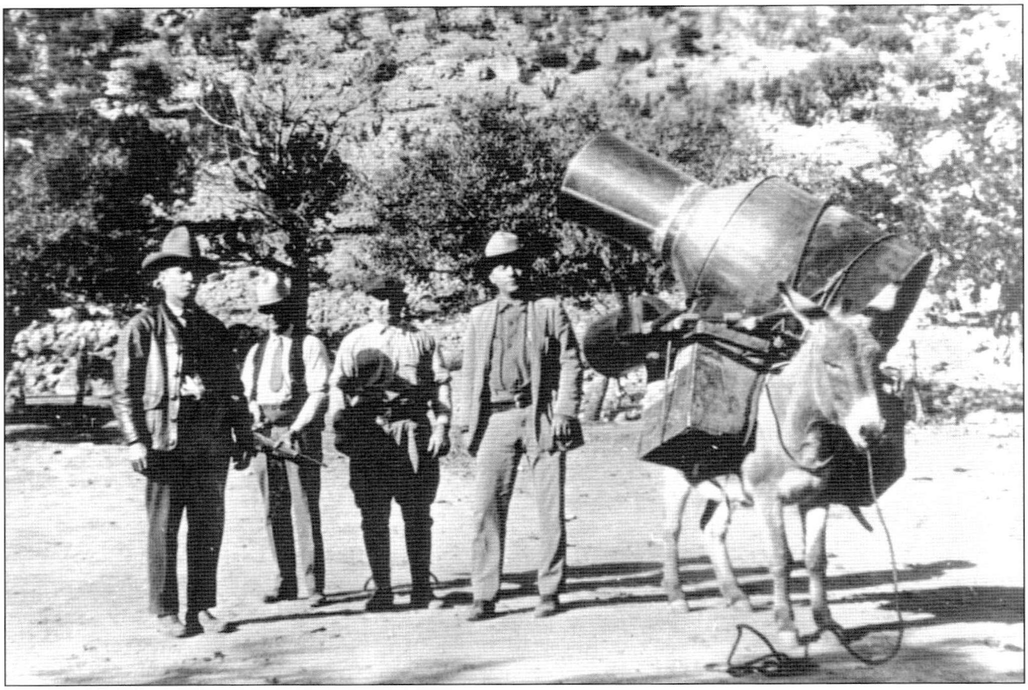

The Prohibition era, which lasted from 1920 to 1933, did little to slow alcohol consumption in Grant County or the making of bootleg whiskey. Pictured above are, from left to right, Grant County deputies Claude Hollis, Roy Taylor, Mike Spaulding, and John St. John as they confiscate an illegal still in Rustler's Canyon, east of Santa Rita, in 1925. Stills were often hidden in rugged canyons near a spring or water source. Moonshiners knew that a still in a remote location, away from a road or trail, was less likely to be discovered by the law. Below, Sheriff John W. Turner (left), Clyde Bloodgood (center), and Prohibition agent Jesse Hill stand next to a confiscated whiskey still in the Silver City Courthouse yard. (Both, courtesy of Don Turner.)

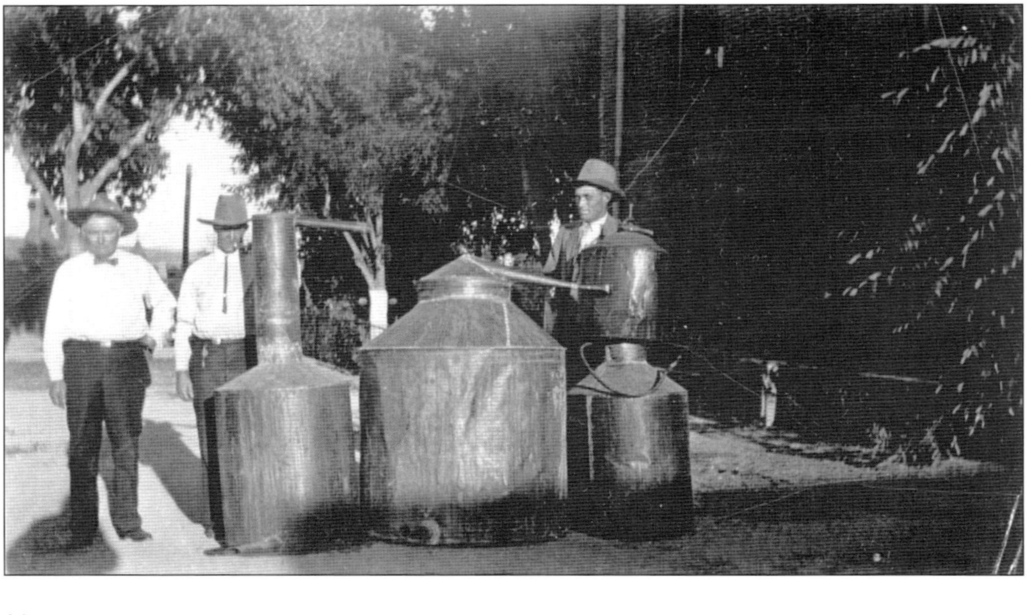

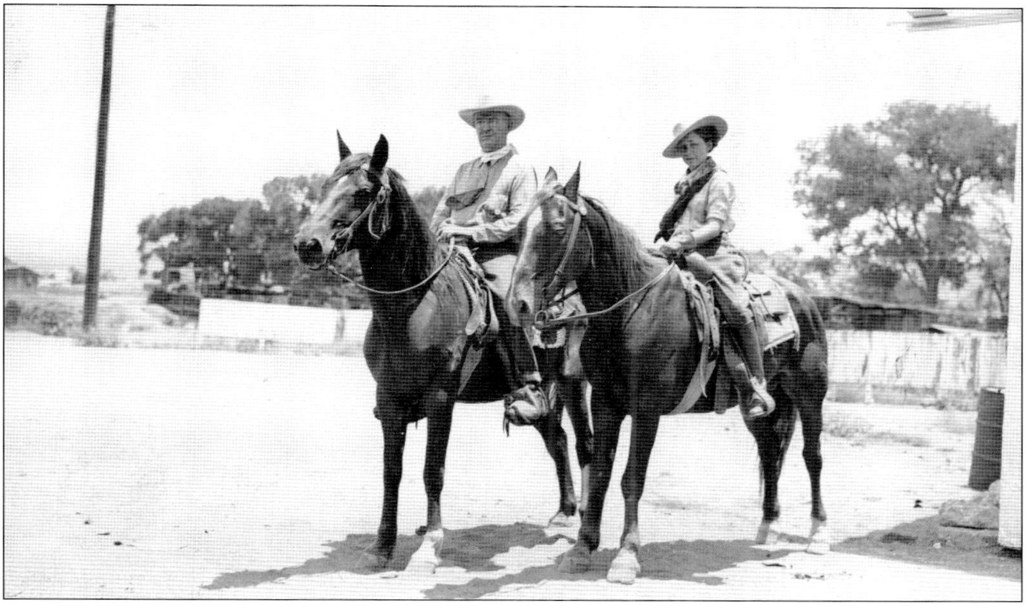

These two participants in the 1935 Fourth of July parade are John O'Leary, manager of the Silver City Chamber of Commerce, and Elizabeth Herndon, riding Shilo. On the back of the photograph, Elizabeth wrote that Shilo was the best horse she had ever ridden. (Courtesy of Don Turner.)

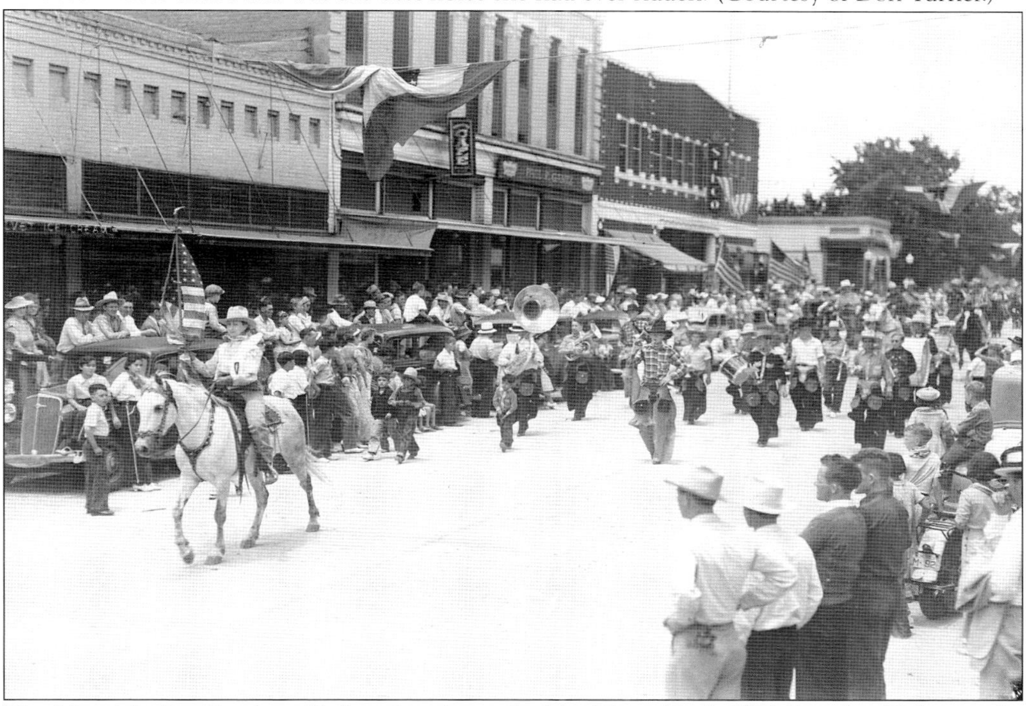

The New Mexico Teachers College band marched in Silver City's 1937 Fourth of July parade, led by Mrs. Frank Druley on horseback. The parade is moving south on Bullard Street. Note that the band members are all wearing Western dress, including cowboy hats and leather chaps. (Courtesy of Don Turner.)

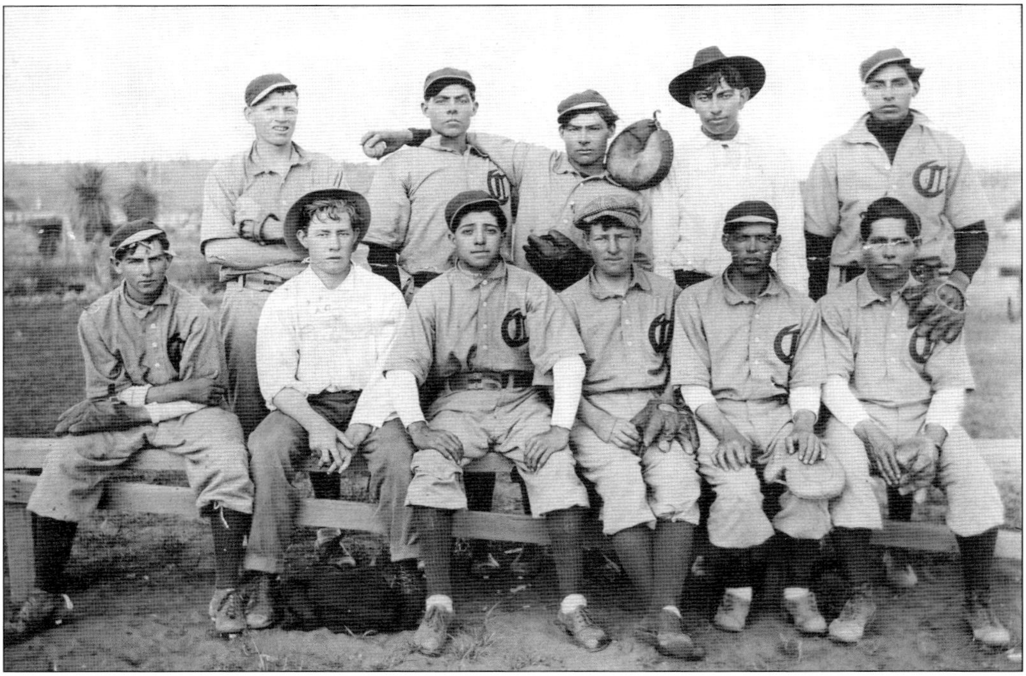

Above, the members of the Central, New Mexico, baseball team from the early 1920s are, from left to right (first row) Norton Moore, Grannell Dickinson, Juan Gomez, Archie Fisher, Esteban Perrez, and Rumaldo Horcasitas; (second row) Francisco Holguin, Panfilo Holguin, Juan Horcasitas, Paulo Horcasitas, and Kenneth Meyers. Below, the Silver City Cubs won the 1927 Southwestern Baseball Tournament, which also included teams from Silver City, Morenci, Lordsburg, Las Cruces, Central, and Santa Rita. Pictured are, from left to right, the unidentified coach, Bill "Shorty" Mrotzek, L. "Eddie" Gomez, Joe Sanchez, Frank Gonzales, Pifie Madrid, Nicho Ortiz, Dan Alderete, Diego Gonzales, Juan Gomez (father of the photograph's donor), R. "Hock" Morales, Tacho Morales, Adolph Carson, and Ben Deck, with batboy Julian Espinosa kneeling in front. The all-star team drafted players from the Central Cubs, Fort Bayard, and Alianza Hispanic Alliance. (Both, courtesy of Genevieve Johnston.)

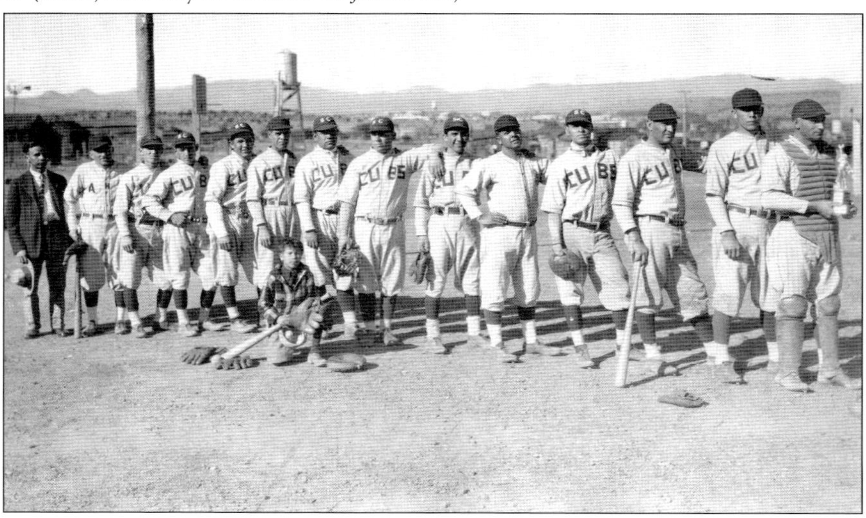

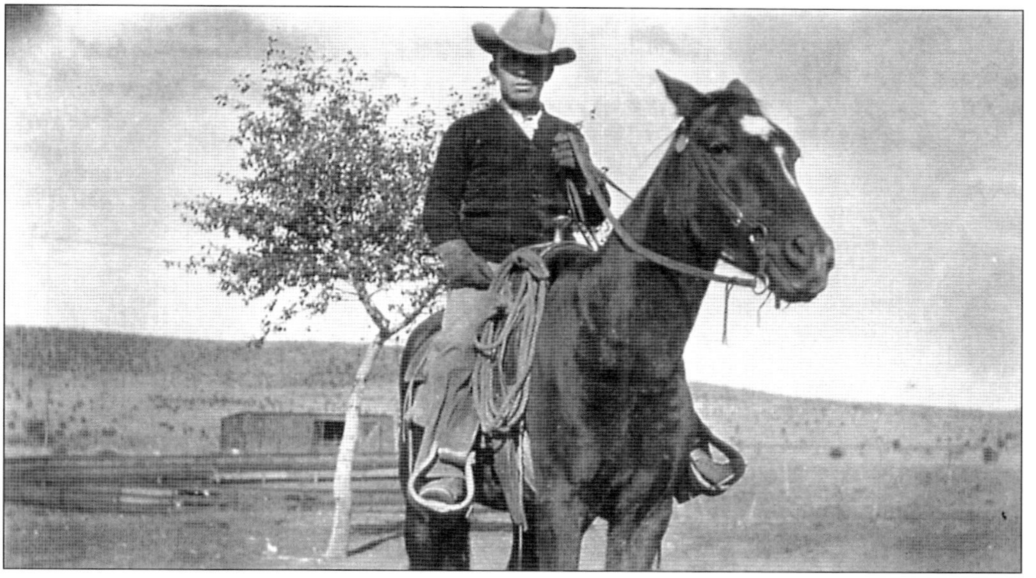

Rosedale Dairy, east of Silver City, was one of the oldest dairies in southwest New Mexico. Established in 1890 by C.G. Jenks, it operated for almost 80 years and was one of the first in New Mexico to have modern, up-to-date pasteurizing. New Mexico rancher and author Agnes Morley Cleaveland, known for her 1941 memoir *No Life for a Lady*, operated the dairy from 1907 to 1908. Cleaveland, who sometimes had more customers than she could supply, added water and butter coloring to the milk. However, an incident in which an incorrect ratio turned the milk pink led townspeople to believe that they were being poisoned. Philip Harsh bought the dairy in 1908, and ownership was subsequently passed down through the family. Fiske Harsh, above, took over management in 1927, and was associated with the dairy until his death in 1974. Rosedale Dairy closed in the late 1970s.

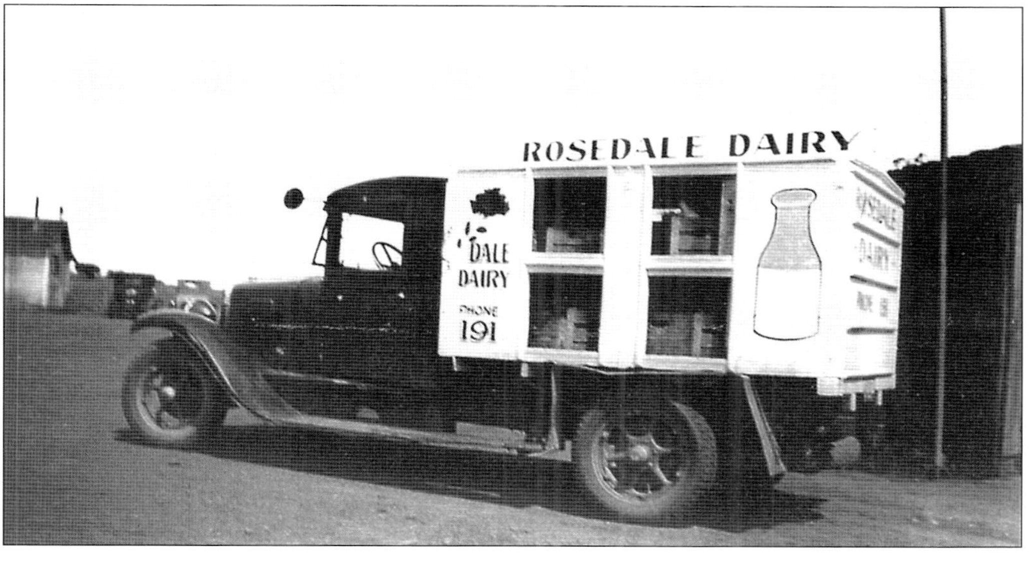

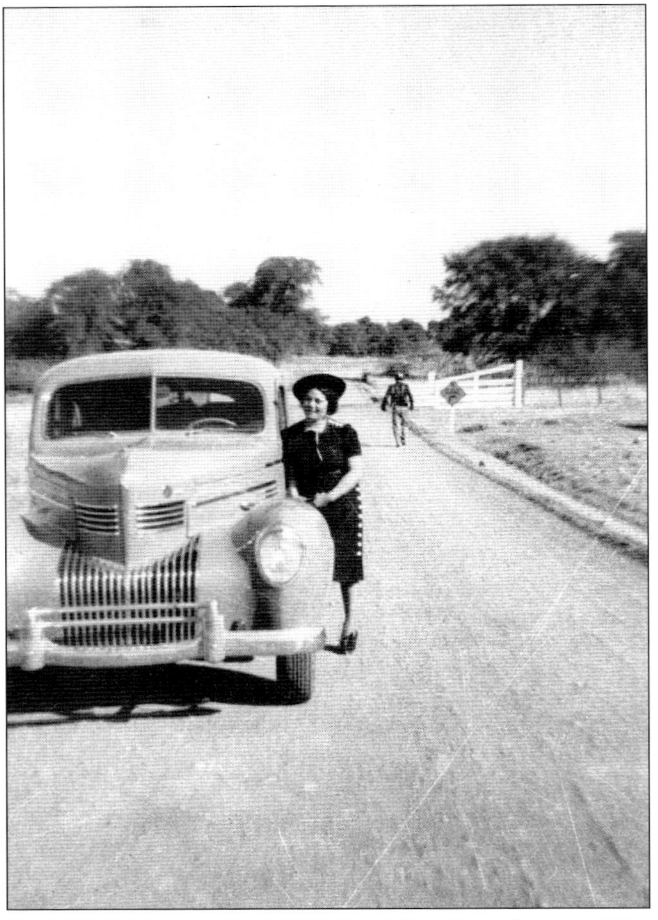

Mildred Clark Cusey, pictured at left, and her sister Florence, orphaned after the deaths of their parents, were sent to the Southwest because of Florence's tuberculosis. At 14, Mildred lied about her age to work as a Harvey Girl in Deming, New Mexico, but turned to prostitution to help pay for Florence's medical bills. Later known as "Madam Millie," she became a successful bordello businesswoman, owning three red-light houses in Silver City and several elsewhere. She also became known for her philanthropy, feeding families of striking miners, supporting local charities, and paying medical bills and college tuition for local youngsters. Millie retired in 1968, but she appeared in public for many years, riding in Fourth of July parades in a convertible alongside a town dignitary. (Both, courtesy of Peggy Wright.)

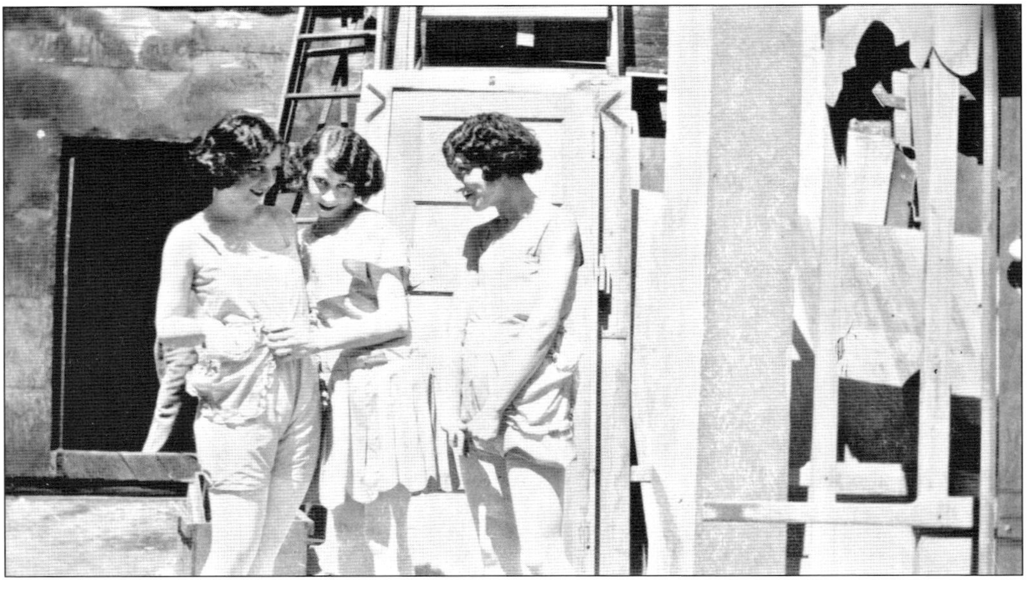

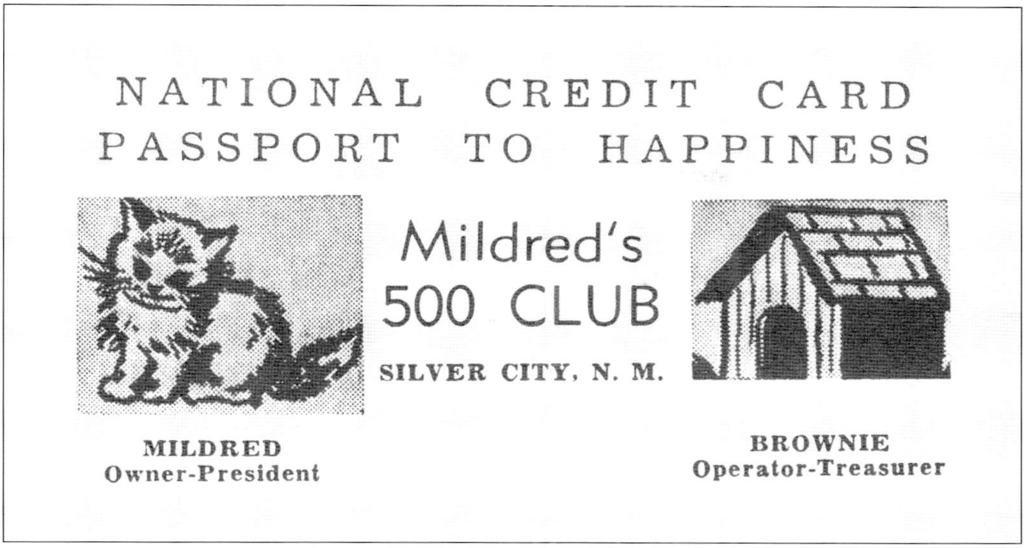

Madam Millie gave business cards, like this one, to potential customers. Mildred's 500 Club referred to the three bordellos she operated on the 500 block on Hudson Street. Some cards carried the phrase "Across the Ditch," referring to the red-light district that was on the east side of the Big Ditch. New girls at Millie's establishments would walk her dog downtown as a subtle form of advertising.

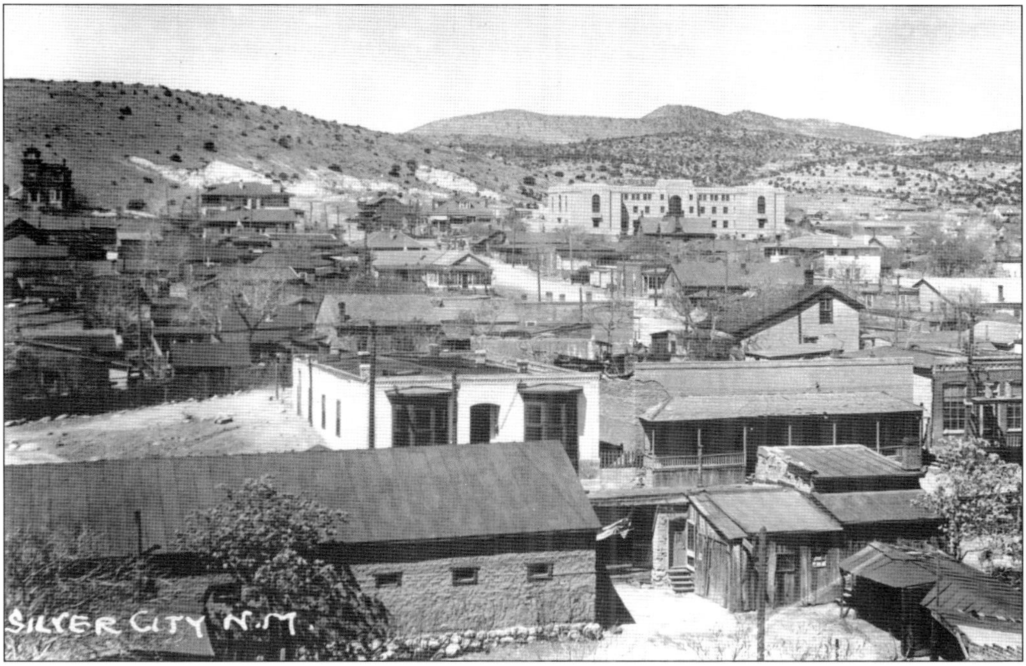

Silver City's original red-light district clustered around the southern end of downtown before its proprietors relocated their establishments across the Big Ditch to Hudson Street around 1905. The white house in the center of the photograph was built on Texas Street in 1883 for Kate Stewart, a prominent early madam, and purchased a few years later by Bessie Harper. Both of these frontier madams were credited with many good deeds in Silver City. (Courtesy of Don Turner.)

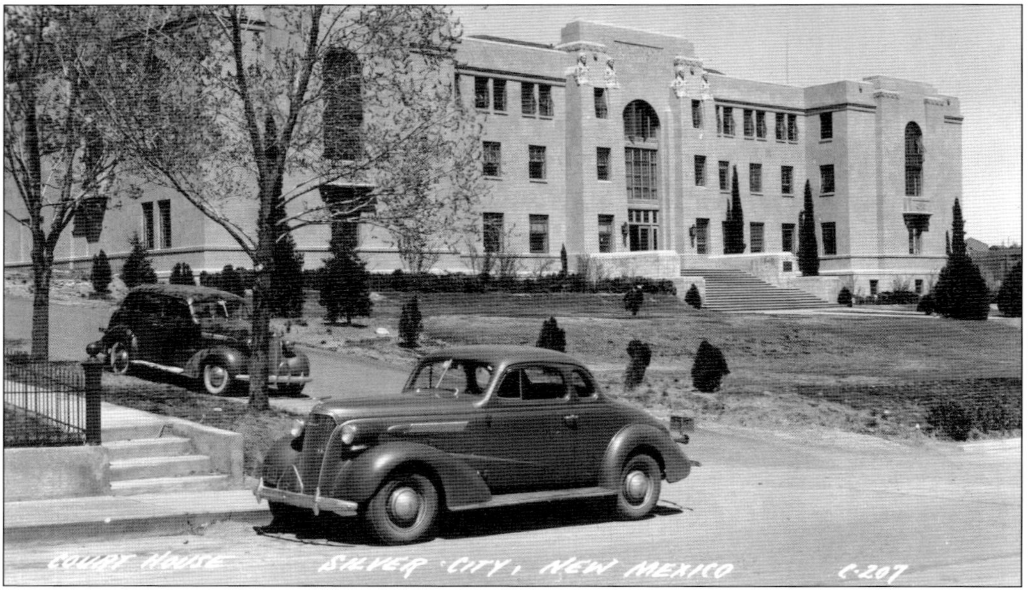

The modern Grant County Courthouse, completed in 1930, was built at the top of Broadway, behind the old courthouse, which was demolished soon afterward. The beautiful facade featured female figures and false balconies, and the third-floor jail had arched windows. Murals featuring local images of mining and ranching were created for the lobby by Theodore Van Soelen, a Santa Fe artist working under the WPA artist's program. (Courtesy of Don Turner.)

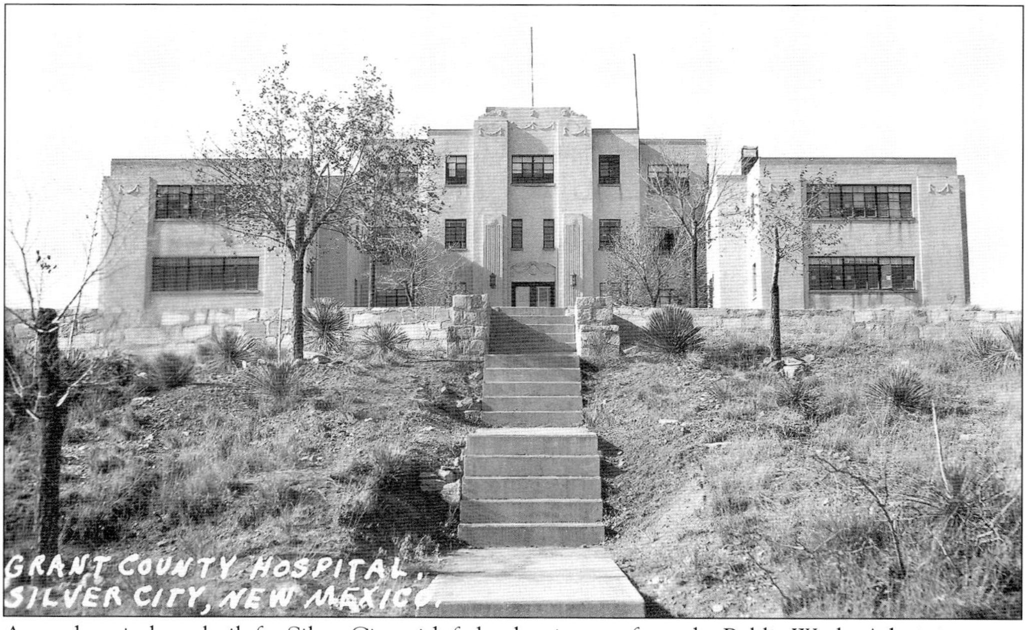

A new hospital was built for Silver City with federal assistance from the Public Works Administration in 1937. Located at the northeast edge of town, near Silver Heights Boulevard and Juniper Street, it held 25 beds. In 1938, it was renamed Swift Memorial Hospital. The facility was enlarged and renamed several times before being abandoned and replaced by the Gila Regional Medical Center. (Courtesy of Gila Regional Medical Center.)

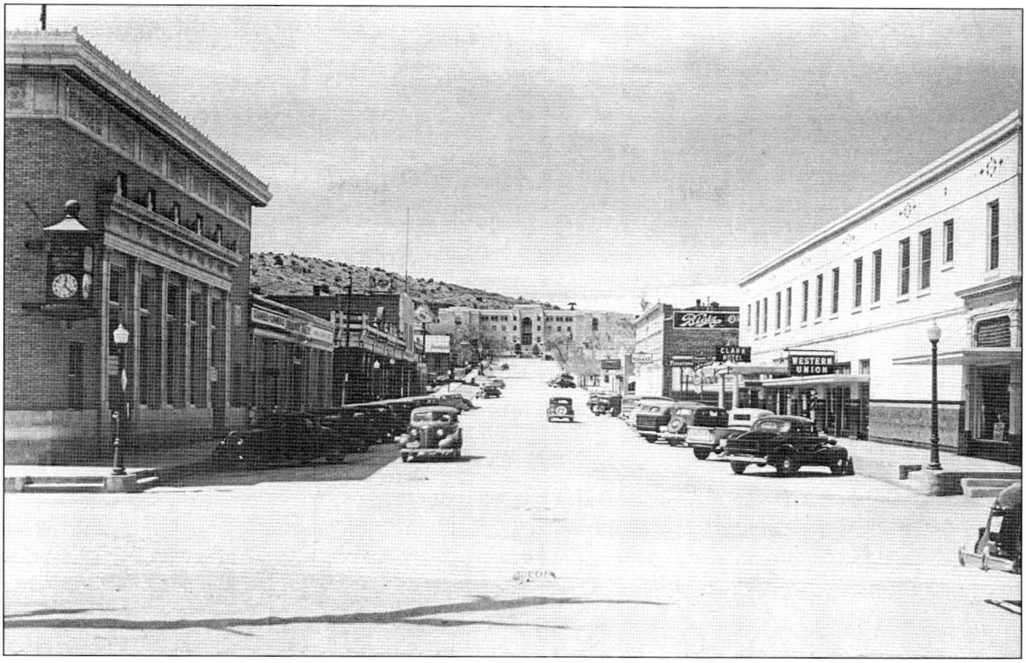

Looking up Broadway from Bullard Street, the new Grant County Courthouse stands at the top of the street. The American National Bank is on the left, and the white building on the right is the Palace Hotel. Below, this 1937 Silver City view was probably taken from the courthouse. St. Vincent de Paul Catholic Church, with its twin towers, is just right of center. The large structure directly behind the church is the 1910 school known as the Central Building. The other large building, left of center, is the former Academy of Our Lady of Lourdes, at that time being used as the Silver City hospital. It was torn down shortly after this picture was taken and replaced with the Manville Building, originally a junior high facility but now home to Sixth Street Elementary. (Both, courtesy of Don Turner.)

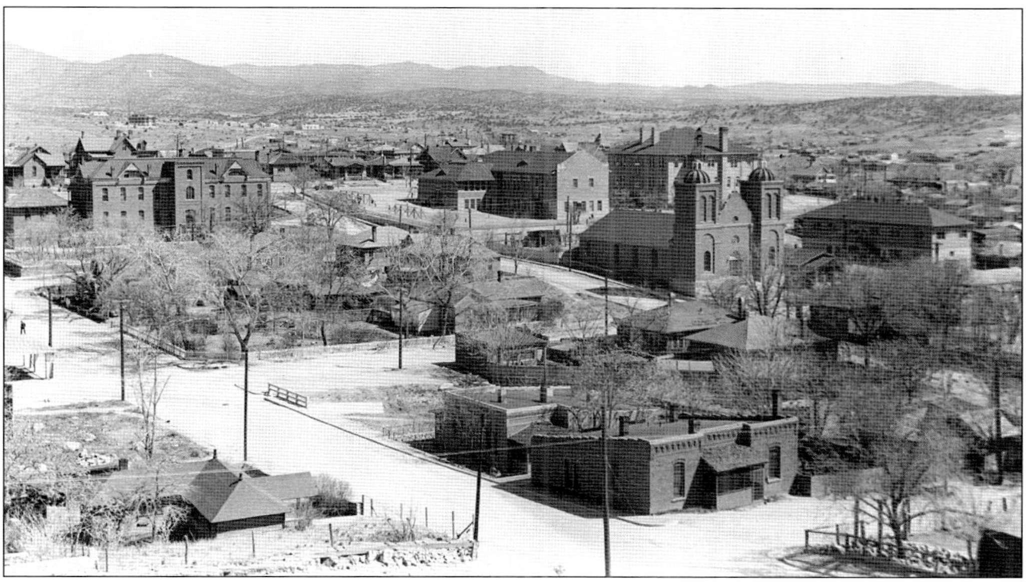

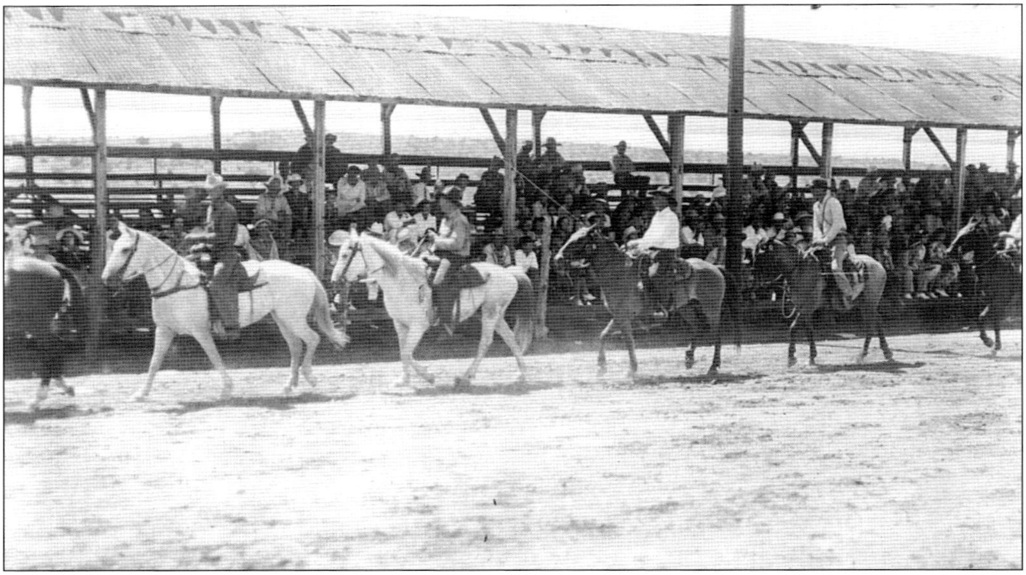

Silver City's rodeo grounds were located east of present-day G.W. Stout Elementary School. The cowboys in this 1938 rodeo are, from left to right, unidentified, Dale McCauley, Jim McCauley, and Otho Woodrow (who was a competitive roper into his 80s). A much-anticipated local event was the Fourth of July Wild Horse Race, where cowboys tried to mount and ride a wild mustang across the rodeo arena. (Courtesy of Connie McCauley.)

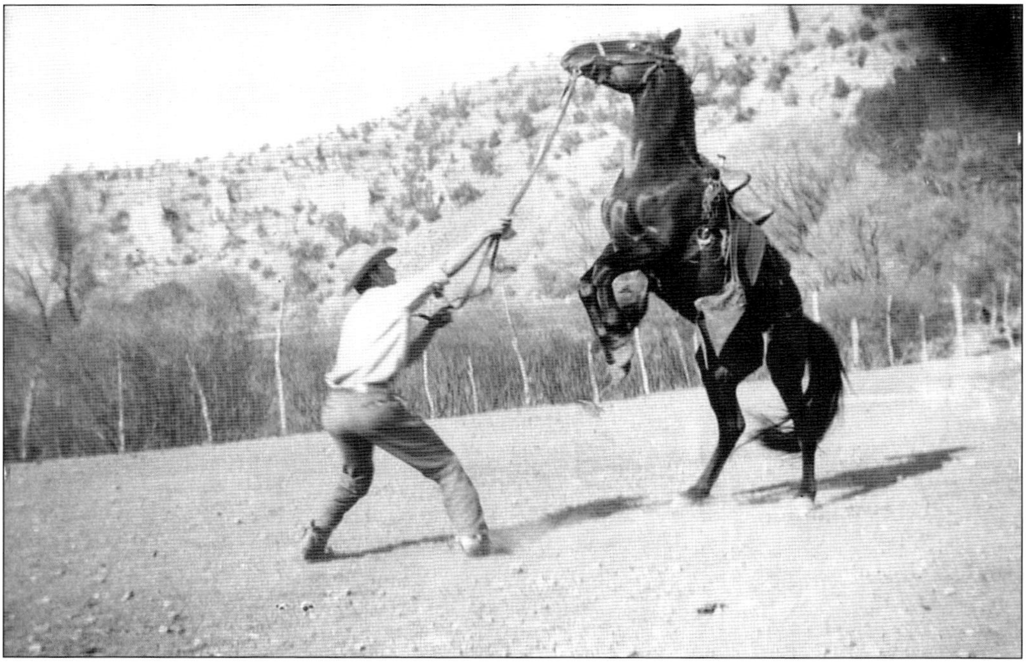

Dawson "Doc" Campbell came to New Mexico in 1929 at the age of 16 and worked for the XSX Ranch. Although his horse, Sharpy, was spirited, he was one of Doc's favorites to ride. Doc saw the last traces of Apache trails through the forest, where travois poles scraped the trunks of the pines, and he knew Nat Straw, last of the mountain men. (Courtesy of Ida Campbell.)

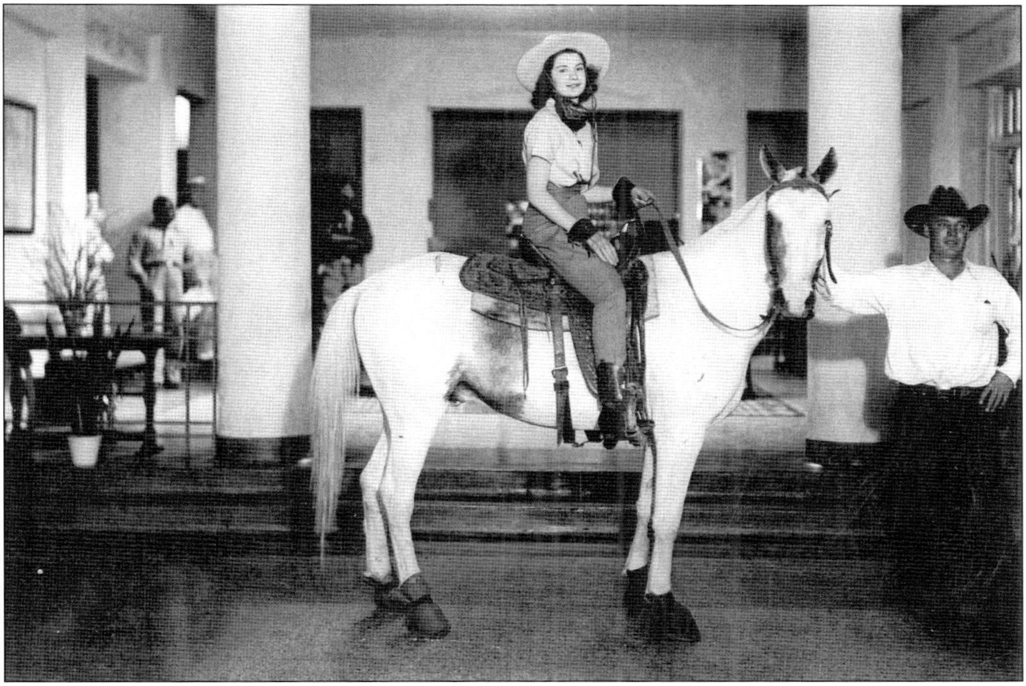

The elegant, modern, five-story Murray Hotel at 200 West Broadway opened in 1938. Jim McCauley rode his horse, Agate, to Silver City from his home at White Signal to attend the Fourth of July rodeo and parade. Martha Ryan, the 16-year-old granddaughter of hotel owner William D. Murray, posed for this photograph with Jim and Agate in the hotel lobby. The horse was wearing socks made from pieces of rubber inner tubes, and Jim McCauley was given a free night for his assistance in promoting the new hotel. (Above, courtesy of Connie McCauley; below, courtesy of Don Turner.)

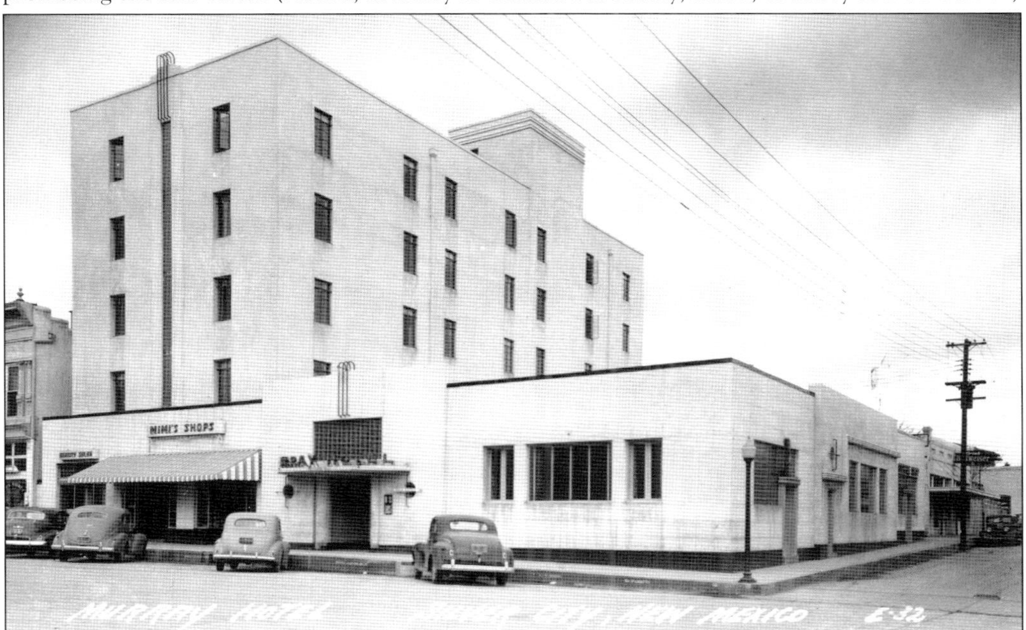

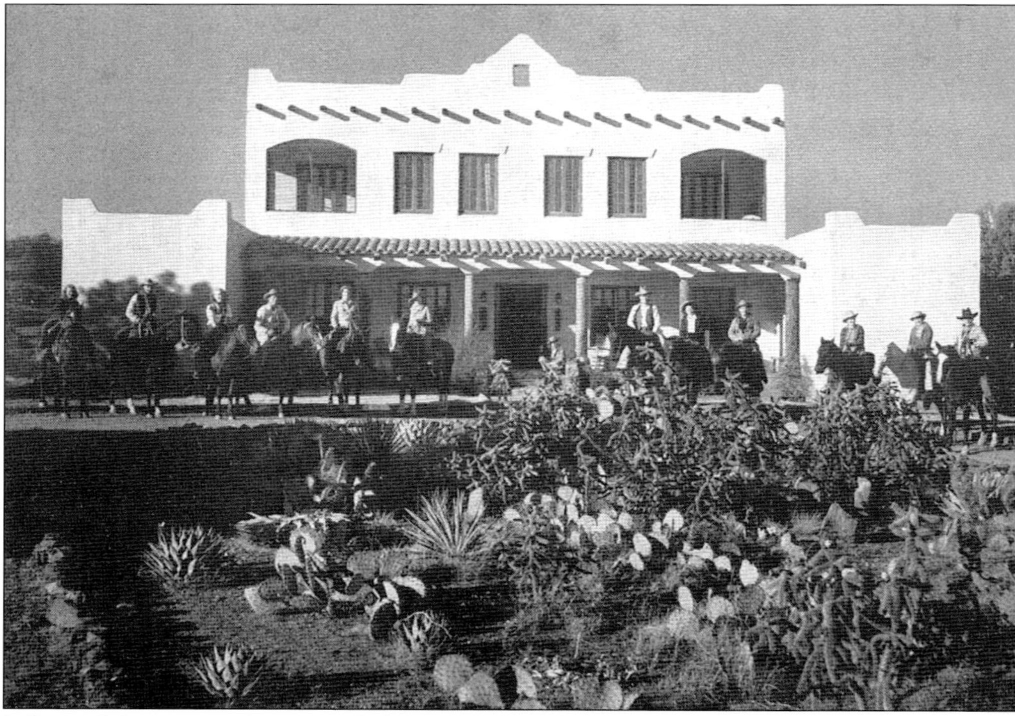

Lillie and Samps Dye homesteaded in a canyon northwest of Silver City in 1910. During the 1920s, their home was purchased by the Franks family, who used it as the headquarters for their cattle ranch. Later, it was a school for "mentally peculiar" (unruly) boys. In 1932, the building was reborn as a country club and hotel, and today the historic structure is Bear Mountain Lodge, a popular guest ranch. (Courtesy of Bear Mountain Lodge.)

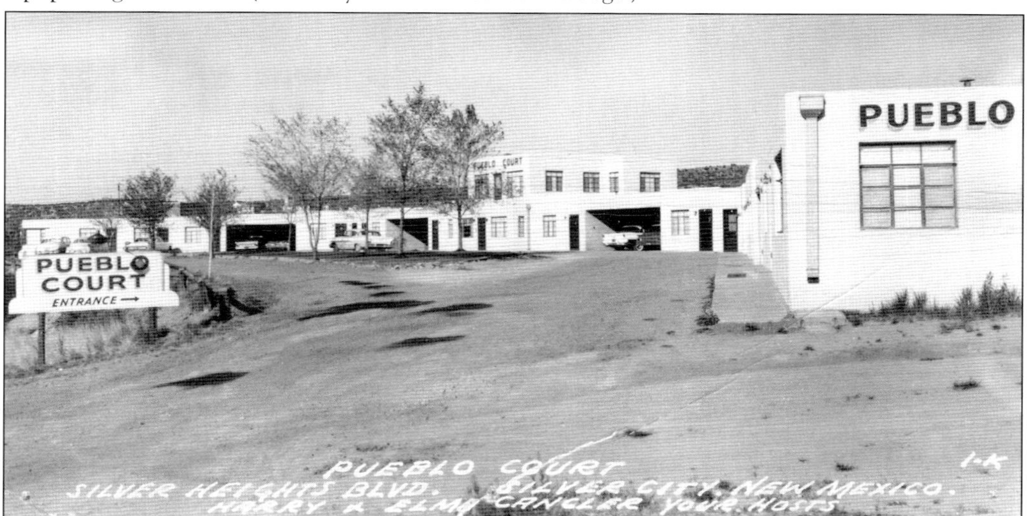

Harry and Elma Cansler operated the Pueblo Court, an early Silver City motel, on Silver Heights Boulevard. The complex included a manager's living quarters, 15 rooms, and small, open carports for automobiles. The structure is now gone, and its former location is the site of a large hardware store. (Courtesy of Don Turner.)

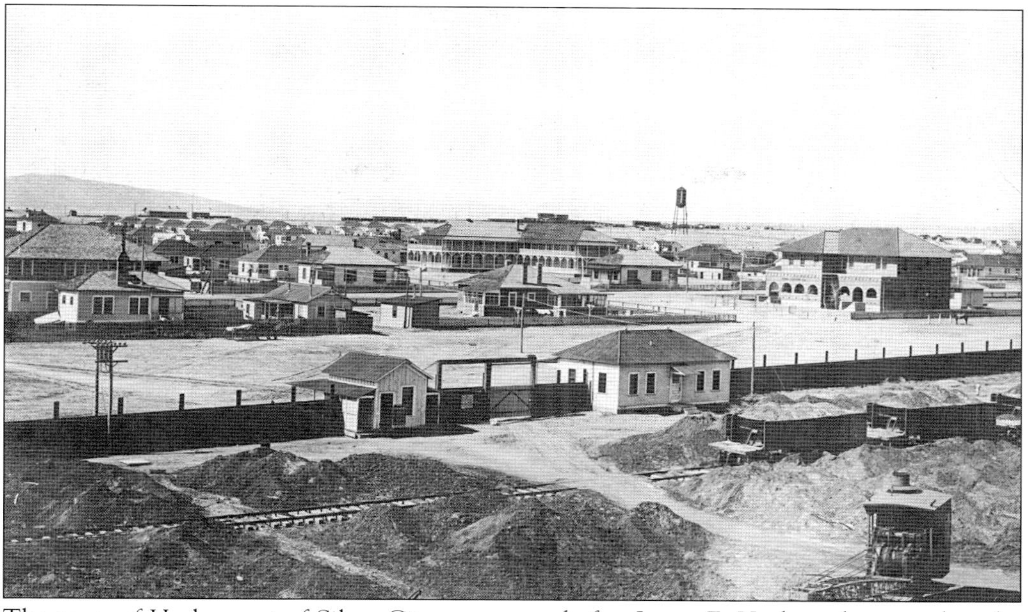

The town of Hurley, east of Silver City, was named after James E. Hurley, who served as the general manager of the Atkinson, Topeka & Santa Fe Railroad until his death in 1910. That year, a concentrating mill and smelter were built here to process the copper ore being mined from Santa Rita, 10 miles to the north. The photograph above, looking west from the mill, shows the plant in 1915. Below, in an eastward view down Cortez Avenue, the Hurley gates are seen in 1942. The tall emission stack, built in 1939, is in the center of the picture. Another stack, even taller, was erected in 1967. Old-timers recall that machine guns were mounted at these gates after Pancho Villa's 1916 raid on Columbus, New Mexico, and also during World War I.

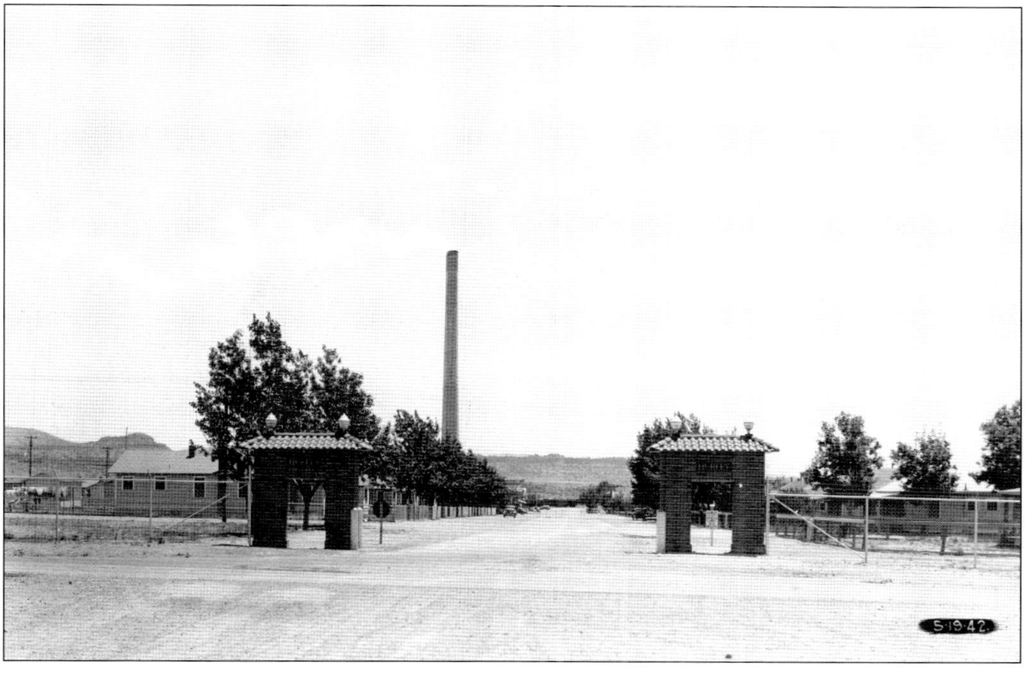

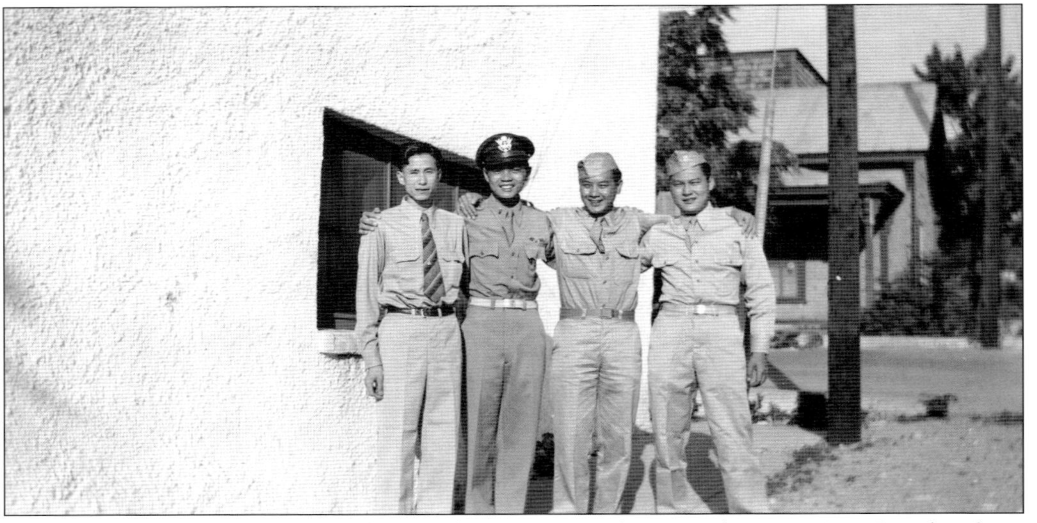

The three Chinese American soldiers in this image were home on leave in 1944. Posed in front of the Lime residence at Sixth Street and Texas are, from left to right, Hom Hong (a cousin), and brothers Yolk Lew, Sinn Lew, and Joe (or Hall) Lew. Yolk and Sinn were both navigators in the US Air Force. Yolk, a second lieutenant, flew 41 B-24 missions out of Italy during World War II. (Courtesy of Don Turner.)

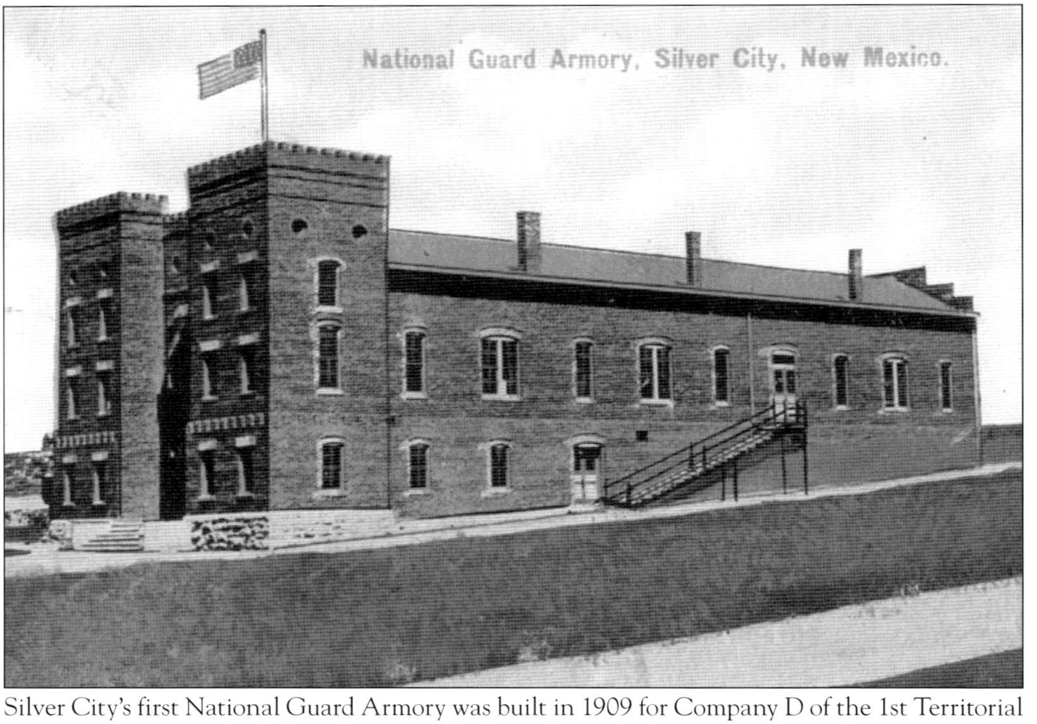

Silver City's first National Guard Armory was built in 1909 for Company D of the 1st Territorial Regiment. Cresting the hill at the east end of Broadway, the building contained rooms for drills, officers, and the battalion headquarters, as well as a reception room used by locals for dances and other social events. Most of the Grant County men who served in World War II trained at the Armory building. (Courtesy of Don Turner.)

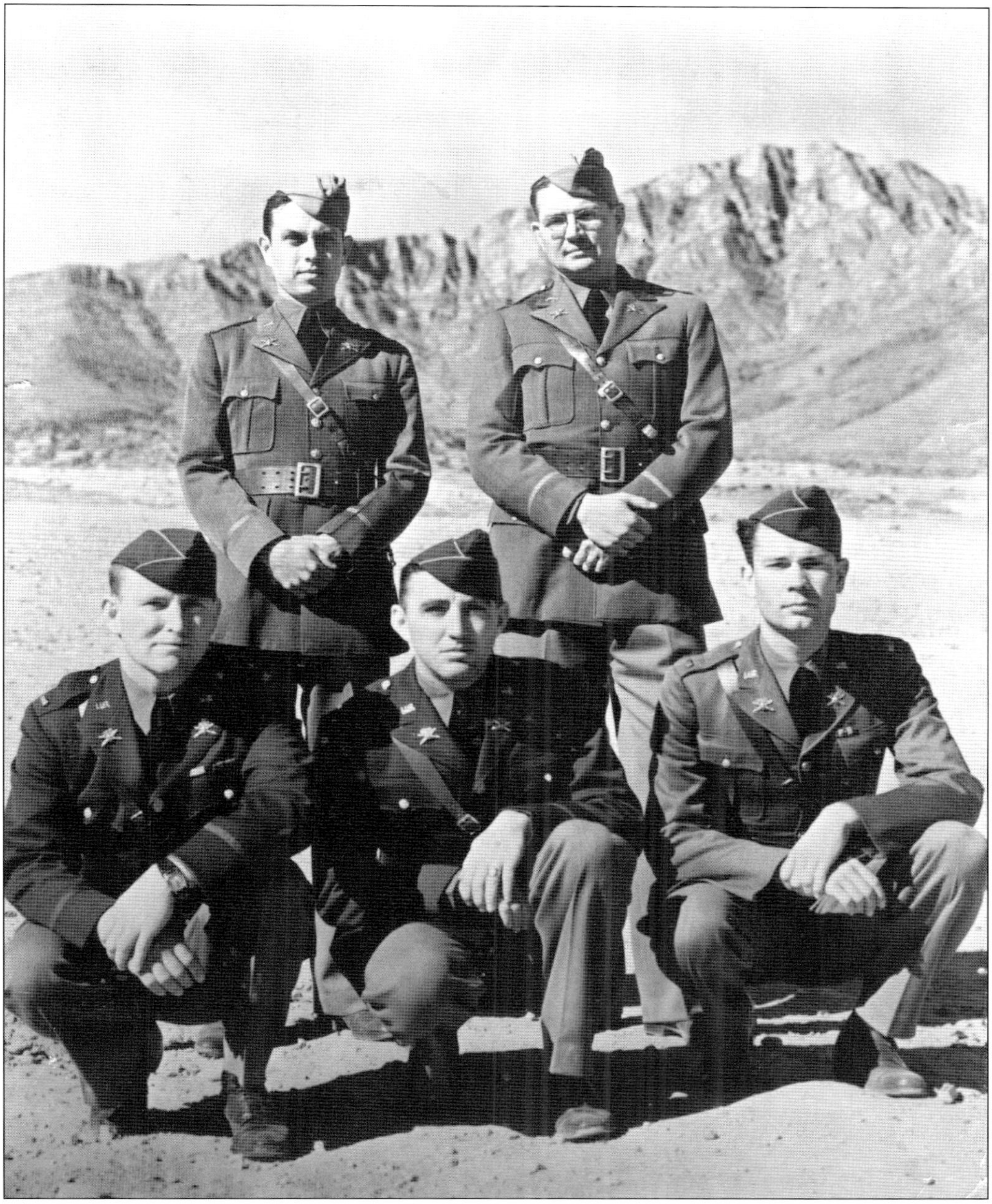

The five officers in this 1941 photograph, taken at Fort Bliss, Texas, were members of the 200th Coast Artillery. They are, from left to right, (first row) Capt. Raymond Thwaits, Lt. Alvin Bayne, and Lt. Jack Ashby; (standing) Lt. Clyde Ely Jr. and Captain John W. Turner Jr. These men all became prisoners of war, and none survived the Japanese hell ships and prison camps. Silver City and Grant County families suffered exceptionally heavy losses in World War II because their National Guard unit was sent to the Philippines and endured the tragedies at Bataan. Less than half the men lived to return home. Some were lost in the three-month battle, or later, the Death March; others died of suffocation or starvation on the hell ships (many drowned when the ships were sunk by US forces), or in prisoner-of-war camps. (Courtesy of Don Turner.)

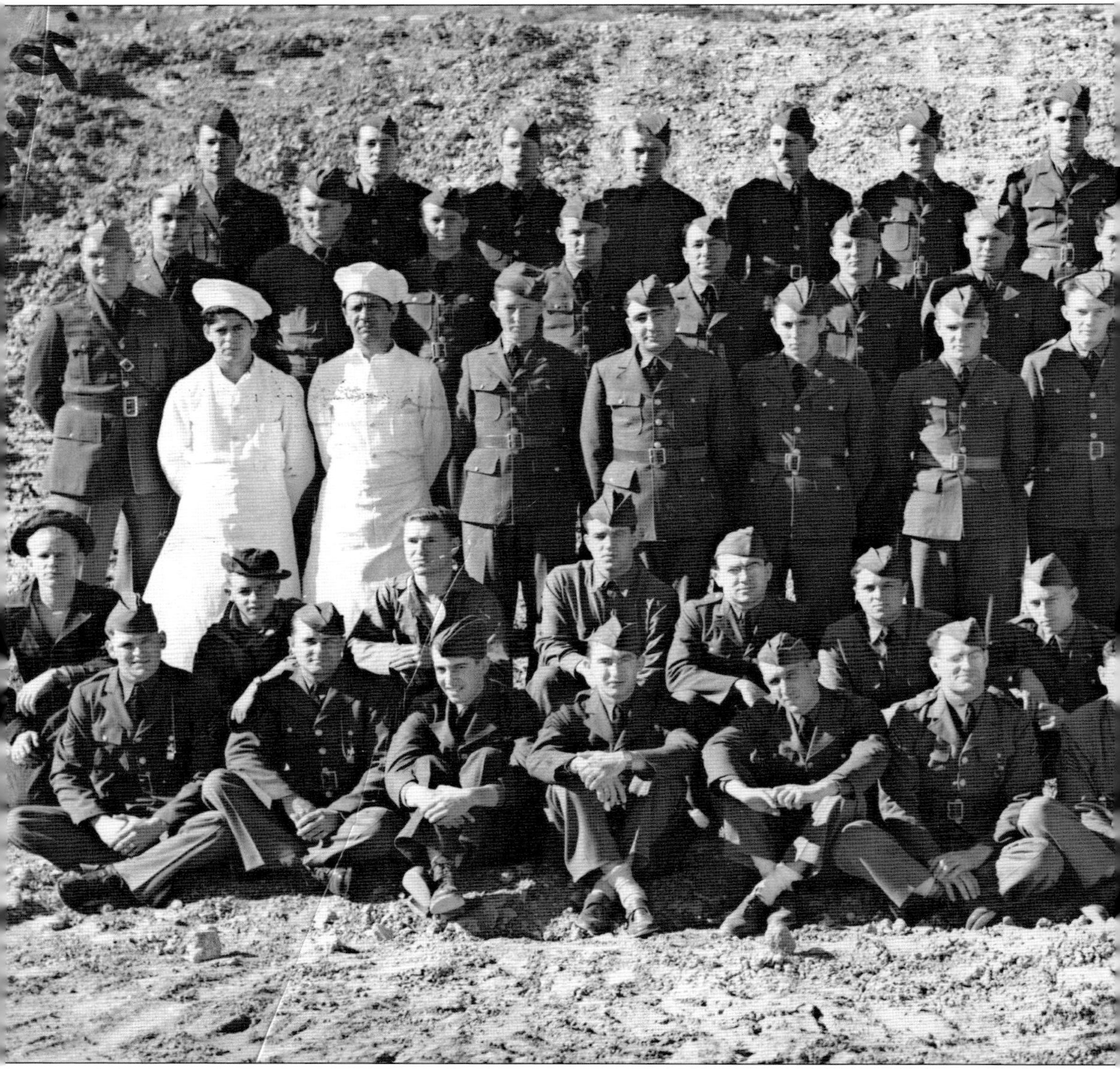

Members of Battery G of the 200th Coast Artillery (AA) were photographed at Fort Bliss, El Paso, Texas, in 1941. These Grant County National Guardsmen served on Bataan, Philippine Islands, in World War II. They were captured by the Japanese in April 1942, and less than half of them survived captivity. Grant County men serving on Bataan included Roman Alderete, Stephan Alex, William Allred, Robert Amy, Pete Armijo, Thomas Barka, Douglas Brown, Jack Burchfield, Richard Burke, Donald Burrell, Rhodun Bussell, Lloyd Byers, Robert Carpenter, Nicholas Chintis, Charles Clark, Louis Clark, Ralph Clark, Kenneth Coffey, Rexal Coffindaffer, Thalias Ray Cook, Baylor Duncan, Joseph Duncan, Frank Eaton, Thomas Foy, Arvil Gale, Walter Gentry, Frank Gonzales, Calvin Graef, Julius Griffin, Pablo Gutierrez, Wallace Hall, Donald Harris, Melvin Harsh, Glenn Haynes, Cipriano Hernandez, Thomas Hodges, Melvin Hulbert,

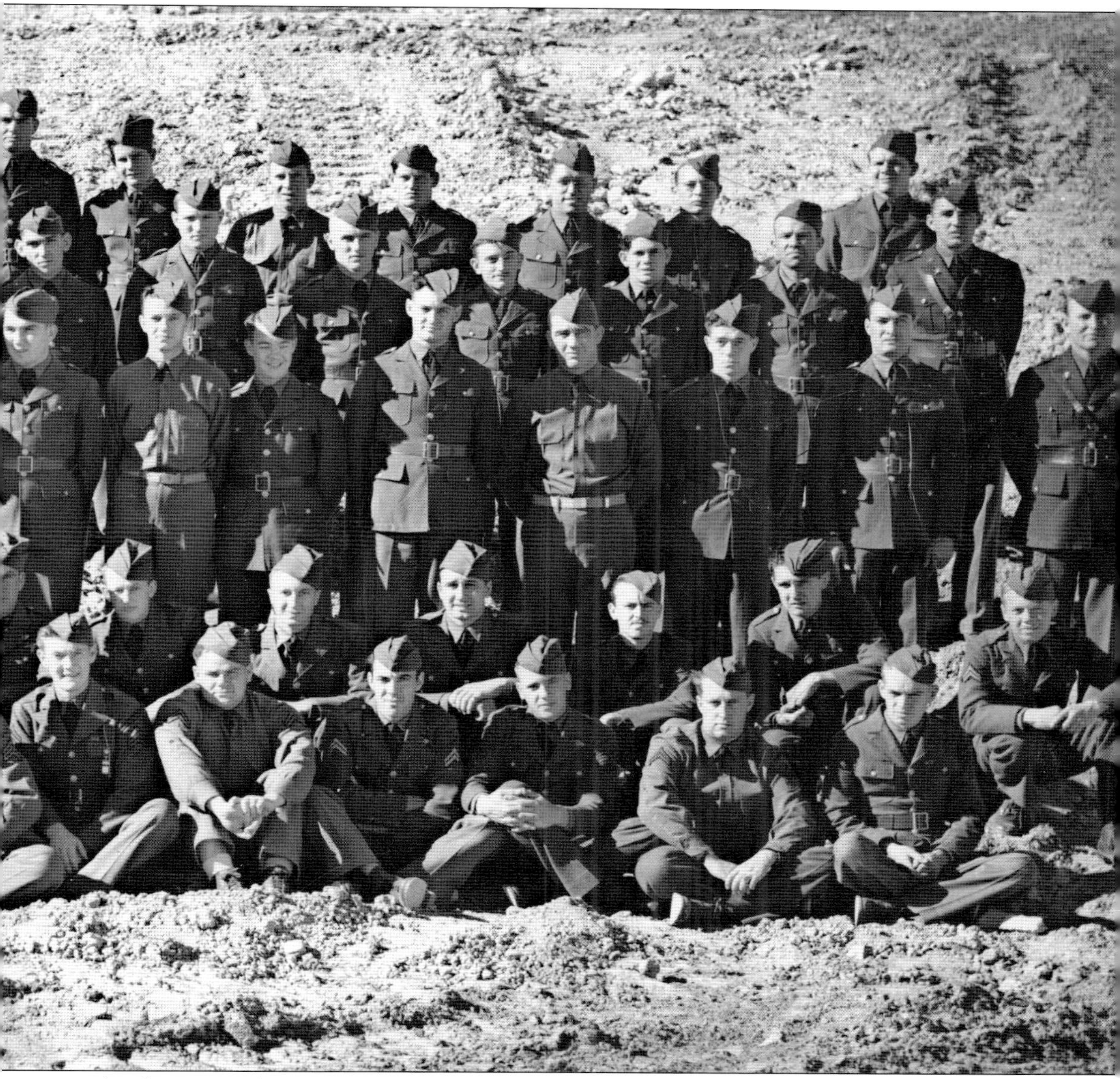

Richard Hunt, Baylor Hunter, Ellis Hunter, James Hunter, Joseph Hunter. George Hynes, Robert Jackson, Billy Jensen, David Johns, Curtis Jones, Harry Kelly, Jack Kennemen, Edgar Long, Robert Luther, Wayne Mahler, James Mayes, Parker McCool, William Mitchell. Manuel Munoz, Lloyd Murphy, Mike Ochoa, Vicente Ojinaga, Roy Owen, Primativo Pena, Richard Pitsor, William Pringle, Barney Prosser, Cipriano Ramirez, James Richards, Joel Rogers, Reynaldo Salaiz, William Salars, Lee Savage, Henry Scally, Winston Shillito, Eugene Snyder, Jack Sprunk, Fred Starnes, Richard Swain, Charles Taylor, William Taylor, Frank Thomas, Prior Thwaits, Norval Tow, Rhea Tow, Walter Upchurch, Max Villalobos, Elmer Worthen, Jeff Wysong, and Vernon Youngblood. (Courtesy of Don Turner.)

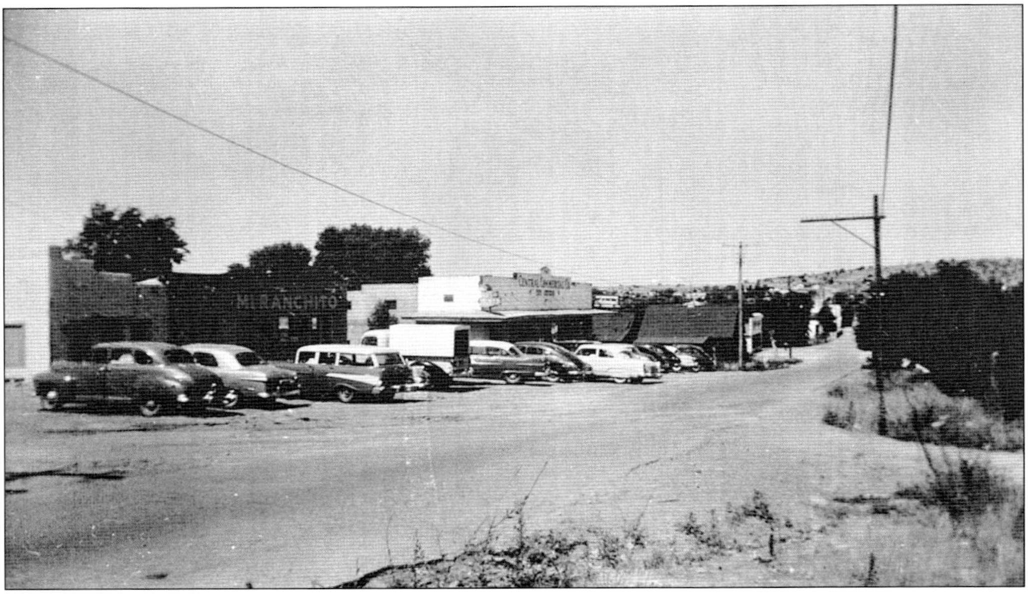

Central, New Mexico, just east of Silver City, is now known as Santa Clara. The Central Commercial Company store, pictured above in 1950, sold dry goods, including groceries, household supplies, and hardware. Below, the Minors Canteen, to the left of the store, served a clientele consisting mostly of miners from the nearby underground mines and the Chino Mine. (Both, courtesy of Anthony Romero.)

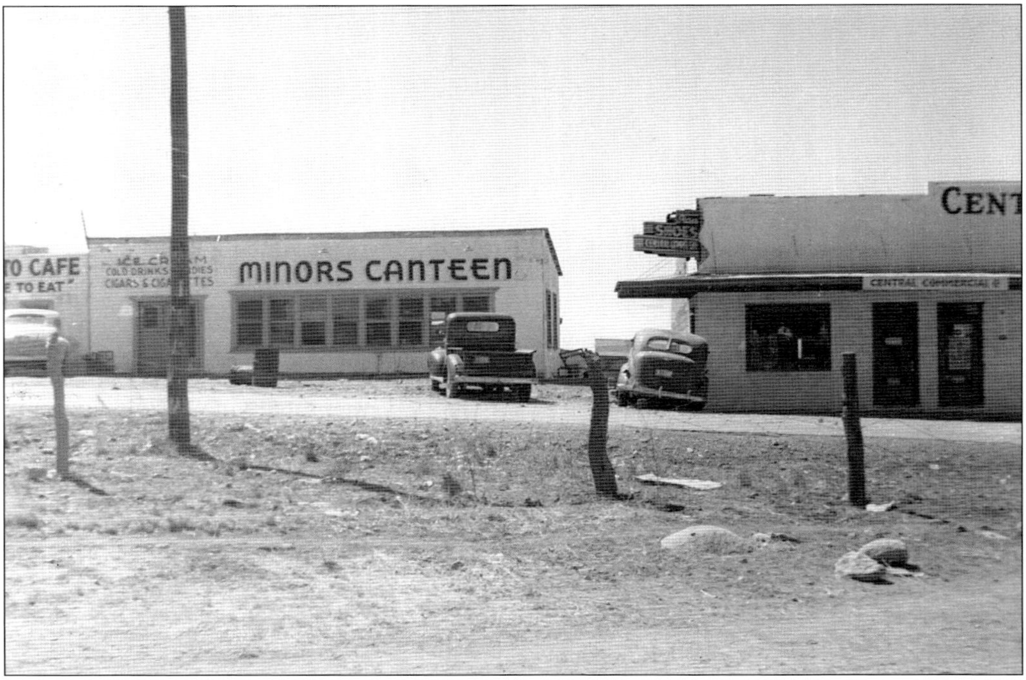

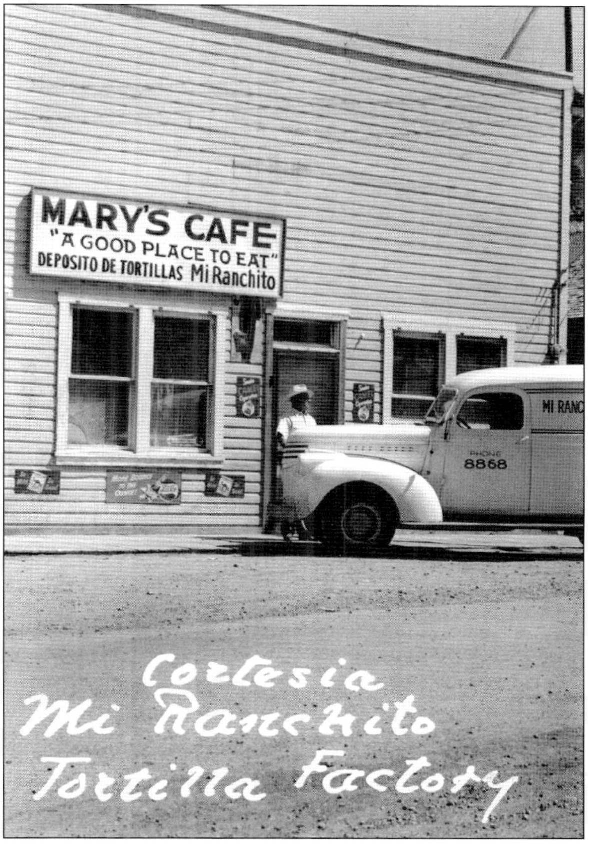

Mary's Cafe in Central City was a popular restaurant that also sold tortillas from Mi Ranchito Tortilla Factory, a business still going strong today in Bayard. Jose Antonio Martinez, below, delivered fresh tortillas to shops and restaurants. His clients ranged from Central to Silver City and all of Grant County. (Both, courtesy of Anthony Romero.)

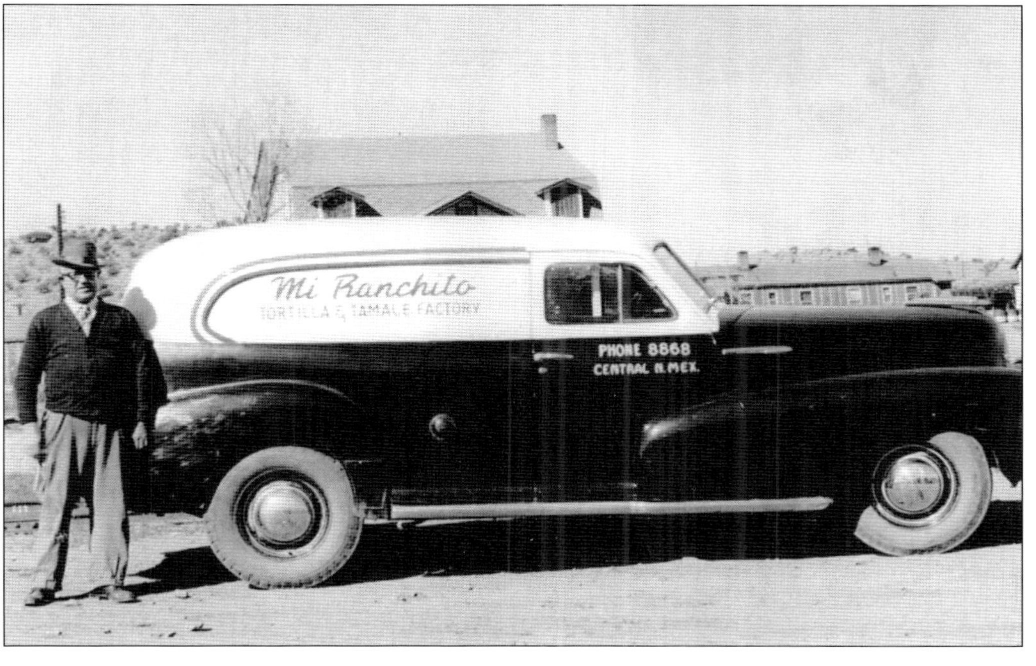

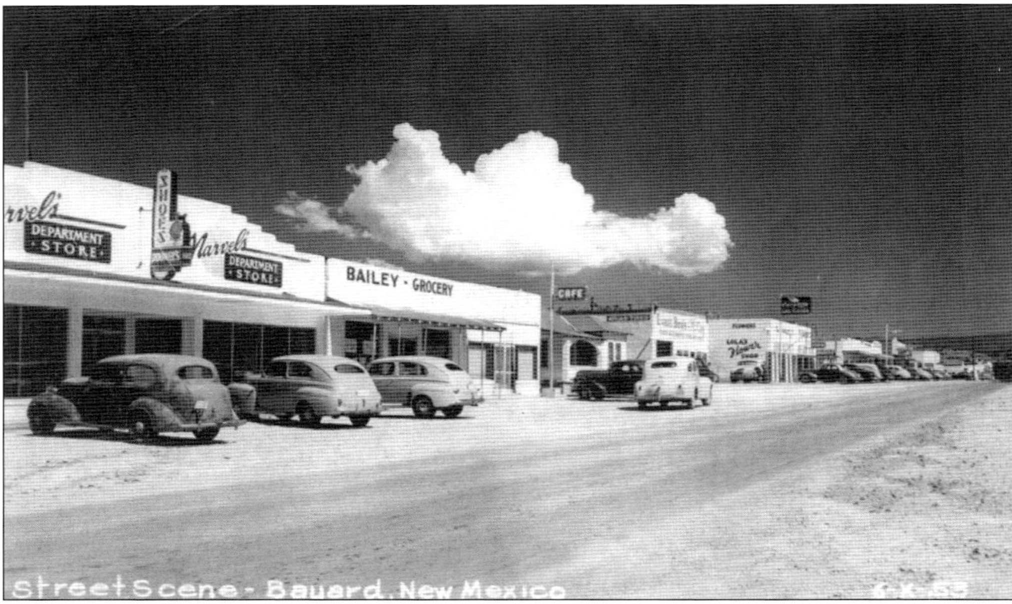

The town of Bayard, east of Silver City, was incorporated as a village in 1938. Originally a cattle ranch and mining claims, when the railroad first came through in 1891 it was known as Hall's Station. When the post office was established in 1902, it was named Bayard Station after nearby Fort Bayard. Above, a 1953 scene on the main thoroughfare, Central Avenue, shows many of the town's businesses, none of which remain today. Bayard even had a chamber of commerce in the 1940s and 1950s. Below, the Bayard Fire Department shows off its fire truck, parked in front of city hall about 1950. Pictured with it are, from left to right, Woody ?, unidentified, Bob Porter, Eddie Evatt (in truck), Doc Woodworth, Bob Himes, Jack Clardy, Baxter Evatt, and Don Smith.

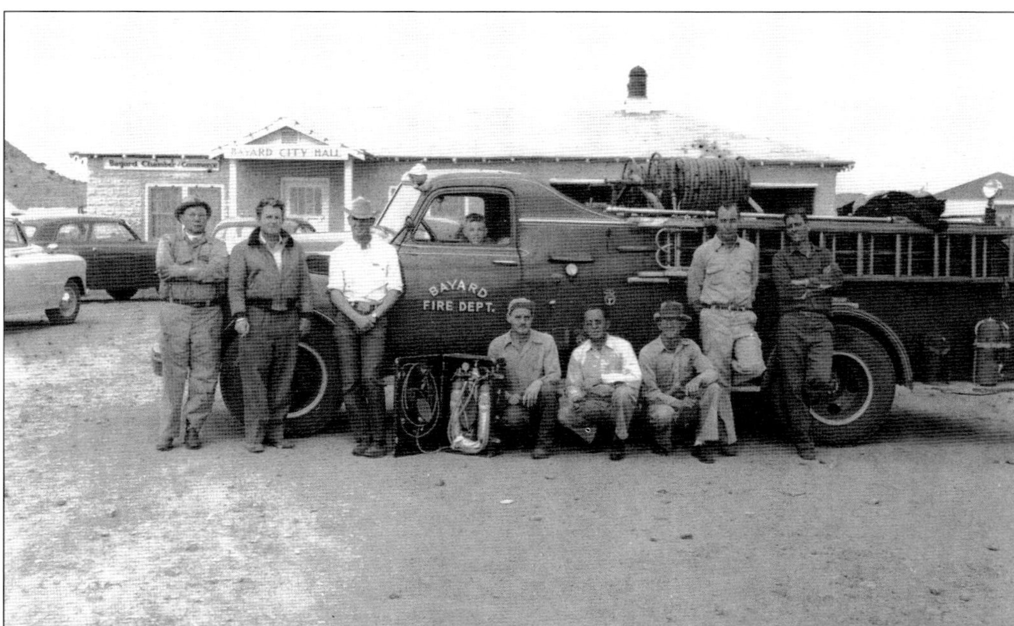

A fiddle player since the age of seven, Forrest Delk started a band in the 1930s called the Gully Jumpers (named for all of the washed-out roads they had to cross on their way to engagements). Shown in this early 1940s photograph are, from left to right, Robbie Arnspiger, Roberta Ramsey, Forrest Delk, Jimmy ?, and Tex Little. Delk was also a prominent rancher until his death in 1996. (Courtesy of Don Turner.)

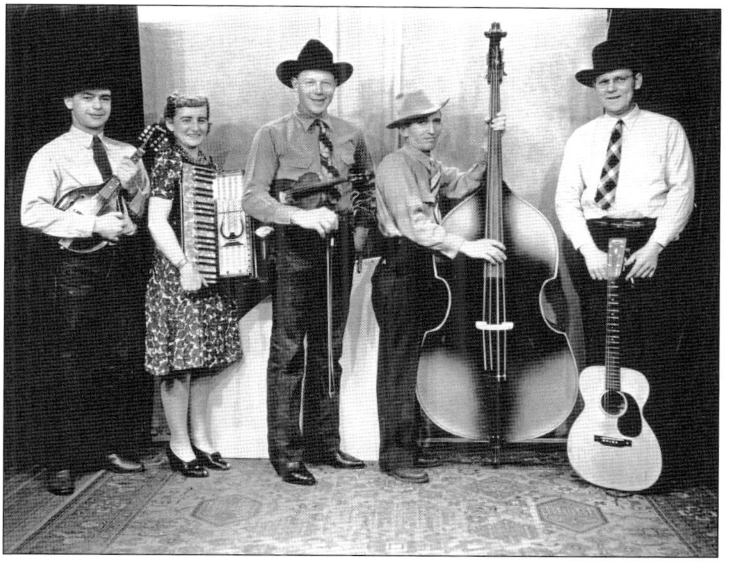

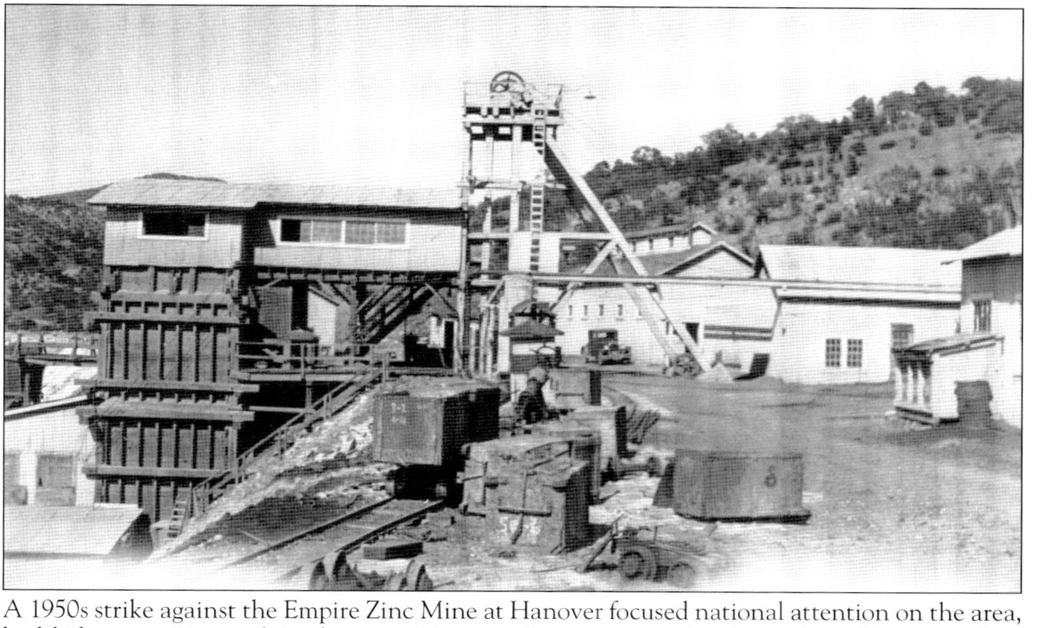

A 1950s strike against the Empire Zinc Mine at Hanover focused national attention on the area, highlighting pay inequalities between Mexican-American and Anglo workers. Women walked picket lines when a court injunction forbade the men from protesting. The cult-classic movie *Salt of the Earth* was produced by blacklisted Hollywood filmmakers in 1954, reenacting the struggle, and was named one of the 100 most significant films of the 20th century. (Courtesy of Don Turner.)

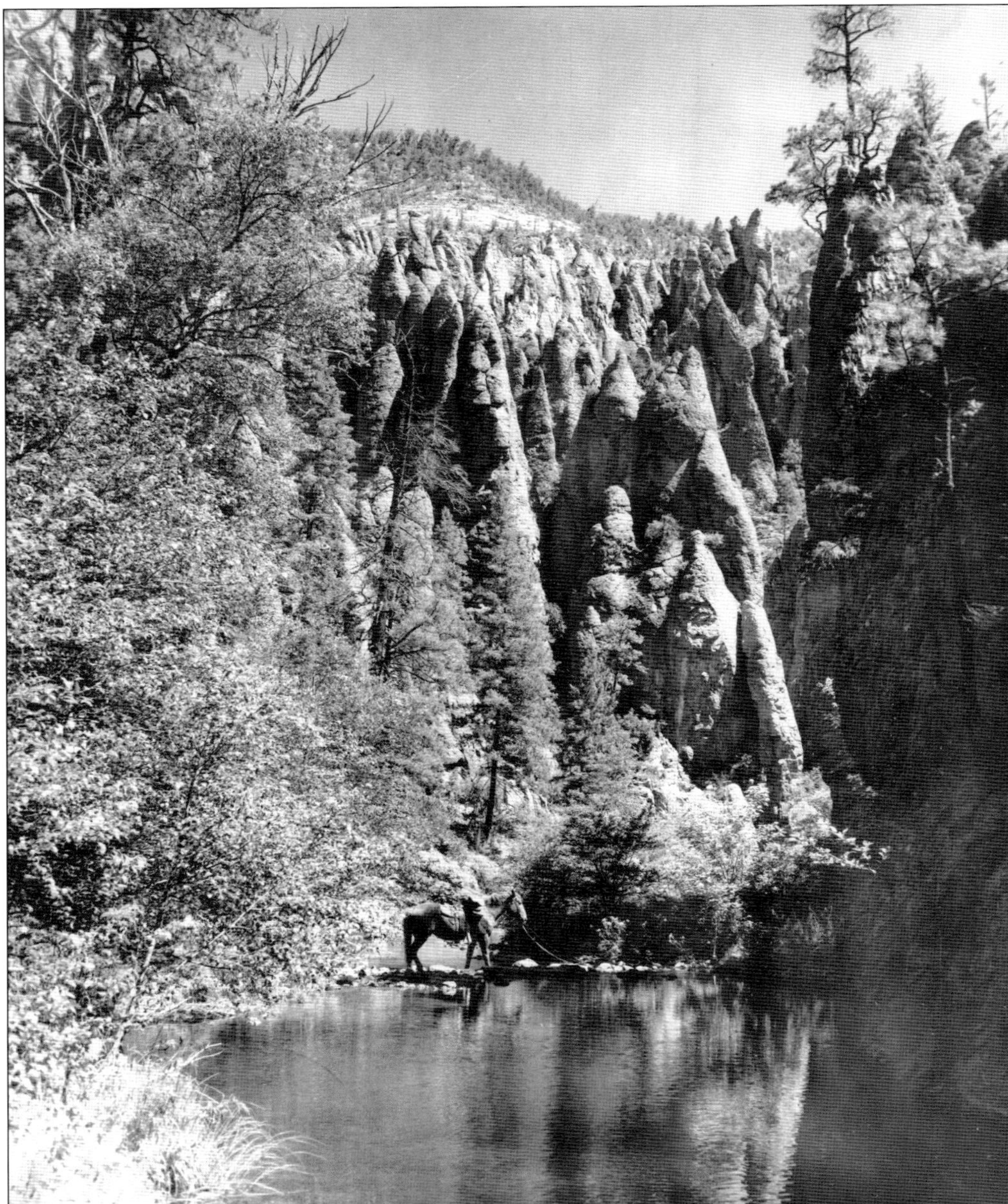

Silver City is at the southern edge of the Gila Wilderness and the Gila National Forest. Established in 1924 on 3.3 million acres of public land, the area encompasses one of the largest and most remote forests in the continental United States and is the oldest designated wilderness in the country. Ranging from 4,000 to nearly 11,000 feet in elevation, the territory contains mountains, canyons, rivers, and caves, and provides beautiful areas for hunting, fishing, camping, hiking, and horseback riding. Most of the region is accessible only by trails and a few dirt roads, and one narrow, winding road to the heart of the area where the three forks of the Gila River meet in the Gila Hot Springs valley. The rider pictured here has stopped on the West Fork of the Gila River to water his horse. (Courtesy of Ida Campbell.)

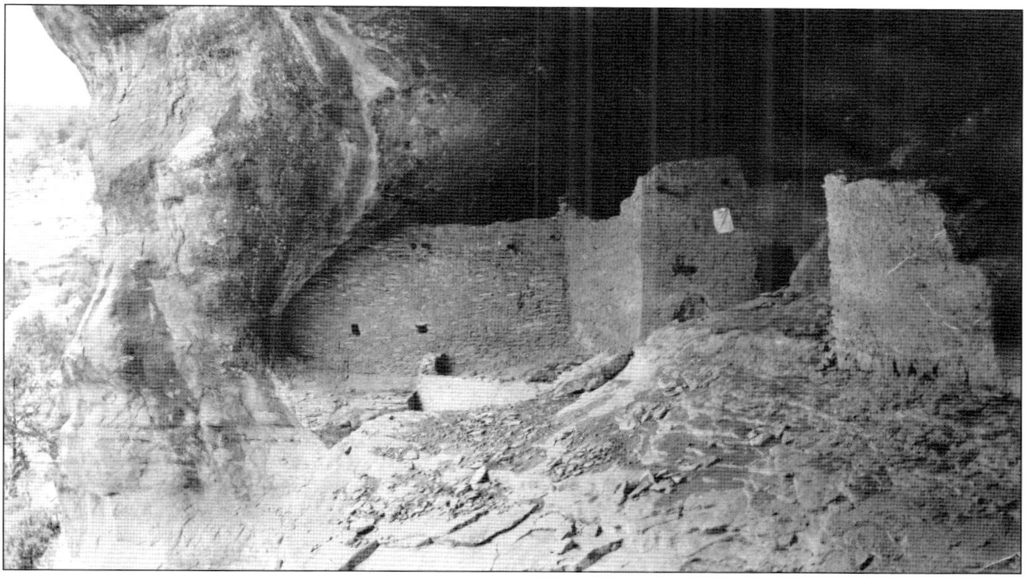

Horseback trips into the heart of the Gila Wilderness were strenuous, but popular, summer outings, and often included a climb to explore the Gila Cliff Dwellings on the West Fork of the Gila River. (Above, courtesy of Jean Eckard; below, courtesy of Jan Blackwell.)

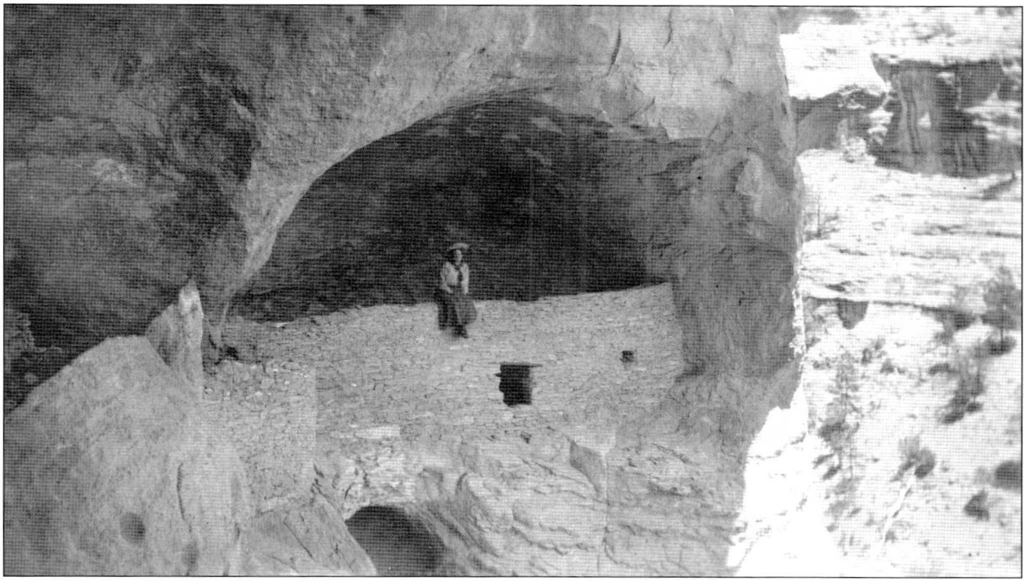

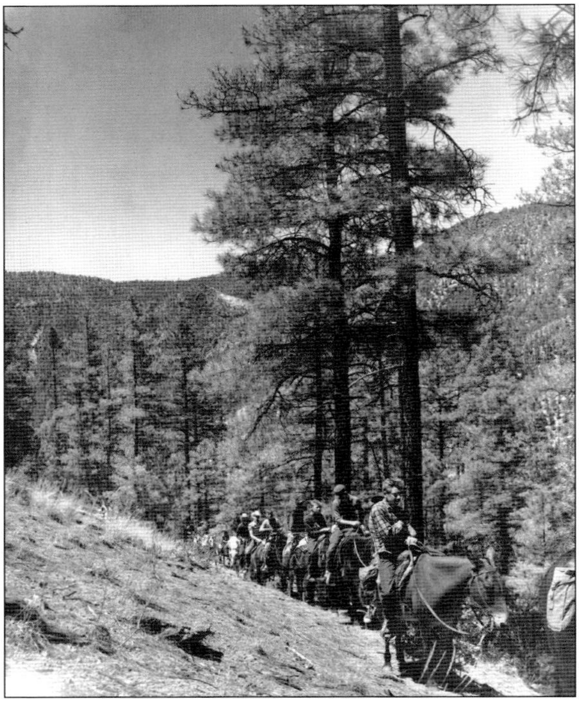

The Gila Wilderness has long been a destination for groups of young people, scouts, church groups, and others from around the Southwest. This 1950s group of Boy Scouts climbed a steep mountain trail to enjoy a refreshing swim in the chilly waters of the Gila River. (Both, courtesy of Ida Campbell.)

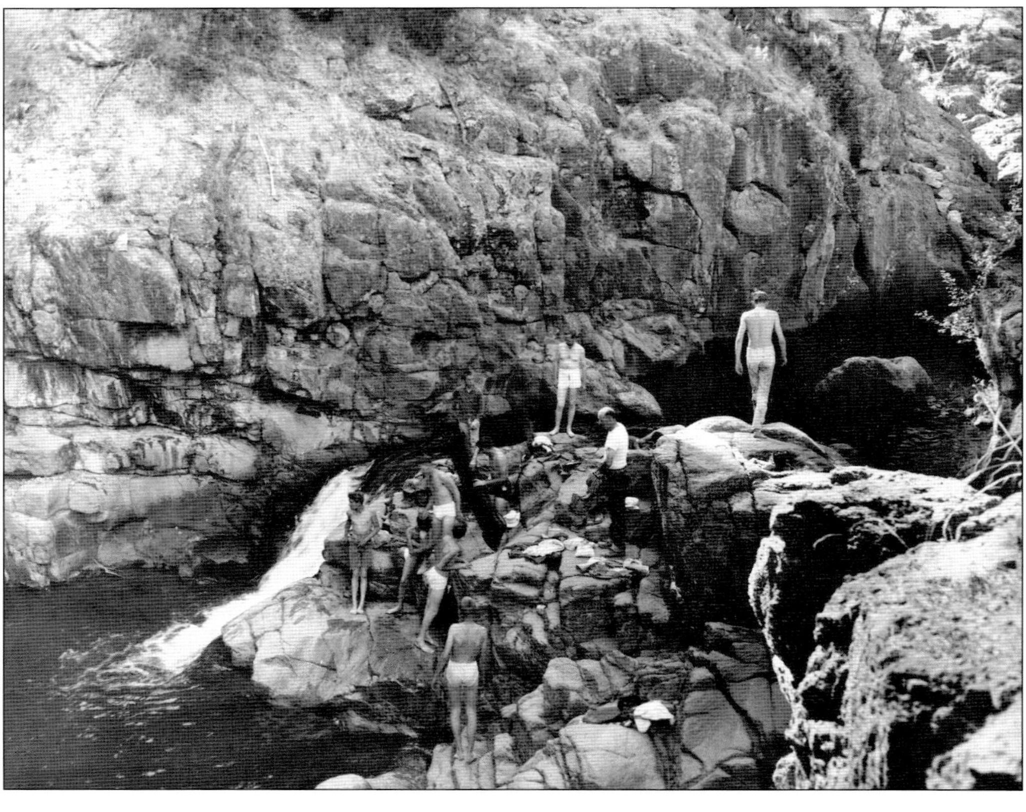

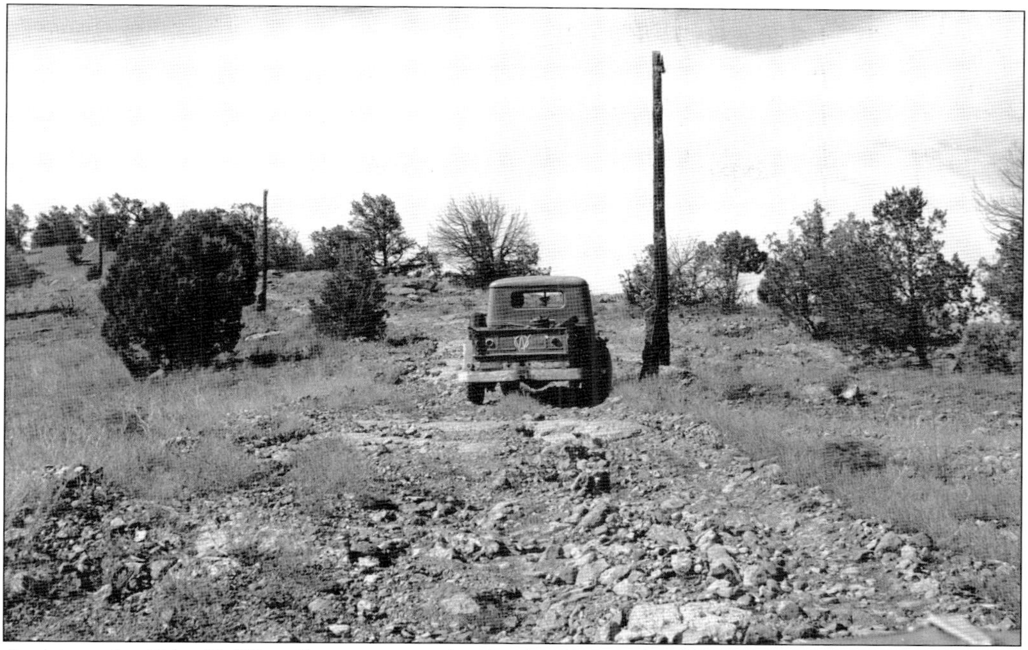

A visit to the Gila Cliff Dwellings was not for the fainthearted. Although this national monument lies just 44 miles north of Silver City, its access road was unpaved until 1967. Earlier the trip required a four-wheel-drive vehicle, and upon reaching the Gila Hot Springs the intrepid driver still faced at least 10 river crossings to reach the dwellings. The driver of the pickup truck below in 1965 obviously did not realize the depth of the crossing at Little Creek. (Below, courtesy of Ida Campbell.)

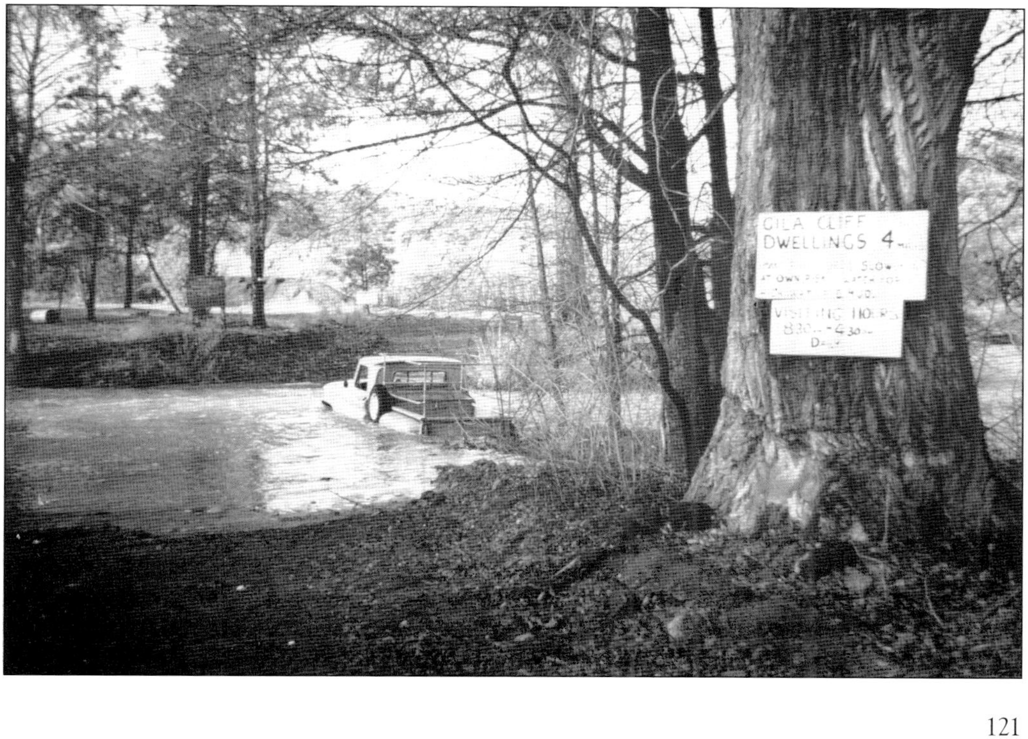

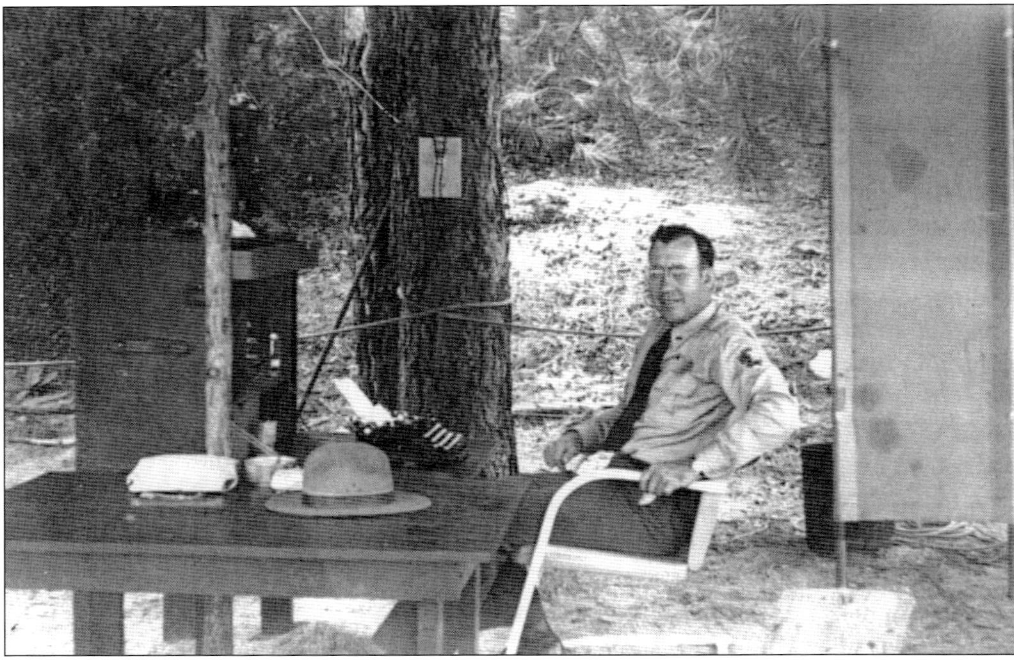

As the first custodian at the Gila Cliff Dwellings, Doc Campbell (above) worked with minimal supplies. The first visitor's center was a tent with an army field desk and a typewriter. Doc had a Forest Service telephone and magneto line that he strung up the canyon. Because the area was so remote, with his $12 annual pay, Doc received approximately $1 per visitor. Doc and his wife, Ida, bought the Hill brothers' ranch, where they raised their children, pictured below from left to right: Angus, Alan, Becky, and Ysabel. Living at the end of a winding mountain road, 44 miles and several hours north of Silver City, the Campbells were self-sufficient, raising their own food in a garden and orchards, while Ida homeschooled the children. A 1948 story in the *Saturday Evening Post* labeled them the "Wilderness Family." (Both, courtesy of Ida Campbell.)

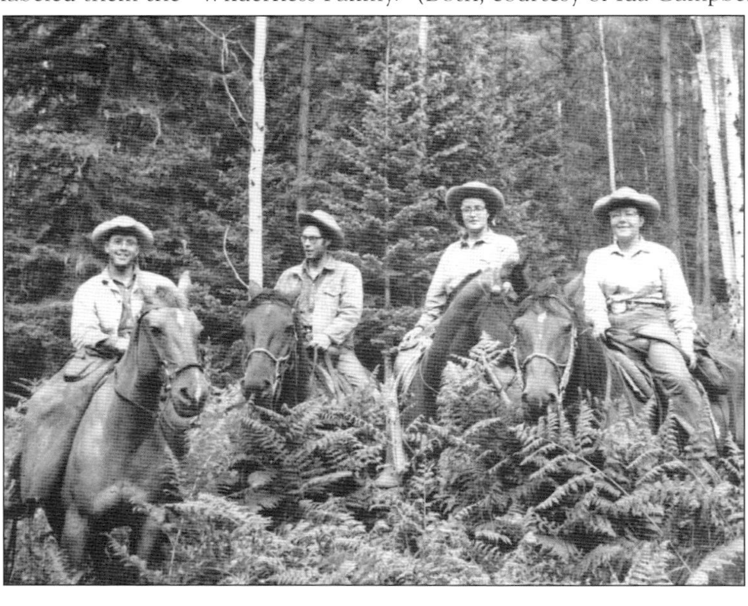

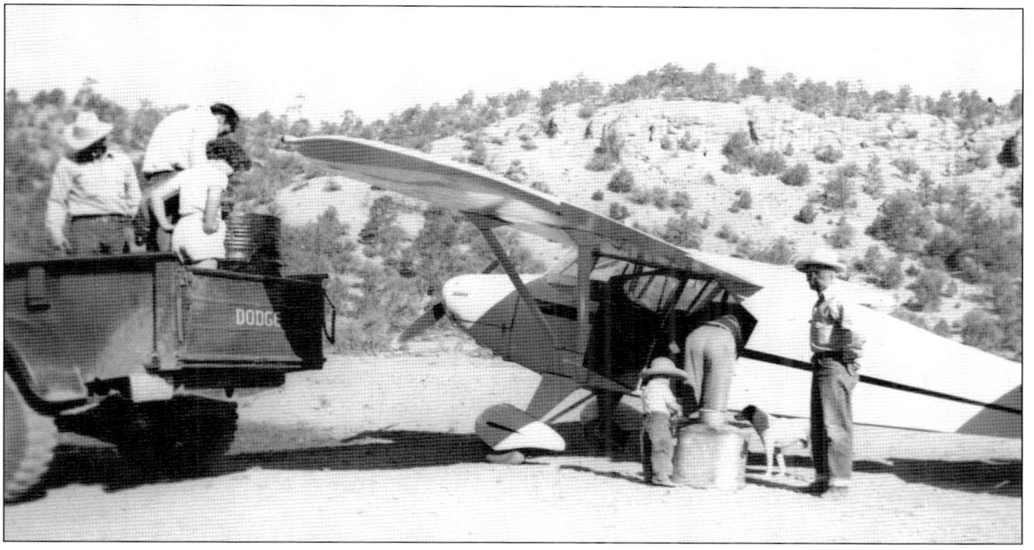

Doc Campbell resided at the Gila Hot Springs at the junction of the three forks of the Gila River. Because he and his wife, Ida, hosted many visitors coming to see the Gila Cliff Dwellings, making the long, difficult trip over the mountain and up the middle of the river, Doc felt that visitors needed to have a quality outdoor experience. In 1950, the Campbells worked with the Game and Fish Department to stock the river with fish. Doc and Ida paid for an airplane to fly in the fish from Glenwood to the airstrip at the hot springs, and 55-gallon barrels of fish were loaded into the back of a truck to be emptied into the West Fork. (Both, courtesy of Ida Campbell.)

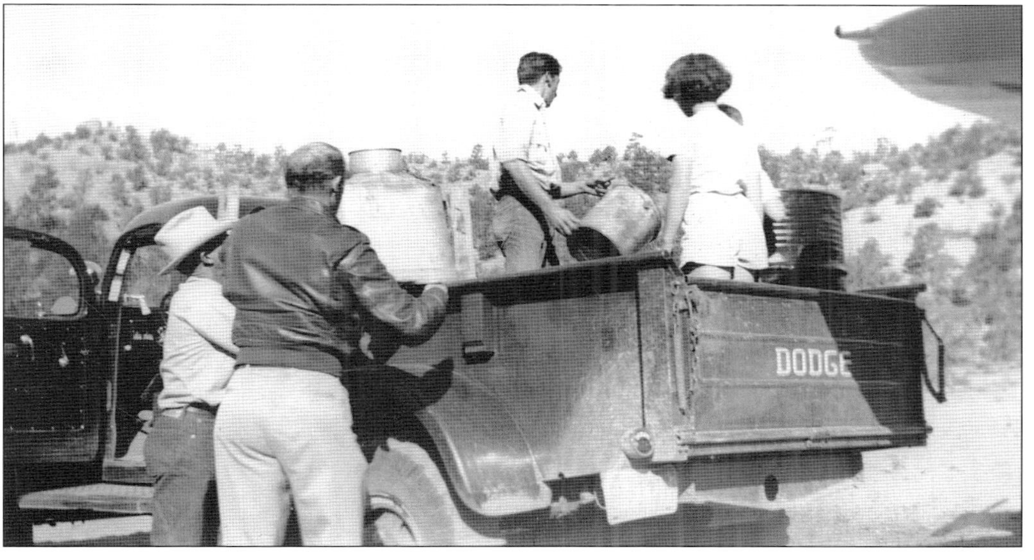

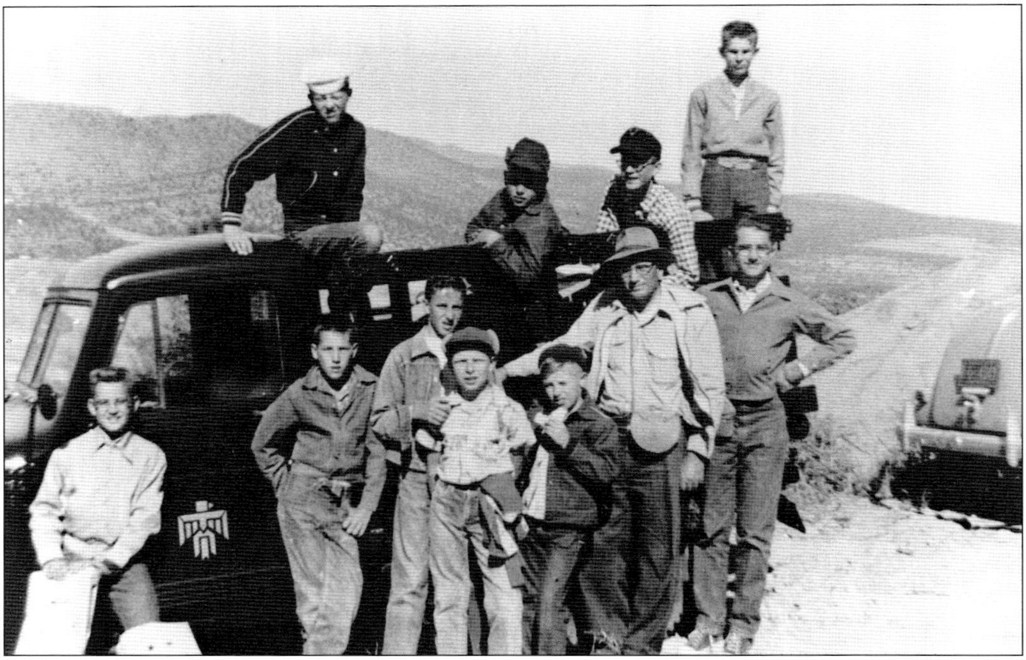

The Kneeling Nun is an ancient landmark on the bluff above the Santa Rita open-pit mine. Visible for 20 miles, the stone monolith has been featured in poems and articles, as well as in historic Apache and Mexican folklore. The best-known story is of an outcast nun who had fallen in love with a soldier and was turned to stone for eternity. For many, the Nun is one of the last reminders of the town of Santa Rita, which was consumed by the copper mine. In earlier years, it was a scouting tradition to hike the 1,500 feet up to the base of the Kneeling Nun, as Boy Scout Troop 105 did in 1955, along with Troop 104. (Below, courtesy of Jane Bardal.)

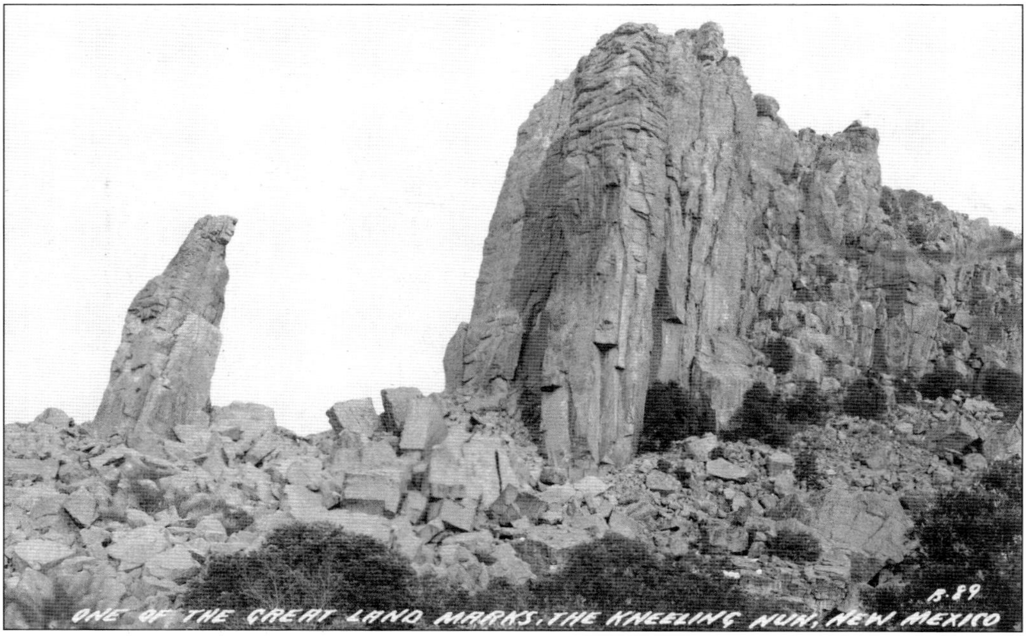

Astronaut Harrison "Jack" Schmitt (right) journeyed into space on Apollo 17 and walked on the surface of the moon in December 1972. It was perhaps prophetic that Schmitt was born in Santa Rita (below), a town that disappeared as it was excavated by the Kennecott Copper Corporation from the 1940s to the 1960s. Schmitt formed an organization called the Society for People Born in Space, for all the past residents who were born in Santa Rita, as the former location of their town is now in midair above the Chino open-pit copper mine. (Right, courtesy of Harrison Schmitt Elementary School.)

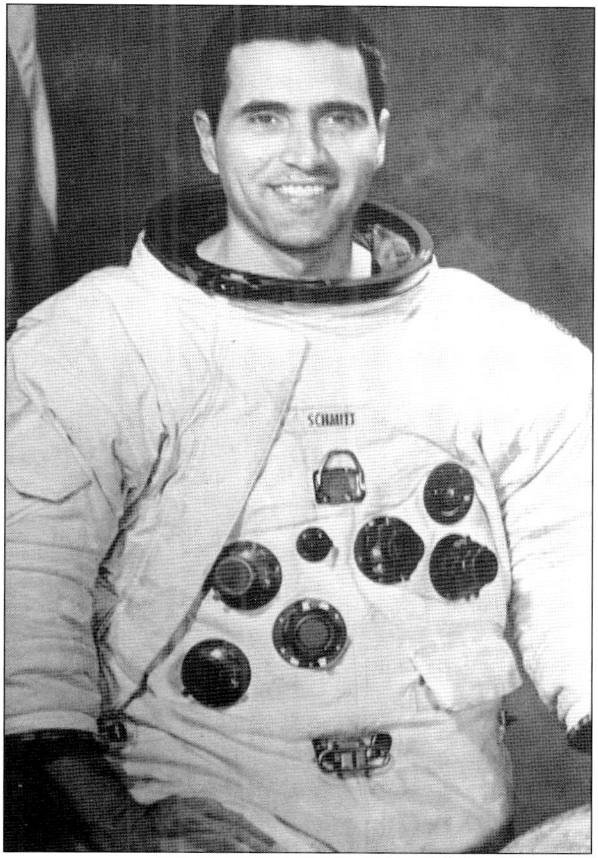

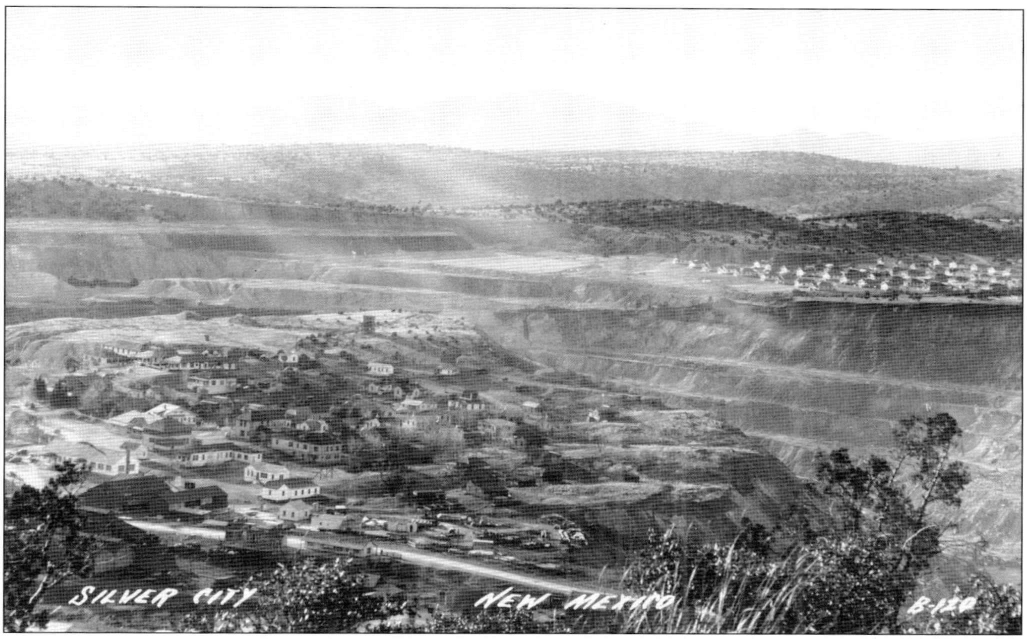

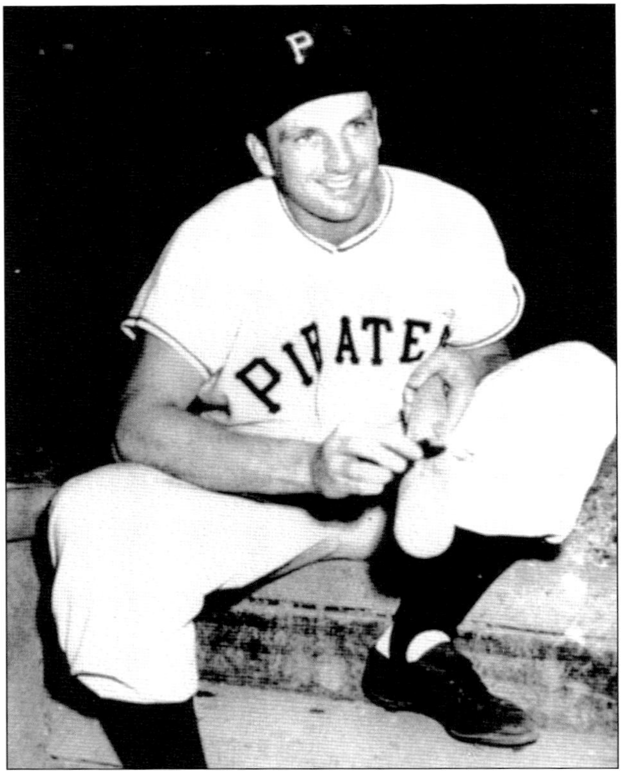

Ralph McPherran Kiner was born in Santa Rita in 1922. He was a Major League Baseball player for 10 seasons, playing for the Pittsburgh Pirates, Chicago Cubs, and the Cleveland Indians and hitting 369 home runs. After a back injury forced his retirement, he became a sports broadcaster and had a pregame show, *Kiner's Korner*. Kiner was inducted into the Baseball Hall of Fame in 1975, and in 1999 was named one of the 100 greatest baseball players. Below, an infant Ralph is pictured with his parents, Ralph and Beatrice Kiner, as they sit on the running board of the automobile. (Both, courtesy of Michael Kiner.)

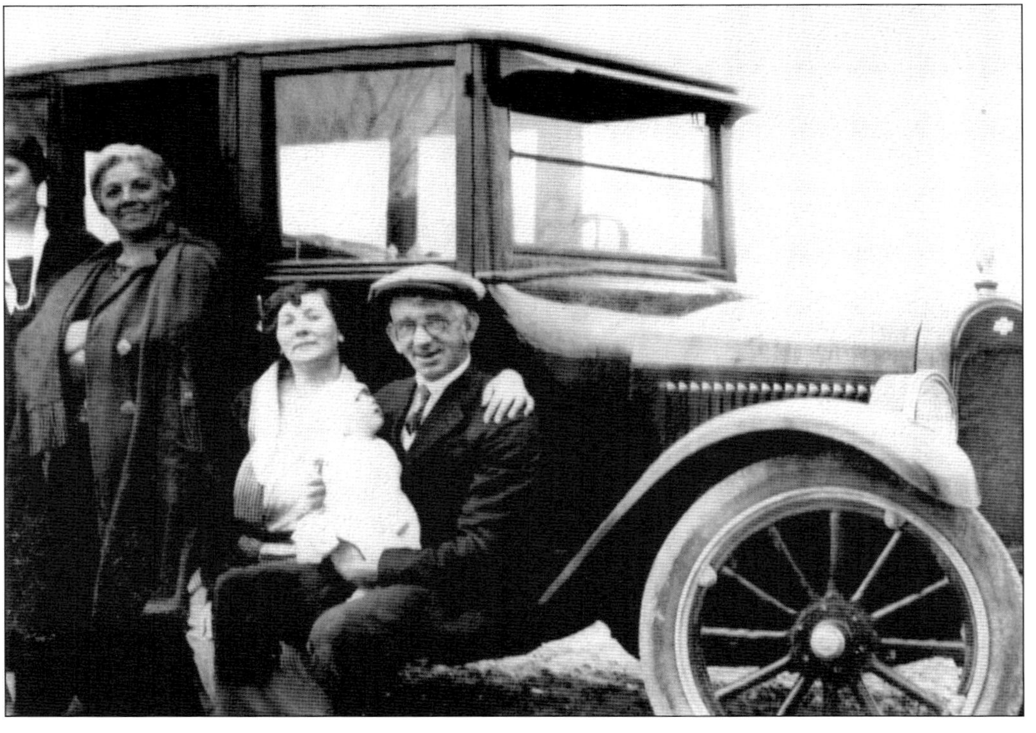

Bibliography

Alexander, Bob. *Six-Guns and Single-Jacks: A History of Silver City and Southwestern New Mexico.* Silver City, NM: Gila Books, 2005.

Alexander, Bob. *Lawmen, Outlaws, and S.O.B.s: Gunfighters of the Old Southwest.* Silver City, NM: High-Lonesome Books, 2004.

Berry, Susan and Sharman Apt Russell. *Built to Last: An Architectural History of Silver City, New Mexico.* Silver City, NM: Silver City Museum Society, 1986.

Campbell, Ida Foster and Alice Foster Hill. *Triumph and Tragedy: A History of Thomas Lyons and the LCs.* Silver City, NM: High-Lonesome Books, 2003.

Cave, Dorothy. *Beyond Courage: One Regiment Against Japan, 1941–1945.* Las Cruces, NM: Yucca Tree Press, 1992.

Davis, Carolyn O'Bagy. *Treasured Earth: Hattie Cosgrove's Mimbres Archaeology in the American Southwest.* Tucson, AZ: Sanpete Publications, 1995.

Davis, Carolyn O'Bagy. *Mogollon Mountain Man: Nat Straw Grizzly Hunter and Trapper.* Tucson, AZ: Sanpete Publications, 2003.

Huggard, Christopher J. and Terrence M. Humble. *Santa Rita Del Cobre: A Copper Mining Community in New Mexico.* Boulder, CO: University Press of Colorado, 2012.

Lundwall, Helen J. *Pioneering in Territorial New Mexico: The Memoirs of H.B. Ailman.* Silver City, NM: Silver City Museum Society, 2008.

Lundwall, Helen J. and Terrence M. Humble. *Copper Mining in Santa Rita, New Mexico 1801–1838.* Santa Fe, NM: Sunstone Press, 2012.

McFarland, Elizabeth. *Forever Frontier: The Gila Cliff Dwellings.* Albuquerque, NM: The University of New Mexico, 1967.

McKenna, James A. *Black Range Tales: Sixty Years of Life and Adventure in the Southwest.* Glorieta, NM: The Rio Grande Press, 1981.

Miller, Darlis A. *Open Range: The Life of Agnes Morley Cleaveland.* Norman, OK: University of Oklahoma Press, 2010.

Pope, Neta and Andrea Jaquez. *The Fort Bayard Story 1866–1899.* Silver City, NM: self-published, 2011.

Romero, Anthony. *Saloons of Central City/Santa Clara, New Mexico.* Santa Clara, NM: self-published, 2011.

Simmons, Marc. *Massacre on the Lordsburg Road: A Tragedy of the Apache Wars.* College Station, TX: Texas A&M University Press, 1997.

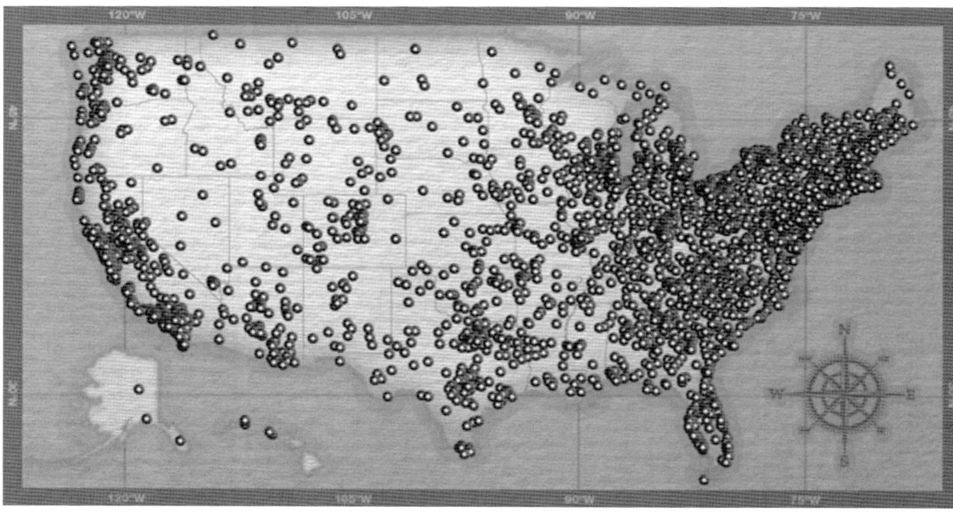